DESTINATION–
The WINNER'S CIRCLE

DESTINATION–
The WINNER'S CIRCLE

DEVOTIONS FOR EVERY LEG
OF LIFE'S RACE

BRAD HENRY

Bridge-Logos

Alachua, Florida 32615

Bridge-Logos

Alachua, FL 32615USA

Destination—The Winner's Circle
by Brad Henry

Printed in Canada.

Library of Congress Catalog Card Number: 2008923866
International Standard Book Number 978-088270-529-3

Scripture quotations are taken from the *Holy Bible, New International Version* ®. NIV ®. Copyright © 1973, 1978, 1984 by International Bible Society. Used by permission of Zondervan. All rights reserved.

G532.316.N.m803.352100

Jamie McMurray Foundation
and *Destination–Winner's Circle*

Brad Henry and Jamie McMurray have at least two things in common—autism and NASCAR. Brad's eight-year-old son, Chase, and Jamie's niece are both autistic. This is why a portion of the proceeds from the sale of each book are being donated to the Jamie McMurray Foundation.

The main purpose of the Jamie McMurray Foundation (JMF) is to promote awareness of and to raise funding for research, education, and support for individuals and families affected by autism. Because of Jamie's involvement as a race car driver in NASCAR, JMF will focus much of its activities on promoting better understanding of autism in the NASCAR community and will seek the financial backing and support of that community.

For more information about the Jamie McMurray Foundation
visit www.jamiemcmurray.com/foundation

You can contact Brad Henry through Bridge-Logos
17750 NW 115 Ave.
Building 200 • Unit 220
Alachua, Florida 32615

If you would like to receive a daily devotional, email Brad at
brad@heavenfirst.com

FOREWORD

Growing up in a football family with my dad as a coach, life was measured in victories and losses. Each weekend there was a battle to prepare for and you knew where you stood after every game. If there was any question, we would just look at the scoreboard. Life isn't quite so cut and dry, however. There are times in our lives when everything seems to be in chaos. There are times when we can do no wrong. Usually, our lives are a mixture of both blessings and struggles. As they say, "Life is hard, but God is good." The older I get, the more that statement rings true.

Brad Henry has a gift and a passion for sharing his experiences and his wisdom with us in a way that everyone can understand. I joke with Brad that someone should make a movie of his life, for more unbelievable things happen to him than anyone I know. God has been preparing him to write this book for a long time. As we travel with him in the race the Lord has put before him, we get a clear picture of how God's grace applies to our lives, as well. Brad has helped me to grasp a clearer picture of how much God loves me and is there for me, as I attempt to run my own race with endurance.

Mostly, this book drives home the truth that this world is a far country from our true home in Heaven. We need to constantly adjust our perspective of ourselves and look at this world through the Lord's eyes. Every morning when I read a chapter from this book, I am encouraged to focus on the things of God, not the things of man.

J.D. Gibbs, President, Joe Gibbs Racing

I'm Done

Trials and tribulations—each day brings new ones. The bathroom in our new house needed painting. The problem was the old wallpaper on the walls. I saw a loose corner I could start peeling. I pulled and it came off so easily that within five minutes I had all the wallpaper off the walls. I was actually pretty proud of myself. I called for Julie to see my great accomplishment, in record time. While Julie was admiring my great work I noticed that there was a little curl of paper again. The closer I looked, the more it became evident that there was another layer glued to the wall. Three days later, I finally scraped the last of it out. Our bathroom looks like something out of Beirut. At one point I just felt like saying, "Enough! I'll paint over the glue!"

Now that we are done, at least for this stage, I have come to realize a couple of things. Circumstances aren't always what they seem. The Christian life is a lot like that wallpaper. Once we are saved by the grace of God, the hard part starts. It takes time, energy, passion, commitment, and love to be a follower of Jesus. Too many times we rely upon our salvation to get us through life. It would be so easy for us to just paint over the glue. No one would ever know, would they? No, you're right. Jesus and you and I would know.

It seems like the tougher the trial, the more of an opportunity we have to draw closer to the Lord. Now I'm preaching to myself on this one, but don't be so anxious to get out of a trial. I thought halfway through this wallpaper ordeal, "Why am I doing this?" I could have paid someone to do it, but the sense of accomplishment is so much better than I had imagined.

That is how we should view our trials. God will not give us more than we can handle. Even though the walls may seem to be coming down, and still may, He *is* in control. The Lord wants us to be strong and the only way for us to be strong is to have adversity in our lives. Let the adversity you are going through now be a chance to let your faith grow. Let it be a chance to let God shine through you. The Christian walk is not a sprint, but a marathon.

Have a great day.
Brad

Stress

S tress! Now here is a topic that we can all relate to. Stress comes in various forms and degrees and people handle stress differently. I can talk to a thousand people and enjoy doing it, but put me on top of a tall building and I'll be crawling for cover. I watch these guys put support beams on skyscrapers and my hands sweat just looking at them.

I believe that unhealthy stress is when we don't have the proper perspective in life. Here is my take on this life:

1. Jesus is in control
2. This life and body are temporary. This world is not our real home.
3. The *only* thing that matters is "Do we have a personal relationship with Jesus Christ and have we trusted Him for our salvation." If we have then Heaven is in our future.
4. We need to look forward to being with Jesus more than anything else in this world.

If we have trouble with #4, then stress will build.

When you and I become worried about our health, our children, our jobs, our finances, our homes, and on and on and on, we are really saying, "Lord, I want to hang onto this or let me take care of that." All of our stress comes from hanging onto this life. Have you ever wondered why some people say, "Cancer was the best thing that happened to me"? When we can truly face death and be okay with it, then and only then can we truly live.

"Do not love the world or anything in the world..." (1 John 2:15).

When you and I love our spouse, children, job, position, and money *more* than the Lord, then the stress will come. I had a great Bible study with a friend of mine this morning and this issue came up. It seems that a friend of his had colon cancer and died two days ago leaving behind a wife and two small children. When our perspective is of this world and the things of this world we will always have pain. It's when we can put all things aside and focus on Jesus that our whole perspective will change.

Since this is not our real home and Heaven is in your future, there is nothing to worry about. For us to feel this way is for us to get to know God better. We can do this through prayer, reading God's Word, having fellowship with other believers, encouraging others in the faith, and making this the number-one priority in our lives. When we can fully understand how much God loves us and what His plans are, we will say, "Lord, I'm ready to go. Take me home." Then the stress will leave. Have a great day and whatever "it" is, don't worry about it.

Keep on Keepin' on

I like stories of perseverance. Keep on keepin' on! So many times when things look the bleakest, victory is right around the corner if we keep on keepin' on. This world is full of troubles, but there is one sure way of having victory. That is to have a personal relationship with Jesus Christ. When you have that, nothing can hurt you. Oh sure, your body will one day wither away, but what really matters is your soul. When you have asked Jesus to come in and take control of your life, *nothing* can snatch you away from His grasp. This should be great comfort to all of us, no matter what we are going through. When we can live fully for Jesus, then we can say to the world through the strength of Jesus Christ, "Bring it on!" Many times we don't do things because of fear of failure, fear of rejection, fear of death, or just plain fear. When we can get to the point in our lives where Jesus means more to us than anything else, *then*, and only then, can we truly live.

God wants us to be warriors. You have to ask yourself, "Why am I still here on Earth?" If you are already saved, then why does God still have you here? The answer is because you have more work to do and it could be something very important. I don't know what it is, but God does and when you stay close to Him, He'll reveal it to you. Who knows, you may be here on Earth to lead the next Billy Graham to the Lord. You may be here to witness to someone because *you* are the only person he or she will listen to. Hell is a place of unspeakable horrors. When we look at all those around us and especially those who aren't saved, we should go out of our way to share eternal life through Christ with them.

You see, we were all destined for hell the minute we were born. For those of us who are saved, we need to give thanks. It's nothing we have done, but what God did in saving us.

Since this is the case, we should not judge others because we were as sinful as everyone else. We need to be truthful with each other and help as many people get to Heaven as possible. Pray that the Lord would give you His words, His power, His love, and His compassion to minister to all those around you. Remember, this life is not a sprint but a marathon and a marathon is run one step at a time. Keep on keepin' on! Jesus could come back today!

The Waves of Life

S ome of you are going through a strong storm. You may be just entering it or you may be on the way out. Wherever you are, storms can be very unsettling. Some might think, "If I could only have God's perspective I could get through this." I believe that we *can* have God's perspective. We first need to know a couple of things.

1. Storms don't last forever.

2. Given the chance, storms make us much stronger, *when* we rely upon the Lord.

3. Pray and continually read God's Word. Having God's Word in your heart enables you to weather the fiercest storm.

4. If you are a Christian, (having accepted Jesus as Savior and Lord of your life), then nothing can hurt you or take you from God's grasp. This is comfort in any storm.

5. God allows certain things to happen to us so we can be dependent upon Him, not ourselves.

6. We are here on Earth for a purpose. The more we pray and read God's Word the closer we are to understanding what that purpose is.

7. The main purpose of life is to come to know Jesus as Savior. After that, it is up to us to lead a life that is pleasing to Him.

Most of us like the atmosphere of a peaceful cove. But in that setting we won't grow. We need to get out of that cove into the deep water. It's tough to let go because we have been taught to hang on. God loves us enough to allow certain things to happen to us that will make us dependent upon Him. The next time the storm rages know that God is God. He knows what is going on and He is always there. Use this as a chance to allow God to work and learn to let go. Why not completely trust in God? He created and owns everything anyway! Think about that one! Have a great day today and if you are going through a storm right now, remember, the power of prayer is awesome and God wants us to pray for each other.

The Passion

A few years ago Mel Gibson produced a movie called "The Passion." To say that this film was a lightning rod for controversy is an understatement. Prior to its release, Mel Gibson was interviewed by Diane Sawyer and he stood firm under her questions. Since the time Jesus started His ministry until He comes back, there will always be controversy when the name of Jesus appears. Why? Because the name of Jesus to some people means peace and salvation, to others it means unbelief and giving up control.

Do not suppose that I have come to bring peace to the Earth. I did not come to bring peace but a sword. For I have come to turn a man against his father, a daughter against her mother, a daughter-in-law against her mother-in-law; a man's enemies will be the members of his own household. Anyone who loves his father or mother more than Me is not worthy of Me; and anyone who does not take his cross and follow Me is not worthy of Me. Whoever finds his life will lose it and whoever loses his life for Me will find it (Matthew 10:34-40).

We are now seeing the same types of discussions that took place when Jesus was here on Earth. Jesus came to be our Savior, not to bring peace. The passage above does not mean we should not love our mothers or daughters.

But, if we love them more than the One who created us, then that is an issue. Any family will have dissension when some believe in Jesus and some do not. The way to Heaven is narrow; it's not a wide road. Either you believe who Jesus is or you don't. Religious beliefs become a heated debate because we are discussing the way to eternal life.

What is your passion? Is it acquiring things or getting to know Jesus more and more every day? "The Passion" is a movie that is graphic in the way it shows the crucifixion. Jesus was beaten, spit upon, mocked, nailed to a cross, pierced in His side, and ultimately died a horrible death so that He could save those who believe in Him. There was no other way. God had planned this before the Earth was formed. It was Jesus' destiny to pay for the sins of mankind. We were the ones who deserved to be on the Cross, not Jesus. But the perfect sacrifice has to be one without sin. Jesus' sinless life was the only one that qualified.

Sometimes shock therapy works and sometimes it doesn't. The Lord can allow anyone's heart to be hardened, but this movie has been a catalyst to bring many souls to Him. Pray that this movie will lead many more people to turn their lives over to Jesus. Pray that many Jewish people will see this and believe. Pray that this movie will show how much Christ loves us. Remember, Jesus could come back tomorrow. Where do you stand?

Do You Have the Right Insurance Policy?

In a worldly sense most of us are worth more dead than alive. Our insurance policies kick in and our families are taken care of financially. But do you have the right insurance policy? There are term and whole-life policies and a number of other policies that help our families when we die. We should be calling this insurance "death insurance," and the insurance I'm going to talk about the "Eternal Life Policy."

If you did not have health insurance and thought you might have a serious illness, you would run right out and try to get some coverage. Here is the sobering thought: We are all terminal; since we are all going to die, what coverage do you have? Are you the person who puts it off until a rainy day only to wake up and find it's raining? In order to figure out what type of coverage we need, let's look at how much we are worth.

"I consider my life worth nothing to me, if only I may finish the race and complete the task the Lord Jesus has given me—the task of testifying to the gospel of God's grace" (Acts 20:24).

We can only begin to really live when we are not afraid to die. In order not to be afraid we need to be assured of where we are going. Do you know? Paul's main concern for you and me is to:

1. Come to know Jesus as Savior and Lord of our lives
2. Share the gospel with as many people as possible.
That is it. Period!

It is interesting that Paul finishes his sentence with God's grace, because that is the only way we can be saved. Going to church, being baptized, teaching a Sunday School class, being kind to others and giving to the poor will not get you into Heaven.

"For it is by grace you have been saved, through faith—and this not from yourselves, it is the gift of God—not by works, so that no one can boast" (Ephesians 2:8,9).

If we could get to Heaven by works then Jesus came to this Earth, died a horrible death for nothing. Jesus did come to this Earth as God in the flesh. He led a sinless life, was crucified, and rose from the dead to pay the penalty for your sins and mine. Whoever asks Jesus to take control of their lives and asks for forgiveness of sins will have eternal life. This is the only insurance policy that really matters. Talk to the Lord today and make sure you are written in the Lamb's Book of Life. No one can do this but you. You can't go through an agent for this one.

Jesus paid the price. The more we consider our lives nothing, not in a sense of worthlessness but in a sense of priority, the more freedom we will have to give ourselves over to the work of the Lord. Don't sweat life, unless you don't have the policy. If you have eternal life in your future you are finally free.

Don't Leave Me

We tried to have a vacation this past week but the weather wouldn't cooperate. Our youngest boy got a bad cold and with bad weather in Florida, we decided to come home. Someone had said that it was snowing in Charlotte, but what's a little snow? As we got about ninety miles from home, I thought someone had turned on a snowmaker. The stretch of road between Columbia, South Carolina, and Charlotte, North Carolina, is not very populated, but it's a good interstate. As the snow began to pick up I said to Julie, "You know it's getting bad when you can't see the white lines." It then became dark and even harder to see. At this point I slowed from seventy down to twenty miles per hour. I had to ask Julie to look to the right to tell me how close the guardrail was. Fortunately a big truck came up alongside us and we pulled in behind him. For the next forty miles our average speed was between ten and twenty miles per hour. We couldn't get off on any exits because the snow was too deep. The two-lane highway was now one lane and cars were all over the place. We just tried to stay in the same tracks that the truck was making. The snow was so blinding that without the truck's lights in front of us, we would have been lost.

Then out of nowhere I started to see flashes of lightning. I thought that if we got stuck now it would be a day before anyone could come to get us. We were in a minivan and at times we were bottoming out. Julie and I prayed openly that we would make it safely and not only did we sense the Lord's peace but also His protection.

We got home two hours late, but we made it home. When we turned on the news the reporter said, "There is something strange happening between Columbia and Charlotte. We have reports of blizzard conditions with lightning." No kidding!! The road we were on received eighteen inches of snow within a short period of time. This capped off a relaxing vacation!

"Trust in the Lord with all your heart and lean not on your own understanding; in all ways acknowledge Him, and He will make your paths straight" (Proverbs 3:5,6).

The truck that I was following was a lot like the Lord. As long as I followed his lights I was fine. There were times that I felt we were going too slow. Once I tried to pass but found total darkness. I couldn't see anything and I mean *anything*. Quickly, I got back in behind the truck again. I thought, " Okay, I'm content to go slower and keep in his tracks. He knows where he is going. I do not."

How many times in life do we think we know better where to go than God does? How many times do we become impatient and step out in our own strength, only to get out and realize we should have waited? Ouch! This truck provided a means for escape on a dark, horrible night. The Lord will always provide a means of escape when we trust in Him and in Him alone. I saw a lot of people try to pass me that night only to see them a few miles up the road in a ditch, or worse. The road I was on became a true metaphor to our lives. Stay on the straight and narrow path and be safe. Get impatient, go it alone and there will be trouble ahead. God wants to dig deep furrows and light our path to guide us. God knows the beginning and the end.

Why not start trusting in God today not only for your salvation, but for all the other things in your life that so easily entangle you? Worry, jealousy, anger, resentment, and pride all happen when we try to go it alone. At times that night the truck would speed up a little and I would say, "Don't leave me." As we got to Charlotte and he got off, we honked our horn at him. He was our refuge in the storm.

In this life, are you still trying to pass that truck all the time? Are you still trying to do it in your own time and in your own strength? Let the Lord lead and I can tell you from experience and God's Word that when you do, your life we be much less hectic and worrisome. You will then be able to enjoy the things the Lord gives to you.

Stay in line, you'll get there when the Lord wants you to get there. Think about that one.

Suffering

The age old question is, "If God is in control why do children get cancer, why are people murdered, why do people have handicapped children, why do people die in the prime of their lives why, why, why?" The only answer I have is that there is no answer. God only knows the why, but the Bible can give us some insight into God's plan.

Let's look at what we do know:

1. Since the fall of Adam and Eve death and sin entered all of our lives.
2. We are all sinners, all of us—Romans 3:23
3. We will all die in our Earthly form.

Many times we are shocked when someone dies, but we all have to die. That shouldn't be a shock. We sometimes fall into the trap that this world is Heaven and forget that living on Earth is just the beginning of life. You could say that our nine months in the womb before we were born is like our life on Earth. We will be born into either Heaven or hell, depending upon our faith.

There are only two reasons we are here on Earth:

1. Come to know Jesus as Savior and Lord of our life.
2. Share the gospel with as many people as we know.

I can tell you from God's Word and experience that nothing else matters. Let me ask you: What can you take with you when you die? Have you ever seen a U-Haul following a hearse? Our house, car, stocks, family, and job will all be left behind. Since this is the case why do you do the things you do? If you are accumulating more than you need, why? You may say, "I want to make sure I have enough to retire on," or "I want to make sure my kids have an education." While this is good, how much is enough? I know kids who appreciated college and made more of themselves when they worked for it. This is not always the case, so please pray and ask the Lord how much is enough. Money is not the cure-all. If you are not ready for money when it comes, it will put you into problems that you never even dreamed of.

So what does all of this have to do with suffering? Money has caused a lot of suffering in this world. It is one thing most of us have allowed, at one time or another, to control our lives and it has produced tremendous suffering because of our mistakes. There are few things worse than being shackled with huge debt.

"Praise be to the God and Father of our Lord Jesus Christ, who comforts us in all our troubles, so that we can comfort those in any trouble with the comfort we ourselves have received from God" (2 Corinthians 1:3,4).

The Lord allows us to go through trials so that not only can our faith be refined, but that we can comfort people who are going though the same struggles. If you say to someone who has just lost a child, "I know how you feel," it's not true if you have not lost a child. But if that person knows you have lost a child, you can provide them comfort with the same comfort the Lord used to bring you through that trial. If someone was rich their whole life they can't say to someone who just declared bankruptcy "I know how you feel" because they don't.

Just think, the Creator of the Universe is using you and me to further His Kingdom—Christian and non-Christian alike. I know of a company whose president is so harsh that he has driven his employees to seek God. The persecution and uncertainty in their jobs have sent them on a search for Jesus.

So why is there suffering? In this life we will have pain and suffering. Part of this is to refine our faith, part is for other people to wake up and sense their own mortality, and part is so we can encourage others as part of the family of God. If we can view Heaven as the ultimate paradise (which we should), we should rejoice and not mourn for those that have died an Earthly death. We mourn because we are left without them. If they could tell us how Heaven was, we would cry no more. So how do we get to that point?

" ... Forgetting what is behind and straining toward what is ahead, I press on toward the goal to win the prize for which God has called me heavenward in Christ Jesus" (Philippians 3:13,14).

In the midst of suffering, we have to strain ahead toward Jesus and Heaven. We have to forget the past. Only take with you from the past what will encourage and strengthen, not that which would hinder and drag you down. I know people that are dead spiritually because they can't let go of the past. Christ died for you and me to give us a new life. When we accept Jesus into our lives, we are new creations.

"Therefore, if anyone is in Christ, he is a new creation, the old has gone, the new has come" (2 Corinthians 5:17).

The old has gone, amen and amen. The Lord can free you from pain, suffering, demons, and addictions. I have seen a lot of prayer requests lately and have sensed the pain of loved ones who are going through some tremendous trials. My comfort to you is God knows what is going on and He will never let you go through more than you can handle. Use this time as a chance to pray, read God's Word and feel the presence of the Lord. I have had some of my best devotions when I have felt the weight of the world upon my shoulders. It is then and only then that I stopped relying upon myself and turned things over to God. Have you turned everything over or are you still holding onto something? When we can turn everything over to God our lives will be refreshed.

"In his heart a man plans his course, but the Lord determines his steps" (Proverbs 16:9).

The Lord is in control, always.

Tired of Life

Do you ever get tired of life? We are in the midst of an election year and I'm already tired of the ads that are running. Children are dying of cancer, there are wars, marriages are breaking up at an unbelievable rate, terrorism is at an all time high, most Americans are saddled with a huge amount of debt and I could go on and on. Do you ever get tired of life and wish Jesus would come back now?

A very good friend of mine died last week and it was sad to not be able to talk with him anymore but we were all encouraged by the strength of his family. You could tell that this family had hope. They knew he was in Heaven with Jesus. Now that is joy, unspeakable joy. Sometimes our actions speak louder than words. In our lives we sometimes think we will live forever and are shocked by the death of a loved one. No matter how hard we try, the statistics are never wrong; a person is born, that person will die. There are only two things between those events that matter. Did you accept Jesus as Savior and Lord of your life and did you share the gospel with others? That is it. This man did and he did it as a humble servant. When I walked past his casket I knew beyond a shadow of a doubt that he wasn't there.

Thirty-five years ago, my dad laid in the same place in the same funeral home. Then, I had no hope. I believed he was still there somewhere in that body, dead forever. Now I know he is with Jesus. Thirty-five years later, in the same funeral home I walked past a casket again and this man was clutching a Bible in his hands. This was his faith, this was his legacy. His grown children were a testimony to faith in Jesus Christ. His legacy will live on because he and his wife instilled what is really important into their children. Jesus is the way, the only way to Heaven and eternal security.

Some people felt that since this man just retired, somehow he had been robbed of the joy of his retirement. How could God do such a thing? Clutching a Bible in his hands gave proof that he was not mad at God, but just the opposite.

The morning I went to the funeral I broke down and cried. This man of God had been my dad's partner in his medical practice. The memories of thirty-five years ago started to come back. I have a knack for being like an ostrich. If I don't like what I see, immediately my head goes in the sand. I can distance myself from the past because I know I can't go back and change anything. In the short run this is good but in the long run I hide too much away. I pulled out the tissue box and then when I used all that up I started on the toilet paper. Where was all this coming from? I finally figured out that I still missed my dad and I was coming home to familiar surroundings that had lasting memories. It's okay to cry. God uses that as a way to cleanse and heal us from past and current hurts. I came home from the funeral mentally exhausted. I had not lost a family member, or did I? You see, I really had not dealt with my dad's death, but it was good to get back to familiar territory and hear stories of him again. This family that lost their father and husband did more to encourage me than I did to encourage them. Their hope in Jesus was a light in a dark world. In the midst of death everyone could see hope.

The next time you get tired of life focus on Jesus. Jesus will never change and will sustain you no matter what the circumstances. Don't get caught up in the trials of everyday life. Jesus died a horrible death and rose from the dead so all who believe in Him will inherit eternal life. We can have victory not only in Heaven, but in this world too.

Don't wait until you get to Heaven to enjoy life. We can have abundant life here on Earth when we realize that we already have eternal life when we are born again of the Spirit. Make sure you are right with Jesus. When you are, the things of this world will fade away, giving us a clear picture of the security and glory that awaits. Let's try to lead a Spirit-filled, joyful life no matter what the circumstances. Start today by being that person that God has created you to be. Be joyful, not tired, pray without ceasing, and give thanks for what God has done and continues to do.

Tired of life? Focus on Jesus.

Why Pray?

This morning Julie said to me, "I'm a little worried. You didn't want to pray this morning." A friend of mine this past week said, "I feel distant from the Lord." In my case, I have been so consumed with other things that I have been distracted from the main goal. I thank the Lord for a godly wife that He uses to help me in my walk with Him.

Yesterday I had a day that I was just plain angry. Our seven year old had a doctor's appointment that I was a little concerned about. I had been gone for a few days and work had piled up and I just felt overwhelmed. Instead of asking the one who created the universe to help me, I decided to go it alone.

In Luke Chapter 22 there are a couple of verses that really stand out on the power of prayer and being focused:

"Simon, Simon, satan has asked me to sift you as wheat. But I have prayed for you, Simon, that your faith may not fail. And when you have turned back, strengthen your brothers" (Luke 22:31,32).

This is an awesome verse demonstrating the battle between Jesus and satan for our souls.

First of all, satan has to ask Jesus before he comes at us with any trial. That's the good news. But in this verse Jesus didn't say anything about stopping satan from sifting Peter as wheat. The only thing Jesus says is that, "I have prayed for you that you faith may not fail, and when you turn back, strengthen your brothers."

We do not learn how to get out of a jam by having someone else get us out. We learn to get out only when we try, fail, try, fail, try, fail, and then succeed. Then and only then can we help strengthen others with the same power that the Lord has strengthened us. When people used to loan me money when I was in debt, that didn't teach me anything. It wasn't until the faucet was shut off and, only then, did I have to start thinking and working for myself. It made me creative and disciplined never wanting to get back in that position again. If people had kept bailing me out, I would have never learned how to do it.

The Lord has given us a great imagination. Use it to glorify Him, not ourselves. Use it to acquire things for the kingdom, not ourselves.

Let's look again at prayer. Prayer protects us from the arrows of the evil one. Let me define "protection" in the way the Lord uses it.

We can pray for our children to be healthy and they could still die of cancer. We could pray for protection for our family when they are driving and an accident may still happen. So if prayer doesn't stop horrible things from happening, why pray? This is what prayer will do:

Prayer will protect our minds and our souls for eternity when we know Jesus as Savior and Lord of our lives.

Whether we like it or not we all have to die a physical death. This life on Earth is not our real life.

What prayer will do is keep us less stressed by allowing God to be in control. It won't be us at the helm. Since God created you, me, the Universe, and everything in it, why shouldn't we give everything over to Him? If we truly believe this, why do we hang onto things? Pride, confusion, and lack of prayer can play havoc with our decision-making.

Satan is asking Jesus all the time what he can do to keep us from the goal. The first goal is for you and me to come to know Jesus as Savior and Lord of our lives. When that is accomplished you are a child of God forever with Heaven in your future. Nothing can take that away from the time you make that decision until the Lord calls you home. But remember, satan doesn't want you to be an influence on any others.

Why? Because satan wants these people in hell for eternity, not Heaven. As a Christian you have the ability through the power of the Holy Spirit to lead others to eternity through Jesus Christ. That makes satan furious. If you aren't in a trial maybe you aren't doing enough for the Kingdom of God. The best thing we can do is to be a target but also be in prayer so our hearts won't be troubled.

Genuine prayer will keep us close to Jesus. Will it keep our family and our jobs safe? Not necessarily. What our prayer will do is let God's will be done for eternity. Let's not focus on the here and now. Lead your life focused on eternity and Jesus. There is nothing on this Earth that matters except salvation and evangelism. This life is a staging ground for us to be saved and to lead as many others to Jesus as possible.

If you are in a trial now, if you feel left out, if you feel the Lord has let you down, then pray. Prayer is nothing more than talking with the Lord as you and I would talk. Remember the Lord has never left your side no matter how lonely you feel. The longer we go without prayer the better chance the evil one has to get a foothold in your life and make you miserable. When we are miserable it is tough to be an effective witness for Jesus.

If you feel lost, without hope, persecuted and tired, pray that the Lord will protect you from the evil one and restore your faith. When we take one step to Jesus, He will take twenty to us. I have seen this in my own life time and time again. Don't let the evil one make you think you are not worthy. Remember, you are a child of the King.

Who's in Control?

Ah, the word, "control." Each of us likes some type of control. I know many people who are afraid to fly because they aren't in control. (I hope the pilots up front are!) Many executives who aren't running a meeting can't stand to take a back seat and listen because they don't feel in control. Having your kids get a driver's license is certainly losing control. Going into surgery is losing control.

So who is in control?

"There is no wisdom, no insight, no plan that can succeed against the Lord" (Proverbs 21:30).

This verse means that no matter how much we plan, no matter how much we play politics, no matter how much we prepare, the Lord's will, will be done. Amen to that. Wouldn't our lives be much less worrisome if we were to take this to heart? So how do we start letting go and letting God be in control?

Faith: Faith is the basis of our Christian walk. We are to accept Jesus Christ into our lives by faith. Thomas said that he wouldn't believe in Jesus until he saw His nail scarred hands. After Thomas saw Jesus, he believed.

"Because you have seen Me, you have believed; blessed are those who have not seen and yet have believed" (John 20:29).

Faith is believing, not only what has been seen, but trusting what the Lord has told us. Faith in Jesus is the only way to Heaven. Going to church every Sunday, putting money in the offering plate, going to Bible study, teaching Sunday School, being kind to others, being confirmed, and being baptized *will not get you into Heaven.*

"For it is by grace that you have been saved through faith, and this not from yourselves, it is the gift of God, not by works, so that no one can boast" (Ephesians 2:8,9).

God doesn't want anyone to boast. If we could earn Heaven by works then Jesus paid a horrible price on the Cross for nothing. We all have sin in our life and the minute we are born we are all destined to hell for eternity. It is only by faith in Jesus and God's grace that we will inherit eternal life. If we ask Jesus into our lives, ask Him to forgive our sins, acknowledge that He died on the Cross and rose from the dead to purchase a place in Heaven for us, then we will live for eternity with Him. Since this is fact, by all means, let's try to let God be in control.

God created the Universe and knew before you were born when you would die. Since we cannot extend our days by what we do, it is futile to think we can extend anyone else's days. I worry about my children. Now I know what my mom went through with my brother and me. We gave her a handful and then some. Unless I'm in the Word constantly and praying, the evil one gets a foothold and I start to doubt the perfect plan of God.

God's plan is perfect and *He* is in control. When we believe this, then, and only then, can we lead a life that is stress free. Sure, there will be times of anguish in trials, but when we know that God is in control we can then say, "Whatever it is, bring it on." If you are a Christian, you are a Christian by faith, not by works. Some may say, "They died too young,"

"They suffered," "How tragic, they were so good," "Why did they have to die?" I hate to tell you, but none of us are getting out of this life alive. Let me rephrase this. We are all getting out alive in spiritual form, not bodily form. Our destination will be determined by what decision we have made about Jesus before we have died an Earthly death.

That should be our only concern in this world. Coming to know Jesus as Lord and Savior of our lives and then leading as many people to Him as possible. Think about all the things that you are worried about and put them down on a piece of paper. There is nothing on that piece of paper that you can control so pray that the Lord would help you with those things. Rip up the piece of paper and throw it away. Since there is no plan that can succeed against the Lord, and if you are a Christian, then rejoice. Sure, there will be trials in this world but hold on to the hope of Heaven. Try to get to the point in your life where you don't hold onto anything of this world and I mean *anything*. Once you can start living like this, your life will start to be forever changed and you will have a huge impact on others who are lost.

Who's in control? It will never be you and me. Start today by asking God to help you lead a life for eternity and not focus on a life that is temporary.

Autopilot

In the early 1980's, I was a pilot for an airline. The airplanes I flew did not have autopilot, so it was quite a task. In the airlines, the captain will fly one leg and then the co-pilot will fly the other. It was my turn to fly this particular leg. We were flying into Indianapolis late in the evening and the conditions were calling for moderate icing. En route, we were picking up quite a bit of ice, but when we started our descent we really started picking it up. All of a sudden the airplane started to shake like it was starting to stall. Years of training had taught me that anytime you feel this coming on you put on full power and if need be, drop the nose to get extra airspeed. When we landed I could see the person directing us in looking intently at the right wing. When we unloaded all the passengers I went out to look under the wing. Under the wing there were ugly looking icicles about eight inches in length hanging under the wing. If I hadn't been well trained, things that evening could have been disastrous.

A number of years ago on a winter night near Detroit, an airplane was experiencing the same condition, trying to land with moderate icing. This crew had the luxury of an autopilot. An autopilot has a knob that you turn and the plane will turn, descend and track the course without you touching the controls. This particular evening the crew was watching the instruments and waiting for clearance to land. A few minutes later the plane started to shake, inverted, and impacted the ground with such force that everyone on the plane died instantly. You see, since the crew didn't have their hands on the controls, they couldn't feel the stall before it happened.

Are you on autopilot in your Christian faith?

It is easy to get up, go to work, come home, go to church on Sundays, pray at night, and think we are close to God. But really what we are doing is putting our life on autopilot. We need to get back where we are hand flying again, not taking our hands off the controls.

"Be very careful, then how you live, not as unwise but as wise, making the most of every opportunity, because the days are evil" (Ephesians 5:15,16).

We cannot take our hands off the controls. Satan is lying in wait for those who drop off, who take things for granted, who wander from the faith, who get lazy. Make this the day that you start taking your life back before it is too late. Ask the Lord to help you come back to Him like you did when you first believed. If you have not accepted Jesus as your Savior, then make this the day. Cry out to Him and ask for forgiveness and that He would come into your life. If life seems too overwhelming and you have given up, start by taking one minute, then one hour at a time. Don't think about everything you have to do or should have done. Jesus always gives us a fresh start.

Trust in Him and He will lead you from the darkness to the light. Get control by letting *God* be in control.

I'm Tired

Have you ever felt that you just can't go on? You may have been there or you may be going through something now that is very painful. Anytime we focus on the temporal more than the eternal we will be susceptible to this feeling of being overburdened.

I love the book of Ecclesiastes. It was written by Solomon, who was King David's son. As King of Israel, God gave him wisdom and unbelievable riches. He had it all, and I mean all. Here are some of the things he had:

1. More gold than you and I could count (25 tons of gold).
2. 4,000 stalls for his horses and chariots.
3. 12,000 horses imported from Egypt and from all other countries.
4. Solomon had 700 wives of royal birth, including Pharaoh's daughter, and 300 concubines.
5. A lavish palace.

So Solomon had everything that his heart desired.

In Ecclesiastes 2:10 he says, "I denied myself nothing my eyes desired; I refused my heart no pleasure … "

Most of us, if we had unlimited resources would probably fall into the same trap. If you and I are not constantly focusing on God and eternity, then we will fall into the trap of worldly possessions.

This is what Solomon says about all that he has done and what it has meant to him:

"Yet when I surveyed all that my hands have done and what I have toiled to achieve, everything was meaningless, a chasing after the wind; nothing was gained under the sun" (Ecclesiastes 2:11).

Here is a thought that will hopefully turn you back if your heart is tuned toward riches.

"I hated all the things I had toiled for under the sun, because I must leave them to the one who comes after me. And who knows whether he will be a wise man or a fool?" (Ecclesiastes 2:18).

Most of us chase after status, wealth, position, and accumulation of things because somehow we think that will make us successful and content. I can tell you from experience, and from what the richest man in the world says, that everything is meaningless unless God is involved.

If you are tired, feel beaten up, have lost hope, and are anxious, take a look at your life and see what you are chasing. Chasing after wealth, status, security, and a host of other things is like chasing after the wind. The wind comes and goes but we can't see it. No wonder we are tired. We are chasing after something that not only we can't see, but that which cannot be obtained.

At the end of the book of Ecclesiastes, Solomon talks about what is the real purpose of life. He has tried it all and here it is:

" ... here is the conclusion of the matter: Fear God and keep His commandments: for this is the whole duty of man" (Ecclesiastes 12:13).

When we fear God reverently, we will keep ourselves in check and not wander off to chase after worldly things that can entrap us. When we follow His commandments our lives will be a lot less stressful. The greatest two commandments are:

"'Teacher, which is the greatest commandment in the Law?' Jesus replied: 'Love the Lord your God with all your heart and all your soul and all your mind. This is the first and greatest commandment; and the second is like it: Love you neighbor as yourself'" (Matthew 22:36-39).

When we love God with all our hearts, souls, and minds then we won't have time to get caught up in acquiring things. We will be caught up in getting to know God so much better and sharing with others what is really important—how to get to Heaven.

Start today by making a note of what is bogging you down and ask the Lord to help you get rid of it. Turn things over to Jesus who created it all. He can handle it, I promise.

Have a great day and don't let anyone steal your peace.

Yank It!

I was eating a pretzel a few days ago and I heard a loud pop. I went upstairs and looked in the mirror and my back molar had split in half. I called the dentist and they rushed me in. Now I don't like going to the dentist. Have you ever taken your pet to the vet? You see dogs being dragged by their collars across the linoleum floor? That's me. Dragging the whole way to the office. My mind going out of control—doom and gloom, drills breaking apart, blood going out of control, the doctor saying, "Oh, no!" My imagination gets the best of me even before I get in the chair.

The first doctor looked at the tooth and said that if he didn't cap and crown the other two beside it, then chances were both would shatter when they got the molar out. Finally, after three hours that work was done. The next morning I went in to get the tooth pulled. They wanted to put me out, but I wanted a local and have them yank it out. "Yank", what kind of a word is that? But it was appropriate and yank he did. Because it was a back molar and dead, it had to come out in three pieces. It reminded me of an old *Three Stooges* episode. Yank, yank, yank, yank, and yank. Finally it was done. Then I had to go back to another dentist and get more work done on the middle tooth. He said, "Hey, you're still numb; let's do more work!" Needless to say, I'm glad it's over.

Yesterday morning before I went in, I was trying to find a Scripture passage to calm my nerves. I wish I could be as attuned to Scripture all the time as I was before my ordeal. In the whole scheme of things—kids with cancer and other horrible things going on in the world, this was a very minor thing; but it definitely got my attention. I asked God to give me peace and a passage. I turned to the Twenty-third Psalm and read something differently than I had ever read it before.

In Psalm 23, something jumped out at me and it was these phrases:

Verse 2   He makes me
            He leads me
Verse 3   He restores me
            He guides me

No matter where we are in our lives, at times God gets our attention to slow down. "He makes me lie down." He makes me slow down, whether I want to or not. It is for my own good. When I can't find my way, He leads me out of the darkness and into the light. Most of the time I have no clue where I'm going. We all like to think we do, but our paths are clearly directed by the Lord. When I'm down and out and frightened God restores my soul and lifts me up, then He guides me to safety.

I am very fortunate to have a godly wife who prays for me. Her prayers also calmed my nerves so when I went into that doctor's office I was ready to say, "Yank it." There may be something in your life right now that you are afraid to tell God to handle. It may be a bad relationship, unresolved conflict, maybe a deal gone bad, or you need to make amends. Once you get to the point where you allow God the freedom to do anything in your life, then you will have the peace that you have been searching for. Pain is part of this life, but we can use that pain to see the power of Jesus at work in our lives.

The Frog in the Kettle

Our government is now debating the marriage amendment. When you get right down to it, we are fighting the corruption of America. The "Frog in The Kettle Syndrome" is this: You place a frog in boiling water and the frog will jump out; if you place a frog in cold water and heat it to boiling, the frog becomes comfortable to the gradual change and doesn't realize he is being cooked until it is too late. This is where we are now in our society. If we were to go back to 1960 and turn the television programs on that we have today, people would be sickened and appalled. Back in 1960, married people on TV weren't even shown sleeping in the same bed.

Now we are talking about allowing same-sex marriages. Before I go any further, let me tell you this. As far as sin goes, I was one of the worst. I lived a very immoral lifestyle for many years and did pretty much as I pleased. It wasn't until Jesus saved me at the age of thirty-eight that my heart was changed and I saw clearly the destructive course of my life. My conversion by the grace of God was very dramatic. It was black and white to me on what I needed to do with my life. The key point was that I couldn't have made those changes without Jesus.

The marriage amendment won't work as long we live in a sinful world. I don't have anger toward homosexuals. I have compassion. Why? Because sin is sin and we are all sinners.

". . . for all have sinned and fall short of the glory of God" (Romans 3:23).

This doesn't say some people sin; it says *all* of us have. Jesus saved me when I was deep in my sin and I didn't deserve to be saved. It was by His grace. If I then judge and don't forgive, then why should God forgive me?

"But if you do not forgive men their sins, your Father will not forgive your sins" (Matthew 6:15).

Homosexuality is a sin, but so are adultery, arrogance, and pride. We don't need more laws, we need our hearts changed by Jesus. That is the only hope for our country and the world. We have turned our backs on Jesus and what do we expect?

"If my people, who are called by My name, will humble themselves and pray and seek My face and turn from their wicked ways, then will I hear from Heaven and will forgive their sin and will heal their land" (2 Chronicles 7:14).

Most of this generation is arrogant and prideful. Arrogance and pride are catalysts for wicked, sinful behavior. When we think we are bigger than God, look out! We are called to not only humble ourselves, but we are called to pray and earnestly seek the Lord. Find Him, by praying and asking for His help and forgiveness not only for others, but, more importantly, for ourselves. After we have humbled ourselves and pray and seek God, then we are to turn from our wicked ways. Many times when we have done something wrong, we feel guilty, we ask forgiveness and then go on doing the same thing again.

God will not stand for this.

After we have turned from our wicked ways, then and only then will God hear from Heaven and heal our land. We thought we were safe in America. The events of September 11, 2001, have shown us that evil is everywhere. Our land will not be healed until we turn from our wicked ways. We have so much prosperity in America that sometimes we think we were smart enough to earn what we have.

We only have what we have because God has allowed it.

It can go away from us just as fast as it came. I'm not saying September 11 was a glimpse of judgment on America. But as you can see, there is no place safe except in the arms of Jesus. Do you know Jesus? Have you asked Him to come into your life, acknowledged who He is, and asked Him to forgive your sins? If you have done this, then you are a child of God and that can never be taken away. If you haven't made that decision and you were to die today then it would be too late. You would spend eternity in hell. Going to church each Sunday, putting money in the offering plate, being kind to others, and doing the best you can will not get you into Heaven.

"For it is by grace you have been saved, through faith, and this not from yourselves, it is the gift of God, not by works, so that no one can boast" (Ephesians 2:8,9).

Going to church, giving money, and being kind are all works. We should do these things out of thankfulness for what Jesus has done for us—not to get into Heaven.

It is only by God's grace that our land will be healed. Let us all pray for a heart change. Please pray that many would come to know Jesus. We can't change people's minds, only Jesus can. Let us become a prayerful people who seek God in everything we do.

Afraid

The Dictionary defines "afraid" as "frightened or apprehensive about something."

I don't like spiders, especially big ones. There are a lot of other things I don't like but, hey, that's me. One night while we were living in Phoenix, I went out to the back porch. On the wall was the biggest black wolf spider I have ever seen. I did what any other mature man would do—I called my wife Julie. Actually, I screamed for her. "You won't believe what's outside," as I handed her a can of Raid and a flamethrower. "There is the biggest spider out there and you are going to have to kill it." Not only did I send her out, but I closed the sliding glass door behind her. Now that is something to be proud of!

What makes us afraid? There is fear of failure, being made fun of, fear of rejection, fear of heights, and fear of death. Subconsciously, a lot of us are afraid to die. We are afraid because the unknown can make anyone a little apprehensive.

Jesus says, "I tell you, my friends, do not be afraid of those who kill the body and after that can do no more. But I will show you whom you should fear. Fear Him who after the killing of the body has power to throw you into hell. Yes, I tell you, fear Him" (Luke 12:4,5).

We can be afraid of a lot of things, but sitting in a hospital in a white gown, waiting for the doctor's results can put fear into anyone. What will the results be? Am I going to die? Not to minimize death, but we are all going to die a physical death.

The saying is, "We aren't going to get out of here alive." At a young age I watched my dad, and my security, die. I became afraid of death. Now that I am saved, I know that the death of my body is just the beginning of what I am really here for. We are here on Earth for two things. The first is to come to know Jesus as Savior and Lord of our lives, and the second is to tell as many people about Jesus as possible. Nothing else will matter or last.

So don't be afraid of the lab results, the horrible boss, the bad neighbor, or spiders, but be afraid of the one who can send us to hell. Jesus has that power. If we have not made a decision to accept Him, have not asked Him for forgiveness, not acknowledged who He is, and what He did on the

Cross, then we have no hope of Heaven. Then we are to be afraid—afraid to the point of death. Remember that being kind to others, going to church each Sunday, being baptized, confirmed, putting money in the offering plate will not get you into Heaven. If works could do it, then Jesus died for nothing.

Make sure today that you have made that decision. This may be the day that Jesus calls you and this is an appointment you want to be ready for.

"Believe in the Lord Jesus and you will be saved ... " (Acts 16:31).

When we can put the fear of death out of our minds, we will all be free to live a life that is worth living. Why? Because there is no end—eternal life starts the minute you make that decision and confess that Jesus is Lord. Don't procrastinate about this one.

Afraid? Bring it on!

Did Jesus Give His Parents Fits?

I thought that would grab your attention. When Jesus was twelve years old, his parents took Him to the temple in Jerusalem for the Feast of the Passover.

"After the feast was over, while his parents were returning home, the boy Jesus stayed behind in Jerusalem, but they were unaware of it" (Luke 2:43).

Verse 44: *"Thinking he was in their company they traveled on for a day. Then they began to look for Him among their relatives and friends. When they did not find Him, they went back to Jerusalem to look for Him. After three days they found Him in the temple courts, sitting among the teachers, listening and asking them questions."*

Verse 48: *When his parents saw Him, they were astonished. His mother said to Him, "Son, why have you treated us like this? Your father and I have been anxiously searching for you."*

Jesus did not sin—He led a sinless life, but that doesn't include Mary and Joseph. Jesus came to earth 100 percent man and 100 percent God, so that by His death and resurrection whoever believes in Him will inherit eternal life. One of the great things about God sending Jesus to Earth was that He got to feel the pain of loneliness, pain of rejection, pain of the death of loved ones, and, yes, His parents' worry.

I like verse 48 when His parents said, "Why have you treated us like this?" They couldn't find Him for three days. What was going through their minds? Have you ever been in a mall and lost your child for a second? All of a sudden you have an inexpressible horror that fills your soul. All you want to do is find that child, and then when you do, you want to take a switch to them. I think if Jesus's parents had had a switch, they may have been inclined to hit and ask questions later. Joseph and Mary weren't 100 percent—or even 1 percent—God. They were 100 percent man and woman.

Jesus got to see the pain and fear in their eyes. Julie and I were at the Baltimore Airport a few years ago, and the kids were playing in a little recreation area. We turned our backs for only a few seconds and our youngest was gone. We went running over and couldn't find him. Could someone have taken him that quickly and put him on a plane? Would we never see him again? All of a sudden a man called out, "Hey, are you looking for a little boy? He has climbed up here." There was an observation tower that had a staircase and he had gone up there. First, we were elated and then we were ready to get the switch out.

Two thousand years ago, Jesus' parents went through what you and I go through. Jesus knows first hand what your heart is feeling. Fortunately for us we have a compassionate God who knows everything. Our God is a God of mercy who understands our pain. Nothing is too small for Jesus.

Each of us has something going on in our lives. Make this the day you start trusting and knowing that Jesus cares about you and your circumstances. Call upon Him to help straighten out the mess, the clutter, and the worries of this life and lead you down a path that is pure and righteous.

I gave my mom fits and even enjoyed it at times. Now I guess it's my turn!

The Trap

This past week we have been having a huge squirrel problem. I think I have gotten rid of most of the culprits, but I still have left the trap out. The trap is steel with a door on each side and a place for food in the middle. Once the varmint gets in and starts eating, it sets off the trap door and slam! they're caught. I put peanut butter in the trap, as that is what was recommended, plus they have to really lick the trigger to get it off. The first squirrel walked in, licked all the peanut butter off and waddled off into the woods. Seems I don't know how to set the trap. I went through a half a jar of peanut butter before I caught one. It pays to read the instructions first.

Yesterday morning Julie woke me up and said, "Brad, there's something big in the trap. I don't think it's a squirrel." I ran down to look at my prize and there was the ugliest possum you can imagine in the cage. Since they weren't the ones eating my roof, I just let him go. I started out the door and I could hear Julie say, "I have to see this." Yea, me too! I opened up the doors of the cage very carefully, because possums are mean. The doors were open and he still didn't want to get out. He had been trained to be trapped and he wasn't moving. I looked at Julie and she was giving me the motion from inside the house to poke it and get it out. Easy for her to say, "Poke it." Well, I poked it and ran and he ran too—back into the woods.

What struck me as unusual was that this possum had given up on escape. He had tried all evening to get out and couldn't so he quit even when the doors had been opened up. Some of us may be caught in sin right now and we have given up. We have tried to get out of it, but can't. This possum couldn't get out; he needed something from the outside to let him go. No matter how much discipline we have, there is a sin that so easily entangles us, traps us, and takes our hope away. Outside this world, there is one person who can defeat the devil and that is Jesus. You and I cannot defeat the devil, but with the power of the Holy Spirit, we can.

"That they may come to their senses and escape from the trap of the devil, who has taken them captive to do his will" (2 Timothy 2:26).

It took me many tries to catch that animal, just as it sometimes takes many tries for the devil to trip us up. He is sly and the sin looks so appetizing, until the doors shut and there is no way out.

Maybe your sin is an immoral lifestyle, anger, greed, or jealousy. These sins will trap you and keep you hostage so that you can never lead the life that Jesus has promised. Make today the day that you turn to Jesus, ask Him to forgive your sins, trust in Him, and ask Him to help you in all the areas of your life. Even if you have an open door to get out, some of us still stay in sin. We need Jesus to lead us out.

What may look appetizing may have a few trap doors attached to it. Be very careful how you lead your life. Pray for the Lord's protection and guidance to see clearly in a world full of trouble.

Trust in Jesus and Jesus alone.

Are You in the Furnace?

Nebuchadnezzar was King when Daniel and his friends Shadrach, Meshach and Abednego were taken from Israel to Babylonia.

"King Nebuchadnezzar made an image of gold, ninety feet high and nine feet wide...." (Daniel 3:1).

Now that is a large and very expensive image. There was a command sent out that when the sound of the horn, flute, and all kinds of music started playing, everyone was to fall down and worship the image. Verse 6 says that "Whoever does not fall down and worship will immediately be thrown into a blazing furnace."

Shadrach, Meshach, and Abednego were true to God and would never bow down to any god other than the true God. When Nebuchadnezzar found out, he was furious. But these three came back with the following statement to the King:

" ... O, Nebuchadnezzar, we do not need to defend ourselves before you in this matter. If we are thrown into the blazing furnace, the God we serve is able to save us from it, and He will rescue us from your hand, O king. But even if He does not, we want you to know, O king, that we will

not serve your gods or worship the image of gold you have set up " (Daniel 3:16-18).

Nebuchadnezzar was so furious that he threw them into a furnace which was heated seven times hotter than normal. The guards who threw them in were killed by the heat. Nebuchadnezzar saw four men in the fire, stood up to look, and called for them to come out.

" ... They saw that the fire had not harmed their bodies, nor was a hair of their heads singed; their robes were not scorched and there was no smell of fire on them " (Daniel 3:27).

The angel of the Lord protected them. He was the fourth person. As was said in verse 18, "But even if He does not" is a very important statement. We could all say, "I know God will deliver me from this cancer, broken marriage, being fired, being broke, but if He does not that won't stop me from trusting in Him." Easy to say, tough to do.

When the fire is raging in your life, are you able to hold onto the truth? The more we train our minds by being in God's Word, praying and worshiping Him, the easier it is to trust. If the only time we talk to God is on Sunday, then when a trial comes it is certainly more difficult to feel peace in your spirit.

Today someone is watching you under pressure. It may be your boss, co-worker, best friend, or worst enemy. King Nebuchadnezzar then believed in God. Amen. But if the men had said, "this is not worth it," what testimony would that have been to Nebuchadnezzar? In the same sense, when someone throws barbs at you or tries to hurt your reputation remember, that the battle is the Lord's and He can overcome anything much more dramatically than we could ever do.

The next time you are threatened with a fiery furnace, will you be a willing servant or one who runs the other way? If you have accepted Jesus into your life, then nothing of this world can harm you, not even death. We are here to share the gospel with as many people as possible after we have made the decision ourselves. Pray that you would be that person God uses to being others to Him. What an awesome honor that is.

31

Hope

"Those who hope in the Lord will renew their strength. They will soar on wings like eagles, they will run and not grow weary, they will walk and not grow faint" (Isaiah 40:31).

I know of a man who lost his wife in childbirth seventeen years ago, now has lost that seventeen-year-old son in a car accident. Cancer, failed memories, failed marriages, being fired, and terminal illnesses can break us down and leave us drained.

Life is full of twists and turns. When you think you have it figured, you get blindsided by something that you never expected. You see, the answer to this world's problems is one thing, but God wants us to have our hope in Him, not in our circumstances.

Let's take a look at hope in:

Family: While it is great to have a family, we are still all sinners. You will be let down by family members, no matter how good their intentions. We will also die a bodily death. Our family can't be with us forever unless they are believers, so don't put you hope there.

Job: While you may have security in your job and money in the bank, it can all be gone in an instant. You may say, "No way," but I have seen it. Riches are fleeting and you are only as good as your last deal.

Christ: Never changing, always there, and He knows the future. He is the only one who can protect, sustain and deliver us from harm and death.

Remember this: None of us will die!

The shell we are living in will waste away at some point either by disease or an accident, but you and I will live forever. The question is, what will your address be?

If you have acknowledged that Jesus died on the Cross and rose from the dead to pay the penalty for your sins and you have asked Him into your life to take control, then you will go to Heaven.

If you have gone to church each Sunday, have been baptized, given money to the poor and to the church, are a great parent, but have not accepted Jesus into your life then your final address will be hell. Eternity in hell; forever separated from God.

Life will always throw you a curve, but when your faith is in Jesus you can have the ultimate hope. Start today by putting all your hope in Jesus. Still love your family, job, hobbies and co-workers, but that is not where your hope is to be.

Each day our strength will be renewed when our hope is in Jesus. Soaring like an eagle is effortless. It just glides in the wind. Let God take you where He wants to take you, don't fight it. If you allow God to take you, you will not grow weary, and you will not grow faint. When you work against God by living in your own strength, you will always be weary.

Renew your strength today by recommitting your life to the Lord. Allow Him to come in and take control. Since God created the Universe and everything in it, shouldn't we at least give the Lord a chance in our lives?

Teamwork

"The Lord said, 'If as one people speaking the same language they have begun to do this, then nothing they plan to do will be impossible for them'" (Genesis 11:6).

"Nothing they plan to do will be impossible" when people of like mind attempt something. This verse comes from the Lord when the men of that age were building the Tower of Babel. Of course, the men were building the tower for the wrong reasons. They wanted to build a tower that reached to the heavens and to make a name for themselves. God doesn't want arrogance.

You see, their plan was great, but their motives were not. How many times in any family or organization do we start off down a road before asking the Lord which direction to go? "Okay, let's send Johnny to Yale Law School," only to find out years later Johnny wanted to be a veterinarian. "Let's get a job where we can make a lot of money so we can give it to the Lord." This is a very popular phrase in today's culture. You see God doesn't need our money to get things done. Giving the Lord our money should be out of thanks for the abilities that He has given us. It's like saying, "When I win the lottery I'm going to build grandma a new house, buy you a new car," and on and on. Most people who win the lottery forget all those commitments, spend it all, and end up worse than they were before.

Don't do things for money; do things because it's right.

If you do what the Lord wants you to do then He will make sure you are taken care of. If you do things for money, it will never be enough.

As for teamwork: In our society it's all about me, me, and me. It is very difficult to have someone give it up for the team. Look at the United Sates basketball team in the Olympics. They had more talent than anyone, but why did they have such a tough time? Because they were *individuals* used to getting the attention. Attention on oneself will not create teamwork. Teamwork means that you need to put the team first, not yourself. Are you willing to do that?

The only way we can become a team is to let the Lord be in control. Once we are able to get rid of self, then God has the freedom to work in our lives. Once He has the freedom to work then He has the freedom to create a great team. The disciples made a great team. Jesus didn't pick the best of the best. He picked the worst of the worst. They certainly didn't know anything about teamwork or time management, but when they caught the vision of Jesus and the resurrection, all that changed. They got rid of self and lived their life for a common purpose and achieved uncommon results.

In your family or business you look to your president as the leader. Let's say you don't view him or her as a leader, but that isn't important. God has put them there.

It is our duty to pray for them and do what they ask of us. Do those things that are morally and ethically right. Don't follow anyone that doesn't follow these parameters. Remember none of us is perfect so quit expecting anyone to be perfect. Teamwork is not one person but a group of people "speaking the same language." Speaking the same language means going after the same goal. Your organization should have a goal and each one should do whatever they can do to make the team strong. The team is only as strong as the weakest link. Instead of ridiculing the weakest link, why don't we all try to encourage the weakest link? We may all be surprised what takes place.

Jesus could have done this alone, but He chose twelve to help Him change the world. Miracles can happen when we put the Lord and the team first. Why don't you give it a chance?

This Ship Is Sinking

Those would be the words I would hear on my first cruise, or maybe "Man Overboard!" I have a unique ability to think of disastrous things that can happen at a moment's notice. Bungee jumping? No, the cord might break and then my neck. Skydive? No, either the chute wouldn't open or the plane would crash on takeoff. Let's go whitewater rafting? Last time I tried that I got held under by a double hydraulic and then was spit out like a seed. No thanks. Hey, what about a roller coaster? Didn't someone get their arm cut off on a ride a couple weeks ago? Let's just go fishing? Last time I did that my friend was fly-casting and caught me in the cheek with a beautiful fly. Yellow and black it was. Saved my cheek, but not the fly.

It's dangerous out there!

I'm not as bad as I used to be in thinking bad thoughts, but I still have a long way to go. You see, a lot of weird, and I mean weird, things have happened to me. Instead of forgetting and moving on, I remember and step back. All right, run back.

I was having one of those bad weeks where all you do is fret. Ever been there? This is what happened in a seven-day period of time.

First—I was living in Phoenix at the time and on my way to work I stopped at a Dunkin' Donut drive through. I said to the woman at the window, "I'll have three cake donuts and a cup of coffee". She started mumbling something that I couldn't hear. I thought she may be able to hear me if she opened that window. It was early, I hadn't had my coffee, and I was getting annoyed. Okay, I was annoyed. Again, cake donuts and coffee, again I hear her mumbling through the glass. I thought, "I'm going to have to stick my head through her window and let everyone know inside the restaurant what I want," and of course I did. I leaned forward to tell her what I thought and smack! She had not forgotten to pull her window open, I forgot to roll down *my* window. I hit my head on my window so hard I saw stars. She started laughing and I can't tell you how embarrassed I was. I finally got my three cake donuts, my coffee, and drove sheepishly away with her still laughing.

Second—I drive up to a McDonald's and tell the box I would like a hamburger, fries, and a large Coke. She said, "That will be $2.75; please pull around to the first window." I pulled around to the first window and paid my money. I was driving down the road and made a sharp turn to avoid a car and also put my hand over to hold the Coke so it wouldn't spill. The only problem was there was no Coke. There wasn't a hamburger and fries either. Apparently, I paid my money and just kept on driving past the window with that person holding food for me. I did go back, and again, instead of one person, there were four people laughing, waiting for the man to come back and get his food.

Third—I needed gas. The pump wouldn't take a credit card so I had to go in and pay cash. Paid five dollars and while I was driving down the road I looked at the gas gauge and thought to myself, "That didn't put much gas in." It would have if I had pumped the gas. I paid, got in my car and drove off without pumping the gas. Again I drive back, the guy smiled; apparently more people do this than at Dunkin' Donuts and McDonald's.

Where was my head, what was I thinking? We have all been to that place where we think we cannot take another step, where we think we cannot go on, where we think we cannot handle it any more. You may be there right now.

When we attempt things in our own strength, we will never succeed in the long haul. We will burn out and not be good to anyone. A couple weeks ago I was fretting about a number of issues. The reason I was fretting about them is that I wasn't praying about those issues. I was trying to handle them in my own strength and not the Lord's. The day I started praying about what decisions to make, not only did things work out, but I had a peace that I hadn't had in weeks.

Why did I wait so long?

Many times we find comfort in trials and pain because that is all we know. Most of us don't go to the dentist till the pain of the tooth is much worse than the fear of the dentist. But by that time so much damage might have been done, that it costs ten times as much than if you went in for a normal checkup.

Do you feel like your ship is sinking? Is the water coming in faster than you are bailing it out? Chances are you are trusting in your own craftiness to get out of this ordeal instead of praying and asking God for help. God loves to help us if we only ask.

"Ask and it will be given to you, seek and you will find; knock and the door will be opened to you. For everyone who asks receives; he who seeks finds, and to him who knocks, the door will be opened" (Matthew 7:7, 8).

If you are troubled, burdened, without hope, and in pain, ask the Lord to keep you from sinking. Ask Him to lift you up on dry land so you will not slip into the chaos that this life brings. We have not defeated satan, but He who lives within us has. Start today by turning your power over to Jesus and let Him reign in your life. Why not let the one who knows the outcome before it even happens, help you in all the decisions you make?

Remember also, if you pay for something make sure you at least pick it up!!!

Think Before You Press "Send"

The tongue can be a wicked thing; also email for that matter. In the Book of James the tongue is analogous to the rudder of a large ship. Let's take for example the "Norwegian Crown," a very, very large cruise ship. This ship is over 600 feet long, more than two football fields, but is steered by a rudder in the back. This rudder in relation to the size of the ship is very small, but the rudder turns the ship wherever it likes. So does our tongue.

"Or take ships as an example. Although they are very large and are driven by strong winds, they are steered by a very small rudder wherever the pilot wants to go" (James 3:3,4).

Where do you want to go? Do you harbor resentment or pride and want to spew out all kinds of evil things? On the other hand, are you and the Holy Spirit working together to encourage others instead of tearing them down? Remember this: We will never tame our tongues.

" ... *but no man can tame the tongue. It is evil, full of deadly poison....* " (James 3:8).

So there is no hope, right? Wrong! Since we can't tame our tongue we need to safeguard against letting out evil from our lips. A lion looks calm in a zoo, but that is because he is locked behind a fence. Let him out and then look out!

I don't like email for discussing important issues. The main reason is that we don't see how the other person is reacting. Sometimes we take an email the wrong way and fire back a volley that we regret. Once the email is sent, it can never be taken back. It's like trying to put toothpaste back in the tube.

" ... *For out of the overflow of his heart, his mouth speaks....* " (Luke 6:45).

Have you ever been with a calm, cool, collected person and someone cuts them off in traffic? All of a sudden there is a loud outburst and they turn into someone you never knew. This isn't because they are mad at the driver who just did that dastardly act! They have anger and rage in their heart that is going to come out sometime and this was the catalyst for it. An email that may seem caustic is sent back with hurtful words because someone has anger and just found a reason to spew. Have you ever read an email and said, "Where did that come from?"

Words cannot only be hurtful, but life lasting. I remember hurtful words said to me over forty years ago. Romans 3:23 says that we are all sinners and will continue to be until Jesus calls us home. The key is to keep damage control to a minimum. The only way to do that is to change our hearts. We do that by:

1. Confessing our sin and asking God for forgiveness.
2. Reading God's Word.
3. Fellowshipping with other believers.
4. Worshipping.

5. Asking God to help us because we can't hold our tongues on our own.

The next time you get ready to say something strong or send an email that may be of a caustic nature, just wait! First pray, not a rote prayer, but pray that the Lord would search your heart and, then and only then, send the email or speak. Most conflict would not happen if were to pray for the Lord's guidance and then talk.

When you can lead a spirit-filled life, you will never have to look over your shoulder and never have regrets. Remember; think before you press "Send"!

Drifting Away

In the spring of 1992, I was to attempt a Half Ironman in Panama City, Florida. The Half Ironman consists of a 1.5-mile ocean swim, a 56-mile bike ride, and then a 13.1-mile run. I know, what was I thinking? The morning of the race, instead of a calm ocean, the waves were breaking hard against the beach. The swim course was marked with buoys that were anchored by heavy blocks. The course was to swim out 1,000 yards, make a right turn past a sailboat that was anchored, make a right turn, swim for 200 yards, and then swim another 1,000 yards back to shore. I was in about the fifth wave to start out. The current was so strong that the buoys were moving off course and the water was so murky that the frogmen were called in to shore. Also the sailboat parked out in the ocean 1,000 yards had to be brought in. This should have sent off an alarm in my mind, but like sheep going to slaughter I followed everyone else in.

The swells were so high that when you were in the bottom of one, you couldn't tell where you were. Everyone in the fifth wave was wearing bright green caps, so we could be recognized by the support people and helicopters, if needed. The first 1,000 yards were great, I made the turn, swam 200 yards and started back in, sighting a pier that we had started from. About five minutes later I looked around and instead of seeing about fifty other green caps, I didn't see *any* green caps. Also, the pier that had been straight ahead was way off to my left. So I did what any elite tri-athlete would do, I started doggy paddling. Where am I? All I could picture was "Jaws" coming out of the water at any time. In my wetsuit I probably looked like a tasty seal. All I could do was keep swimming, so that is what I did. Instead of being in the water for thirty minutes, I was in the water now for fifty-five minutes.

As I got closer to shore I could feel the current trying to pull my legs down. Finally, I came out of the water. I was so far off course that there were families sunbathing where I came out. I actually didn't know which way to run to get my bike. To tell you the truth, I would have been happy at that point to go back to the hotel. After kissing the sand and being thankful for getting on dry land I got on my bike, rode the fifty-six miles and then started the run. Five miles into the run I started seeing three of everyone. I saw a man watering his lawn, so I sat down and said, "I can't believe I paid to do this." The race staff came and got me and took me to my hotel. I came up eight miles short and didn't finish. Hey, I was lucky to be alive!

That day, the professional swimmers started first and when they saw the conditions of the sea they came right back in and never did finish the swim. There were over twenty-five amateurs that had to be pulled to safety that day because of a huge riptide. Riptide, what was that? Up until this ocean swim, I had been practicing in a pool in Pennsylvania. On the way back in, I had gotten to the farthest point on the course and that is when the riptide caught me. If I had been close to shore I would have seen immediately what was going on. I was so far out that I couldn't tell I was drifting and I didn't know which way to go.

Our Christian walk is the same way. Not reading God's Word, not praying, or not going to church starts us drifting away. Satan is the riptide which takes us away into the things of this world.

" ... *let us throw off everything that hinders and the sin that so easily entangles, and let us run with perseverance the race marked out for us. Let us fix our eyes on Jesus, the author and perfecter of our faith....* " (Hebrews 12:1,2).

You see, the race of life is marked out for us just as that swim course was marked that day. That race was a perfect metaphor for life. Hardly anything ever goes as planned. We constantly need to make mid-course corrections. A riptide (death of a loved one, divorce, health problems) sometimes forces us off course. If I had focused on that pier, I would have known where I was. I didn't trust what I was seeing that day. If I had checked before the race,

I would have known there was only one pier. That would have led me to safety. There is only one Jesus who can lead us out of eternity in hell and give us eternity in Heaven when we trust in Him and Him alone.

This life will throw you off course. The closer you are to Jesus when you are thrown off course, the quicker you will realize it. Don't let the sin of this world let you drift off. Jesus never loses sight of you but there are many times we lose sight of Jesus.

If you are drifting away because the things of the world are more important to you than staying close to Jesus, then stop. You are in a riptide that will take you to places that are full of trouble. Stay close to the one who can protect, sustain, and restore you to the life you were called to live.

Stay close to the Lord, don't drift, and you will have tremendous peace that only Jesus can give.

Jealousy

The dictionary describes "jealous" as: Envious; feeling bitter and unhappy because of another's advantages, possessions, or luck.

Not being content with our own lives can lead to feelings of jealousy. We look at our own lives when we aren't content and then start wishing we had what others had.

"Anger is cruel and fury overwhelming, but who can stand before jealousy?" (Proverbs 27:4).

Anger and fury are no match for jealousy. Jealousy can eat away at your inmost being. It can consume your every thought and make you a bitter person. In this life at one time or another we all experience the sin of jealousy.

We may want:

The job someone else has.

The house someone else has.

The money someone else has.

The wife or husband someone else has.

41

The constant in this is, "What someone else has."

Let me get back to the definition: "Feeling bitter and unhappy because of another's advantage, possessions, or luck." You may say, "I wish I had the money Bill Gates has;" "I wish I won the lottery like ____ did;" "I wish I ...." So how do we get off this treadmill of envy? Let me give you a true scenario.

Let's say someone is worth $30 billion.

Let's say another person has a beautiful home and three cars.

Let's say another person has a beautiful wife and children.

For the sake of discussion, let's say the only thing you have is your salvation. This means that you have asked Jesus into your life, acknowledged who He is and what He has done, and have turned your life over to Him.

In this life it may seem like you don't have many wordly goods, but let me show you where we will all be going.

The minute we take our last breath, we will all stand before God. It won't matter if we had five cars or just a bicycle. It won't matter if we were the president of the largest company in America or the janitor. It won't matter if we had ten children or we didn't have any, and it won't matter what we had in our bank account.

The key word in this is "had!"

I like what someone once said: "You have never seen a U-Haul behind a hearse." Whoever you think is the most important person in the world now, or who you may be jealous of will not matter. Why? Because all of us will be standing before God with nothing. The only thing that will matter after our life here on Earth is: Are you saved by Jesus Christ? If you aren't and you want to make that decision when you see God, it will be too late.

Instead of being jealous of other people, feel sorrow and compassion for those who seem to have everything worldly, but don't know Jesus. Can you put aside your agenda, and your pride to look at people a different way? Can you stop trying to be a big shot or trying to hang out with one? A big shot is someone who thinks they or other people are more important than Jesus. Yikes, that's frightening.

Having things does not make people happy. It just prolongs the inevitable. Without Jesus life will be miserable.

Start today by looking at others with compassion no matter how good they have it and how bad you think you have it. Don't get excited about hanging out or trying to feel important by knowing important people. Get to know the one who created people, and that is Jesus.

When our view of Jesus becomes more important than things, we will feel like a huge burden is lifted. Think about the eternal instead of the temporal. Ask Jesus today to help you in this matter of jealousy. Jesus can and will forgive and help you change your heart when you come to Him with a repentant spirit.

Live this life as if it were yourr last day on Earth. Make the most of every opportunity for the Lord.

Don't worry; Jesus is on your side. What more could you want?

He Won't Remember It

When our first boy was born, the doctor said that he would wait a week and then do the circumcision instead of doing it in the hospital. The day arrived and I took Bryce, now seven days old, to the doctor. Our time came and we walked back to a room (which was soundproofed). That should have told me something. The doctor came in with what looked like a little board with Velcro straps on it. The doctor said it wouldn't take long and then proceeded to tie Bryce's hands and then legs down so he couldn't move. It looked like a modern day crucifixion. The doctor had a couple of instruments that didn't look too friendly. He took one instrument and started shearing back the skin in a very sensitive area. Bryce started screaming at this point. After that was done, the doctor took out a pair of sharp scissors and started cutting skin. I will never forget the scream that Bryce let out. It was just awful. I told the doctor, "This is hurting him." The doctor said, "He won't remember it," and I said, "Well, he remembers it *now*!" What an ordeal!

The Bible talks about circumcision of the heart. I now understand. Our heart, in theory, is made up of many different layers. We have layers of pride, resentment, hurt, selfishness, and a host of other issues.

" ... *Circumcision is circumcision of the heart by the spirit*" (Romans 2:29).

As in real circumcision, the Lord at times will painfully peel back the layers of one's heart so we can see Jesus and see ourselves more clearly. The process can take months or a lifetime, but we are all in process. Are you willing to be strapped to a board being helpless and let God work in your life? In other words, are you willing to let God be in total control? Or are you only willing to let God work on you until the pain is too bad and then you run off? How long will the pain of the heart's circumcision last?

"... He who began a good work in you will carry it on to completion until the day of Jesus Christ" (Philippians 1:6).

This means that the Lord will never give up on us. No matter how painful a trial may seem, the Lord is using it to strip away the layers of our heart so we can see Jesus more clearly. When we see Jesus more clearly the things of this world will not seem that important and we will view the things of Jesus as a priority. The things of Jesus are sharing the gospel with others, being kind and not evil, being a servant instead of wanting to be served, being meek in the sprit of God, not prideful. Jesus is the only one who can save us from an eternity in hell. Are you trusting in Him or are you trusting in you?

There are seasons of trials and there are seasons of triumph. Pray that the Lord will help you to see this as one season where you have joy no matter what the circumstances are around you. In order to do this we need to get to know Jesus. Jesus could have gotten down from the Cross and destroyed everyone in this world. Why take the shame? Why take the punishment? He did that so that you and I could have eternal life and forgiveness of sins. Let's try to be men and women who would put our lives out there for Jesus. Let us give up control and let God take over. Are you ready to start that journey today? Once you do, your life will take an incredible turn.

Have a great day and keep praying.

Is Death All That Bad?

It depends if you are the one in pain or the one offering comfort. In this life, unless Jesus comes back for us, we will all have to go through this event. When you are at the end and no one can help you anymore, then you are finally alone. No Earthly one to help, that is! If you know Jesus as your Savior, you have hope. If you do not, then the gates of hell are ready. What a horrible thought that is.

"Why all this commotion and wailing? The child is not dead but asleep" (Mark 5:39).

In the verses before this statement, Jairus, a synagogue ruler, came to Jesus pleading for Him to come put His hands on his daughter and heal her. Jairus's little girl was dying. Jesus went to Jairus's house, and on the way, a woman who had been bleeding for twelve years wanted to see Jesus. She thought, "If I just touch His cloak, I will be healed." When she did touch His cloak, Jesus felt power leaving from Him. Jesus turned around and said, "Who touched me?" The woman came forward and fell at the feet of Jesus and told Him the whole truth." Jesus said,

"Daughter your faith has healed you. Go in peace and be freed from your suffering" (Mark 5:34).

I don't know about you, but if one of my children were dying the last thing I would want was Jesus to stop and help someone else. "Jesus, I asked you first; my child is dying. If you don't get there in time she may die. Hurry, hurry, hurry." I would be pushing people out of the way. Of course, that would be me!

While Jesus was still speaking, some men from the house of Jairus came and said, "Your daughter is dead. Why bother the teacher anymore?" Instead of Jesus looking startled, He said to Jairus, "Don't be afraid, just believe."

My friend from my house just tells me my child is dead and Jesus tells me not to worry. This is tough to swallow. But when Jesus got to the house, His first words were,

"Why all this commotion and wailing? The child is not dead but asleep" (Mark 5:39).

"Brothers we do not want you to be ignorant about those who fall asleep, or to grieve like the rest of men who have no hope. We believe that Jesus died and rose again and so believe that God will bring with Jesus those who have fallen asleep in Him" (1 Thessalonians 4:13, 14).

None of our souls will die, and our souls are what make up who we are. Our outward appearance is just a tent to house our soul. Jesus saying, "Don't mourn." No! Mourning is a process to get over the loss of a loved one, but that loved one is not really dead. If your loved ones know Jesus, they are now in Heaven. Jesus is telling us it's all right to mourn, but don't freak out about death. To get to Paradise (and I don't mean Hawaii) we need to leave this Earthly body. Heaven is an awesome place, so in theory we should be joyful for those who are now with Jesus. If you don't believe that in your heart yet, then you need to get to know Jesus better.

Jesus brought the girl back from Heaven so He could show the power He has over death and I believe that He also saw the pain on the family's faces. Jesus wept when Lazarus died because he was not only a friend of Lazarus, but also a friend of the family. Grieving is part of healing, but if we were to see and experience where our loved ones were, we would be saying, "Jesus get me out of this world, I'm ready to go and be with You."

When you were in your mother's womb, if someone were to ask you, "Do you want to leave that nice warm, comfortable spot?" you would have said, "No way!" But you were born into a beautiful world with many things to experience. You don't even remember that time in the womb. So it will be in Heaven. You will see people you know who have believed. Since there is no pain, suffering, death, and sin in Heaven, most of the things you experienced on Earth will be long forgotten.

So with a strong faith, death will not be bad when you consider what death brings.

For the Christian believer, it brings you face to face with Jesus. Just think, face to face with Jesus. If you want to wail and mourn, wail and mourn for those family members and loved ones who aren't saved.

Have a great day and don't sweat this life. Jesus is walking with you every step of the way until you meet face to face in Paradise.

Do You Worry About
What People Think of You?

It is human nature to want to be liked by others, to be in the "in crowd," to be invited to all the best functions. We all hate to be left out of the group. Where does this desire come from? I think a lot of this is our insecurity. We don't want to be left out; we don't want to be looked at as weird or not up to date on fashion and status. But what are we really insecure about? Are we insecure that people will go around the office and say, "Did you see what she or he was wearing?" "Did you see what they drove up in?" "Do you see how they think they are better than anyone else?" No matter who you are you will never have it all together.

The key issue in all of this is that you have to get to the point in your life where you are fine with saying, "Who cares?" Easy to say, tough to do.

Bartimaeus was a blind man and a beggar. You can't get much more insecure than this. Can you imagine the things said to him? "Get a job." "Quit begging." "What sin did you commit to lose your sight?"

" ... *a blind man, Bartimaeus, was sitting by the roadside begging. When he heard that it was Jesus of Nazareth, he began to shout, 'Jesus, Son of David, have mercy on me!' Many rebuked him and told him to be quiet, but he shouted all the more, 'Son of David, have mercy on me!' Jesus stopped and said, 'Call him.' So they called to the blind man, 'Cheer up! On your feet! He's calling you.' Throwing his cloak aside, he jumped to his feet and came to Jesus. 'What do you want me to do for you?' Jesus asked him. The blind man said, 'Rabbi, I want to see.' 'Go,' said Jesus, 'your faith has healed you.' Immediately he received his sight and followed Jesus along the road"* (Mark 10:46-52).

Picture this: you are sitting in darkness with people talking and saying, "Here Jesus comes." You have heard of His miracles, but do you have faith to actually call out. In darkness are you willing to even open your mouth? "What will people think, will Jesus even hear me?" All of a sudden you get the urge to yell out. "Son of David have mercy on me." I'm sure people were saying, "Shut up you beggar, don't bother Jesus. Jesus doesn't want beggars bothering him." But Bartimaeus had made up his mind that he wasn't going to listen to insults. He was focused. Many people beside him told him to be quiet, but guess what? Again Bartimaeus shouted out even louder, "Son of David, have mercy on me." Chances are Bartimaeus didn't even know in what direction to yell since he was blind. All he knew was that Jesus was near and he didn't care who else heard him. As long as Jesus heard him, that was all that mattered. Jesus stopped with a huge crowd around him, and because of Bartimaeus's faith, Jesus healed him.

You may be sitting in spiritual darkness, the darkness of depression, the darkness of guilt, or anger or the darkness of insecurity right now. No matter what others may think, are you willing to cry out to the Lord and ask Him to help you, save you, and restore you? If He doesn't answer the first time and your friends are saying, "You aren't trying to get religion are you?" are you still going to keep trying until you get an answer from Jesus? It's always easy to give up when you get the jeers of others. But, if you focus on Jesus all of that junk called insecurity, pride, and boastfulness will go by the wayside. When we are willing to be okay with who we are in Jesus, then it won't matter what people say about you.

Listen very carefully; one day we will all stand before God and the only thing that will matter is your salvation. Did you make the decision before you took your last breath on Earth to trust Jesus as Lord and Savior of your life? Did you ask Him into your life for forgiveness of your sins and acknowledge that He rose from the dead so that you could inherit eternal life? If you did, then you have no worries. Don't worry about insults from others. If you are a child of God, you now have the power through the Holy Spirit to feel compassion, yes, compassion for those who are saying awful things to you. No more feeling mad or insecure. No matter how angry you may feel against someone, it will be nothing compared to the awful feeling of knowing someone who did you wrong ending up in hell.

Can you put aside the petty differences of this world and focus on eternal life? Jesus forgave us when we were dead in our sins. How much more should we forgive those who sin against us? We can't accept the forgiveness of Jesus and then not forgive others. Make this the day that you turn all insults, persecution, troubles, and concerns over to Jesus. The evil one would like us to handle that on our own and we will always look bad if we do. Live this life in the power of the Holy Sprit and then the evil one will look bad.

If someone insults you today, remember Jesus is sitting right beside you. Are you going to trust in Him or are you going to trust in your own flesh? Pray before you strike back with any remark that is not pleasing to

Jesus and then you won't have a problem. Since you are already the child of a King, what can be better?

Angels

I love to hear stories of encounters with angels. Angels are as much in force today as they were in Old Testament times. There are different angels. The angel of the Lord named Gabriel must be an awesome figure. Most of the time when people saw Gabriel they either fainted from fear or were speechless. The angel Gabriel usually says, "Don't be afraid … " when he meets someone. Now there are other angels sent by God to Earth every day.

On August 13, 1976, I was celebrating my twenty-first birthday. I went out with a group of fraternity brothers to a bar in Youngstown, Ohio. I had to drive about sixty miles on Interstate 80 to get to this particular spot that evening. My friends told me, "Brad, drink as much as you want because we will drive you home." Sounded good to me. Well, 2:30 A.M. rolls around and I'm the only one who is even close to being able to drive. I had a van at the time and everyone piled in the back and went to sleep. I started driving back to Pennsylvania, but was in no shape to drive. I was so tried I knew that if I could just close my eyes for a few seconds I would be okay. Ever been there? All of a sudden I remember waking up facing the guardrail with the car still in drive. Now picture this: I was driving on an interstate and the smart move would have been to just pull off—which meant I would have been parallel to the guardrail, not facing it. In order to get in the position I ended up in, I would have had to back up on the interstate and to put the front of my van against the guardrail. When I woke up, I was staring straight at the guardrail. I was twenty-one at the time and it took another seventeen years until I was saved, but an angel either parked the van for me that night or lifted up the van and put it there. All I thought at the time was how odd that was. It wasn't until I became a believer and looked back over my life did I realize what happened.

"Are not all angels ministering spirits sent to serve those who will inherit salvation?" (Hebrews 1:14).

This means that those who have encounters with angels will go to Heaven. It seems that the Lord has angels to protect those who will inherit eternal life. There was a racecar driver that recently had an accident and his car caught on fire. When he got out of the fiery wreckage he said, "Who pulled me out?" His agent said that no one pulled him out of the car. This man could actually feel someone lifting him under the arms. This was no aberration; this was an encounter with an angel. If this is the case, then this man will come to know Jesus as Savior before he dies if he hasn't made that decision already.

My wife has had an encounter with an angel and so have countless other people who I have spoken with on this subject. This is not some type of hocus pocus, fortuneteller stuff. *Angels are real.* Angels are ministering spirits that either take on the form of a human or work by the spirit. They are to serve God's purposes and to serve those who will inherit salvation. Don't worry if you haven't seen one, because not everyone who inherits salvation will see an angel. But, you may have an angel protecting you until the day you finally ask the Lord into your life. If you look back on your life, you may think of an instance where the only answer had to have been the ministrations of an angel.

In this modern world today, we all want proof. We want to see it on paper, we want to see it on video, and we want to have other people see it for us just to make sure. The luxuries of this life have sometimes clouded our judgment of godly things. Like doubting Thomas, we say, "Show me proof; I want to see your nail-scarred hands!" Jesus showed Thomas His nail-scarred hands when He could have said to him, "Either you believe or you don't." But Jesus said, "Because you have seen Me, you have believed, blessed are those who have not seen and yet have believed" (John 20:29).

Can you believe in Jesus and His angels without touching His nail-scarred hands? Jesus is creating miracles in your life everyday if you would just slow down long enough to reflect.

" ... *and besides all this, between us and you a great chasm has been fixed, so that those who want to go from here to you cannot, nor can anyone cross over form there to us"* (Luke 16:26).

This verse talks about Heaven and hell. Fortunetellers and psychics would like us to believe that we can still talk to loved ones in Heaven. No we can't, but if our loved ones are saved, the minute we take our last breath on Earth we will be able to talk with them again.

This message was on angels, but as strong as angels are there are also demons in this world. Just know, "He that is in you is greater than he who is in the world." We cannot go this life alone. We need Jesus and He will use whatever measure appropriate to protect you, sustain you, and lead you to a saving knowledge of Him.

"Do not forget to entertain strangers, for by so doing some people have entertained angels without knowing it" (Hebrews 13:2).

Have an awesome day.

What Could Have Been

I had a 6:00 A.M. flight yesterday from Washington, DC, back to Charlotte, North Carolina. I got up at 4:00 A.M. and was at the airport by 4:30. Plenty of time, I thought! Well, security didn't open until 5:00 A.M., so the line was long, to say the least. Once security opened at 5:00, it seemed that things were going unusually quick. I took off my shoes, belt, laptop, watch, and anything else that might beep. I made it through without a problem. When I got to the end of the security check, things began to get out of control. It reminded me of a classic episode of the *I Love Lucy* television show, which aired many years ago. Lucy was in a chocolate factory and all she had to do was put a wrapping paper on each candy. The belt sped up and it got ahead of her. All of a sudden she was eating more than she was packing. Well, this morning the trays that you put your garments in were shooting out on that conveyor as fast as those candies. They were going on top of each other and it was tough to tell what belongings went to which person. All of a sudden a security man came over and started the task of getting things in order. He was picking, pulling, running, and getting things back to normal.

What makes us want to say something smart or funny? Is it our need for attention? I was going to say, "You look like a one-armed paper hanger," but something in my spirit held me back. All of a sudden, he turned towards me, and I noticed that he didn't have a left arm! Yikes, what a blunder that would have been for me to tell him he looked liked a one-armed paperhanger. He would have thought I was making a joke about his disability. Thank you, Lord, for keeping my mouth shut. I said, "Thank you," to Him and moved on thinking what could have been.

"Do not let any unwholesome talk come out of your mouths, but only what is helpful for building others up according to their needs, that it may be beneficial to those who listen" (Ephesians 4:29).

What is unwholesome? Unwholesome is anything that is not pleasing to God. Gossip, slander, cutting remarks, cursing, making fun of someone are all things that are unwholesome. I could have easily said something that would have changed the whole perception of what that man thought about me in an instant. Here is the real problem:

What I said would have been in full view. How many times do we make remarks, not knowing that they are cutting someone to the core? As Christians, there has to be a difference in the way we lead our lives compared to that of the way unbelievers do. Many unbelievers are looking at us. If there is not a difference they will say, "Why do I need God if that is what Christians do?" When trials come your way, there has to be something to hold onto. As the streams of life turn into a torrent, we all need a rock to cling to. The rock is not a family member, a job, a church, or a friend. The only Rock is in the person of Jesus Christ. There are only two reasons to be on this Earth:

1. To come to know and accept Jesus as Savior and Lord of your life.
2. To share the gospel of Jesus with as many people as possible.

Other than these two things, *nothing* else matters, does it?

So when we open our mouths, remember that one word can have a drastic influence on the way unbelievers see Jesus. Since many people don't go to church, read a Bible, or have fellowship, their only view of Jesus may be through something you do. That is a very important responsibility.

We can only hold our tongues by asking the Lord to help us in this area. "Building others up according to their needs" is a very important task. With one word, we can destroy what may take a lifetime to build. One word may also lift someone up when they are at their lowest point. The next time you try to be witty or come out with a clever remark, just stop, and pray that the Lord would give you the right response. It's better to say nothing than to say the wrong thing.

There are many times in our lives that we wish we could only "take that back." Trying to call back the words that have been spoken is like trying to get toothpaste back in a tube. It can be a huge mess. If we are always looking to build others up then the chances of this happening will be minimal. If we are looking out for ourselves more than others then the chances of this happening will be greater.

Pray today and ask the Lord to reveal to you what you need to change. Jesus is there all the time so let us all call on His strength and not our own.

Why Aren't Things Working?

"If you are willing and obedient, you will eat the best from the land; but if you resist and rebel, you will be devoured by the sword" (Isaiah 1:19,20).

In the days of Isaiah, you couldn't purchase a boat, a plane, or a car. What you could purchase were necessities; one of which was food. What does it mean to be willing and obedient? Since God has given us a free will we can chose to follow God's commands or we can choose to keep God at arm's length. Once we are willing to accept Jesus as Savior and Lord of our lives and have asked for His forgiveness, then and only then can we be obedient. In this life, it is impossible to be obedient without the Holy Spirit living within us. That is because in this life we will face trials of many kinds. To live an obedient life for Christ we need His supernatural power to overcome this world.

If you had known me before I was saved, you would have seen a much different man. Since I didn't know Jesus, I was not convicted by the sin in my life. I tell my wife Julie about the things I did and both of us just say, "Who was that man?" I believed in abortion, I believed in sex before marriage, I believed in half-truths, and I was as far from the Lord as anyone could get. Fortunately, the Lord was not far from me. I resisted and rebelled to the commands of the Lord for thirty-eight years. One night when I was at the end of my rope, Jesus sent an evangelist to share the gospel to me and that night my life was forever changed. I asked the Lord into my life, I accepted who He was and what He did on the Cross and I asked for forgiveness of my sins. I can't tell you the change that came over me. It was immediate.

"Therefore, if anyone is in Christ, he is a new creation, the old has gone, the new has come!" (2 Corinthians 5:17).

Amen and amen to that. I started to see things in a much different light. You see, when you accept Jesus into your life, He sends His Holy Spirit to live inside you. That is amazing isn't it? That's why we are changed, not because of anything we have done, but because of the one who now lives inside of us.

I used to go to bars every night and after a couple months that desire went away. I used to have sex without being married, but now felt remorse for what I had done. I used to tell half-truths and now I needed to be totally truthful. I am going to be very blunt in my the description of obedience. Before I do, I want to emphasize that I am not judging you because I was doing what everyone else was doing. I understand where you are.

If you are having sex outside of marriage the Lord will not bless you. If you are drinking and causing others to stumble because of this the Lord will not bless you. If you are telling half-truths the Lord will not bless you. If you are putting material possessions or anything else before the Lord, the Lord will not bless you.

If you can't find peace anywhere in your life, then you are not being obedient to the Lord. Just because everyone else may be drinking and having sex outside of marriage doesn't make it right. Why aren't things working? All it may take is a quick look in the mirror. I am saying these things out of love because you haven't been as bad as I have. I know how the Lord blessed me when I became obedient to Him. Is it tough to do? Absolutely! Is it worth it? I shudder to think where I would be today if I had kept up my previous lifestyle. Are you willing to be obedient to Jesus instead of the sinful things of this world? If not, then look out! The pain you feel now will not let up. What will it take for you to cry, "Uncle?"

I have seen people who have come under tremendous pressure. But thank the Lord that this is where God wants them so they can say, "All right, Lord, I can't take it anymore. Please take over my life and I will live for You and You alone."

Where are you today? Are you willing and obedient or are you resisting and rebelling? You can come to Jesus just as you are. You don't need to clean up your act to have Jesus come into your life. No matter where you are, no mattter what you have done, Jesus not only forgives but He forgets when you come to Him with a repentant heart. Make this the day you stop letting the evil one control your life. Make this the day you start living in peace and freedom.

Pray and then pray some more for guidance, forgiveness, and hope.

God Would Never Forgive Me

I was sharing the gospel with a former Navy Seal one evening. He told me of unspeakable things that he had done that he believed God could never forgive him for. When fighting for one's country, there are decisions every day that would never be made in peacetime. This man had a tremendous amount of guilt that he had harbored for many years. All of the servicemen and women who have fought for our country deserve our deepest respect. They have seen and done things that had horrible consequences, so that we can live in freedom.

When someone comes to the Lord with a repentant heart and asks for forgiveness of sins, God not only forgives, He also forgets. We may forgive someone, but we hardly ever forget. Satan wants us to keep bringing things up and throwing them back in that person's face.

" ... as far as the east is from the west, so far has he removed our transgressions from us" (Psalm 103:12).

" ... for all have sinned and fall short of the glory of God" (Romans 3:23).

Moses and David were men of God. Moses killed an Egyptian who was fighting with an Israelite, and David was responsible for the murder of Bathsheba's husband, Uriah.

I say this in order to make you understand that *we are all sinners*. When we start thinking we are better than someone or we haven't been as bad as the next guy, then we are saying we are righteous. The Bible says in Romans

3:10: "There is no one righteous, not even one." It is *only* by God's grace and forgiveness that we are saved and forgiven.

I hear people say, "If I walked into church the walls would fall down." I understand where they are coming from. People who think they are righteous have probably made other people feel this way. Church is for the sinner, not people who think they are righteous.

I told this former veteran that no matter what he did, God could, and would, forgive him. It was now up to him to acknowledge who Jesus is, what He did on the Cross, and to ask Jesus for forgiveness of his sins. He made that decision, but that is only part of faith. This man was now guaranteed a place in Heaven, but in order to get rid of the guilt of the past, he had to pray and ask God to rid his mind of these things. Satan always wants to bring up our failures and our shortcomings. He doesn't want us to be effective witnesses to others. Jesus not only forgives, He can also restore.

The next time you think you have done something that God cannot forgive, remember Jesus came to this Earth and died a horrible death so that whoever believes in Him will not only have eternal life, but will also be forgiven of their sins. As many of our veterans have died for our freedom, Jesus died so that we could have the *ultimate* freedom of forgiveness of sin and that we could inherit eternal life.

Don't let anyone tell you that you are nothing. Remember, if you are a Christian, you are the child of a King. What an awesome thought that is!

Don't let anyone steal your peace.

It Can't Be

"Naked I came from my mother's womb, and naked I will depart. The Lord gave and the Lord has taken away; may the name of the Lord be praised" (Job 1:21).

Yesterday a horrible plane crash in Virginia claimed the lives of ten people. In the accident were one man's brother, son, and twin daughters. This is the type of pain that cuts to the core of your soul. There is nothing that can be said that will give comfort. We can talk about how awesome Heaven is, but right now, we need to pray for the family and all those affected by this deadly crash.

When we read Scripture, many times we can read a passage without giving it much thought. We can either think, "That won't happen to me," or "That is too outrageous to comprehend." The only thing Job had left was his faith. He lost all his sons and daughters in an accident. When his friends came to see him after the accident, they didn't say anything to him for seven days.

"Then they sat on the ground with him for seven days and seven nights. No one said a word to him, because they saw how great his suffering was" (Job 2:13).

The only thing we can do is pray. Prayer is the only thing that will comfort people in tragic times of loss. This is because prayer starts the angels in Heaven on missions that we cannot even comprehend. Jesus, through the power of his Holy Spirit, will comfort in ways that we cannot understand. I'm not going to say anything that minimizes this pain. We all know the right things to say about salvation, heaven and, that at some point, we have to die an Earthly death. But sometimes, the right answers don't need to be spoken. As a body of believers, we need to lift hurting people in prayer.

I didn't know this family personally, but I feel in my spirit a deep sadness for those involved. I know what it's like to lose a loved one before their time. Of course, that is *my* timing and not the Lord's. Nevertheless, the pain will not go away with sleep or time. If anything, this tragedy has taught us is that life is short. Don't put off today what needs to be said to your loved ones. If there is any conflict between you and anyone, resolve it now. We aren't guaranteed having even this afternoon.

Yes, the Lord has given us life and families, and the Lord will take away our life and families when it's the Lord's time. Jesus wept when Lazarus died. How much more should we be able to weep for those that are not here with us any longer. Don't be afraid to cry. God knows your pain and He will give you comfort to get you through the most dire circumstances.

Please start by praying now and lifting up hurting people in your prayers. Pray that if you are used to help, the Lord will give you His words to say.

Left Behind

There is a best selling series of books known as the *Left Behind* series. Set in the present, it's about Jesus coming to take believers back with Him to Heaven. There are over twelve books in this series, and they are all based on the Book of Revelation. I would urge you to read this series.

Recently, there has been a tragedy in the NASCAR community. There was also the slaughter in Russia where terrorists took over a school and murdered innocent children. A couple of weeks ago in Russia, a man lost six of his children in a flood. If you are a believer in Jesus Christ and have accepted Him as Savior and Lord of your life, then you are saved. If God has called you home, you are in glory. No more worries and no more pain. Being able to walk the streets of gold with Jesus and all your loved ones who have gone to Heaven before you.

But what about those "Left Behind"—fathers, brothers, children, mothers, sisters, and friends? It is easy to say they are in a better place, but that does not give much comfort to those who will feel this loss for some time. When our hope is in this world we will always suffer pain. Why? Because the things of this world come and go.

"The world and its desires pass away, but the man who does the will of God lives forever" (1 John 2:17).

I have written many times that none of us in this world will ever die. We live in a body that is decaying every day and at some point, we will shed this body for another. What makes you, you, and me, me is not our skin and bones. What makes you and your personality is your soul. Your soul will live forever. What we need to be concerned about is what our final address will be. If we are saved by a saving faith in Jesus Christ, we will spend eternity in Heaven. If we have not made that decision and we die, then we will spend eternity in hell.

All the things of this world will pass away.

Often, we get so comfortable in our own world that we forget about the pain of others. My wife and I were talking this morning about the man who lost his six children in the flood in Russia. We were also talking about the recent plane crash. Both of these events have tremendous pain associated with them. A new perspective should be what we take away from these events. We need to live each day like it is our last day. Instead of thinking your children are annoying you, look at them as a blessing to cherish. If you are at odds with your spouse or a co- worker, make amends before it is too late. Time on this Earth is short. We need to get ready for Heaven, but make the most of every opportunity while still here on Earth.

Please pray today for all those left behind. Pray that the Lord will comfort and heal their wounds. This is true pain that wracks the center of the soul. The Lord is the *only* one in this instance Who can give comfort. Pray that through the death of so many, people will be gripped with the reality of this life. Pray that many would make decisions for Jesus, since this is one of the main reasons we are on this Earth. God allows painful trials so we can trust in Him instead of trusting in things, which will always disappoint us.

Love Everyone, Yeah, Right!

I don't care if you are the most godly person in the world we all have a sinful nature. It is tough to love those who either hate us or who just give us a hard time, isn't it?

"If it is possible, as far as it depends on you, live at peace with everyone" (Romans 12:18).

This doesn't say as far as it depends on others, it says as far as it depends on *you*. You see, we can never control other people's emotions or their feelings for us. Since we have grown up in a performance-based world, most people's love or friendship for us is based upon "What have you done for me lately?" On the other hand, there are those who you could spend all your waking hours trying to please and it still would not be enough for them to like you. So how do we love them?

First of all, we have to understand that when we were away from God and maybe even hated or disliked God, God still loved us. He loved us so much that when we were dead in our sins He sent His only Son Jesus to die a horrible death so that whoever believes in Him will have eternal life. Since God loved us first, even when we were deep in our sin, how much more should we love others? If you are saved by God's grace then Heaven is in your future and that should be enough for us to live a joyful life. Just think, Heaven is guaranteed to the believer.

So then, no matter how many people dislike or mistreat you pray that in your heart you can get to the point where it doesn't matter. Our only concern should be to help others get to Heaven and help lead them to Jesus. Don't let your pride get in the way of helping those who may dislike you. If someone dislikes you and you haven't done anything to provoke them, don't worry. The issue is not with you, but with them. They may be harboring so much jealousy and frustration that they may resent the peace that the Lord gives you. Remember where your strength lies and who protects and restores.

In the Book of Romans, Chapter 11, it talks about being grafted into the branches of a tree. The analogy is that the root is God and the branches are His offspring. When we are grafted in to the branch we are saved, but other branches may have been cut off.

"Do not boast over those branches. If you do consider this: You do not support the root, but the root supports you" (Romans 11:18).

I used to drive a hearse as a part time job when I was in college. During one trip, I needed to load up the flowers in the hearse and get them to the cemetery before I went back to get the casket. It was an old country road and I was daydreaming as usual. All of a sudden I missed the dirt road to the right and slammed on the brakes—big mistake! All the flowers and arrangements came flying forward along with a tidal wave of water. As I pulled up to the gravesite, the back of the hearse was a mess. I was putting blue carnations on yellow stems and yellow carnations on blue stems. What a mess! After the funeral, those carnations had already begun to die. It wasn't because they had broken off of the stem. They had been broken off from the root. We can never live when we are apart from the root.

There are other branches all around you, but only one root. Don't worry about the other branches; just be glad you are connected to the root. Since you have the ability to control your own emotions and not the emotions of those around you, be careful not to judge. Only worry about the relationship between you and God. If you love the Lord with all your heart, soul, and mind, then you will have the ability with the Lord's help to love those who may be at odds with you.

"Love everyone," and yes, you can do that when you focus on Jesus instead of focusing on your circumstances.

The Cancer of Arrogance

I have never seen an organization with an arrogant leader ultimately succeed. From the leaders of the Old Testament to the leaders of Enron, the human heart has not changed. Cain felt betrayed and murdered his brother Abel. King David was "a man after God's own heart," but arrogance led him to adultery and murder. Judas sold Jesus into the hands of His captors for money. Some top executives in this country feel that they are above the law and operate under their own laws. Why is this?

"Knowledge puffs up, but love builds up" (1 Corinthians 8:1).

Knowledge can be a blessing and knowledge can be a curse. Knowledge becomes a curse when we start to believe that our promotions, our wealth, our stature, and our abilities are things that *we* have created. The more important we become in the eyes of the world, the less accountable we also become. Most people who rise to great heights start to surround themselves with "yes" people. "Yes" people are those people who will only build you up no matter what you are doing. The problem with major organizations today is that a lot of corporate CEO's have their friends on the board. This is also true with professional athletes today. Most professional athletes have people around them who will never tell them when they are doing anything wrong. They will always be on the side of the money train. Ah, the "money train." Why does it always come down to money? Well, in today's world, money is power and power leads to arrogance if your perspective is on the things of this world. If we are not accountable to others in a godly sense, then arrogance can and will take over our lives. We can start out with the best of intentions, but when people start to say how great we are or what great things we have done, if we are not well grounded in the Lord, we will start to believe that *we* are responsible for our gifts.

As cancer starts out with one cell and spreads throughout the body destroying everything in its path, so does arrogance in a family or a corporation. It is very easy to forget God when people are constantly telling you that you are great.

Jesus came to this world and could have been a king. He could have lived in a palace , destroyed all those who didn't agree with Him, and lived a lavish lifestyle beyond anyone's imagination. Instead, Jesus came to this Earth with a separate purpose. Jesus came as a servant and instead of living in a palace, He hardly ever spent the night in the same place. He could have lived richly, but only had a robe that was gambled for when He was crucuified. He could have boasted of His power, but He never did. He gave all the glory to God. Why was Jesus the perfect example? Partly because He was God in the flesh, but also because love empowered His actions.

Love can cure so many wrongs. But when someone is arrogant, they will never admit a wrong. It is always someone else's problem. Are you willing to admit that you have been wrong? Ouch! Lets look at the traits of love:

"Love is patient, love is kind. It does not boast, it is not proud. It is not rude, it is not self-seeking. It is not easily angered, it keeps no record of wrongs. Love does not delight in evil but rejoices with the truth. It always protects, always trusts, always hopes, always perseveres. Love never fails.... " (1 Corinthians13:4-8).

God's Love	Worldly Viewpoints
It is patient	We live in a world where patience is rarely used.
It is kind	A lot of us get angry at a moment's notice.
It does not boast	Can you stop taking the credit and give credit to others and to the Lord instead?
It is not proud	Can you think of others as better than yourself?
It is not rude	Can you get over your insecurities and quit putting others down to cover up your wrongs?

62

It is not self-seeking · Can you look out for the interests of others more than your own interests?

It is not easily angered · Can you stop thinking of how you have been wronged? Can you give your life over to Jesus?

It keeps no record of wrongs · Yikes!

It does not delight in evil · No matter what someone has done to you, remember we are all sinners; don't judge others; be thankful for your salvation; and pray for others.

It never fails · Pray that the Lord would give you the strength to run the race of life with perserverance and finish strong, never, ever giving up!

The only way we can love unconditioanlly and not get puffed up with our accomplishments is to have the Spirit of God living within us. We cannot do this in our own strength. Even if we are saved and have the Spirit of God in us, we still have a sinful nature. We have to constantly be in God's Word, be praying and having fellowship and accountability to other believers. This life is short so we need to make the most of every opportunity. We can't be an example of Jesus when we exude arrogance and anger. We can show Christ's love no matter what people do to us when we know to whom we are ultimately accountable. Don't lose sight of the goal and don't take your eyes off Jesus. When you focus on these two things you can't help but love those around you, no matter what they may or may not do to you.

Thinking Like Chase

When you first have a child, God lets you go in steps. My wife was great about getting up in the middle of the night and letting me sleep. I still need to thank her for that. Actually, a bomb could go off outside and

I wouldn't hear it. So leaving the baby monitor on for me to get up would be a challenge! When you first bring a baby home, fortunately they just lie there. They have to be fed every three hours, but at least no matter where you leave them, they are still there when you come back. At around three to four months, they start rolling over and then you have to be a little more cautious. Once they get up on all fours, look out! Life will never be the same.

Once we have given ourselves over to evil things life will also never be the same.

"In regards to evil be infants, but in your thinking be adults" (1 Corinthians 14:20).

Since the days of Adam and Eve, what God has made good, most of us have perverted. The first account of murder was because of jealousy between the first two brothers on this Earth, Cain and Abel. Cain was jealous of Abel's blessing and he killed Abel. God made sex to be between a husband and a wife. Since the days of Sodom and Gomorrah until now, the human heart has not changed. Homosexuality, adultery, pornography, and all sorts of evil have come from what started out as pure and good.

Money can be a very good thing when used with the right motives. Money can also be a curse when used with intentions of acquiring instead of giving. Power and status are a gift from God. Whether you know it or not, it is not your abilities that got you the job you are in today. The Lord has not only given you talents, but He has also placed you in your job. We turn this around to think we are the crafty ones and then we let the power go to our heads and start treating everyone as our servant.

You see, evil doesn't start out as evil. Evil starts out as pure and then we let the worries and concerns of this world creep in and tarnish what God has made perfect. So how do we stop the cycle?

"In regards to evil be infants." When you are an infant you have no desire for perversion. You have not been tainted with the evil desires of the world. You take everyone at their word and trust completely. Our five-year-old son Chase, who is autistic, is one of the most loving children I have ever seen. On one side that is good, but he trusts everyone because he doesn't understand evil people. A car pulled up in our driveway last week and a girl got out to sell us cookies while her mother waited in the car. The next thing we knew Chase had opened the door and was in the backseat of this stranger's car. No fear there! He has no idea of consequences, or of what people are capable.

What if we could live our lives like Chase with that innocence? We would:

Wear our hearts on our sleeves

Love everyone around us

Not look for the bad, but the good in everyone

Not think, "What can you do for me?"

Not judge by outward appearances.

Not be tainted by what evil people have done in the past; we can forgive, but it is very difficult for us to forget.

Feel real compassion for other people's pain. When our other son Bryce gets hurt or cries, Chase starts crying too. His compassion knows no boundaries.

Look at what God has made pure and stop there.

Take one hour at a time, don't look back and don't look forward, live in the moment.

Put others first.

" *... but in your thinking be adults.* " Even though Chase lives in a world that is somewhat different than ours, we all need to be wary of evil people. Our world is not pure and satan is the prince of this world. It is very tough to live this life with a pure heart when we have seen what evil has done to those around us. Fortunately, " *... the One who is in you is greater than the one who is in the world"* (1 John 4:4).

Pray that the Lord will be able to rid you of whatever perversion or addiction that has held you captive in the past. I know from experience that the Lord can redeem and restore a perverted mind, but only with the grace and power of Jesus Christ. If you don't want to change, then you are a slave to this world and the things in it. But remember Jesus died a horrible death so that you and I could not only have eternal life, but also have the power of the Holy Spirit to live freely. Start today by asking Jesus to break those chains of evil and start to take on the pure thoughts of our Lord.

Just Another Day, or Is It?

Have you been in a rut where one day turns into a week and before you know it a month or a year has passed by? You look at your life and say, "Where did it go and what have I done?" It is very easy to get into a rut. We wake up, get the kids off to school, go to work, come home, make dinner, do baths, read or watch TV, and then off to bed to start another day. What can we do differently to make each day count? What can we do to make our lives count?

"Whatever you do, work at it with all your heart, as working for the Lord, not for men" (Colossians 3:23).

When you get your children ready for school, instead of going through the same routine, tell them about Jesus, and pour the bowl of cereal with a smile. It is easy to get into a routine and we do things without a joyful spirit. A joyful spirit and a smile are contagious. So are scowls and harsh words. So since we do work for the Lord and not for man, how is this day any different? First of all, we need to change our perspective toward this day. The only way to do this is to start our day with prayer. Your prayer doesn't need to be a thirty-minute, eloquent dissertation. Prayer is just speaking to God as you would to a friend. But even though we can speak to God because of what Jesus has done on the cross, remember that God is God and nothing is impossible for Him.

So even though we may get a paycheck from our employers, our CEO is still the Lord. Why? Because the Lord has put your boss in control of where you work. If you are the CEO, you are there not by your clever ways, but because the Lord saw fit to put you there. So we go to work, but how can our day be different when we work for Jesus instead of man? First of all we can start by:

1. Having a joyful attitude. (How many of you right now are just plain mad at the world or some of your co-workers? Remember, today you are not working for them, you are working for Jesus.)

2. Forgiving—Don't hold grudges. Someone may be giving you a tough time at work, but chances are they are under tremendous pressure from someone else. Even though they may be harsh with you, cut them

some slack. Remember, everyone is perfect until you get to know them. We all have problems so have compassion, not contempt.

3. Remember teamwork—Jesus had twelve disciples and He tried to get them to work together. Even though they had an argument on which one of them was the greatest, they tried to work as a team. This should give us some comfort. Here were men working directly with Jesus and they still had pride issues. Don't be hard on yourselves.

4. Not dwelling in the past—What's done is done. Forget it and move on. Let Jesus be the leader and don't try to rely on yourself to get things done. You can never keep all the balls in the air no matter how hard you try. Jesus not only knows the beginning and the end of each day, He created the world and everything in it. Don't rely on your own understanding, call out to the Lord, and He will give you the direction you need to go in and the attitude to do it in.

5. Having a sense of urgency—Don't be complacent. Is this just another day or is it your last day? What would you do differently if you knew that the Lord was going to call you home today? You would probably make amends with those you had problems with. You would probably be a little nicer and less hurried at the breakfast table, and your prayer life would certainly be more meaningful. How many of those who die ever think that would be the day? Like a thief in the night, so comes death. For the believer, a great experience and a new beginning await. For the unbeliever who has never asked the Lord into his life, hell awaits. If you haven't done so, make this more than just another day, call out to the Lord and you will be saved.

6. Praying for all those around you, not just those who can help you—Many times we get caught up in only helping those who can help us. Let's show compassion and spend time with those who have no bearing on our lives and who cannot help us climb the corporate ladder. Jesus could have spent all His time with kings, but chose to live with the common man. How much more should we live by His example.

To get out of the rut most of us are in we need to view this day differently. *This is not just another day*, this is the first day that you can make a difference or it may be the last day God has allowed you here on this Earth. Don't be complacent about anything you do. Do everything to the best of the ability the Lord has given you, even if it is getting a glass of water for a co-worker. You are God's disciples, each and every one of you.

Let's start today by going out into the world and showing the love of the Lord, not the jealousy and pride of satan. Remember, God is in control and His will *will* be done. Don't fret, but give of your time and your heart to others. When Jesus was on the Cross, He could have called His angels to rescue Him, but we would never have had the chance to be saved. Instead of calling for help, Jesus didn't think of himself, but said to God, "Father forgive them for they do not know what they are doing" (Luke 23:34). Can you forgive others today? In the whole scheme of things, they don't know what they are doing either. Love the Lord with all your soul and strength and the rest will fall into place. This is the day the Lord has made, rejoice and be glad in it.

Heal Me

Healing only comes from the Lord. We have great doctors all over the world, but if the Lord desires us not to be healed, no medicine or doctor will have the right cure. So does illness come from doing something right or wrong in the eyes of the Lord? Eating a cheesecake every night can make you overweight, but in general, no! In the Gospel of John, the people asked Jesus about a blind man and who had sinned for the man to be born blind—his father or mother?

"As He went along, He saw a blind man from birth. His disciples asked Him, 'Rabbi, who sinned, this man or his parents, that he was born blind?' 'Neither this man nor his parents sinned,' said Jesus, 'but this happened so that the work of God might be displayed in his life'" (John 9:1-3).

You may be in the midst of a tough trial right now with a life threatening or a chronic illness. You may have prayed and prayed and prayed some more, and you wonder what you have done wrong. You may feel guilty and blame this on something in your past. If you are doing this stop! I know it may be difficult, but feel privileged in having your infirmities because Jesus feels that you are strong enough to handle it so that the work of God might be displayed in you. When you are in the hospital for chemo, or at work with a chronic illness, people are watching how you handle it. If you handle it in the strength of the Lord, you will encourage others, not only those in the faith, but those who are searching for the Lord and don't know it. Being strong in the face of adversity is contagious. Rely on the Lord's power and strength and He will do great works in your life.

In the Old Testament when Israel was rebelling against the Lord, the people wanted kings to rule over them. During that time, Elijah and Elisha were prophets of the Lord. There was a valiant soldier called Naaman who had leprosy. Elisha wanted him to know that there was a prophet in Israel, so he had him come to his home. Elisha said:

"'Go wash yourself seven times in the Jordan and your flesh will be restored and you will be cleansed.' But Naaman went away angry and said, 'I thought that he would surely come out to me and stand and call on the name of the Lord his God, wave his hand over the spot and cure me of my leprosy'" (2 Kings 5:10, 11).

"Naaman's servants went to him and said, 'My father, if the prophet had told you to do some great thing, would you not have done it? How much more then, when he tells you, 'Wash and be cleansed!' So he went down and dipped himself in the Jordon seven times, as the man of God had told him and his flesh was restored and became clean like that of a young boy'" (2 Kings 5: 13,14).

Faith is not works. We do good works as thankfulness for what Jesus has done for us, not as a way to get into Heaven. Here was a man who had a perceived notion on how to be healed. Most of us have perceived notions on how to be saved. Listen to this very carefully. Going to church, being baptized, confirmed, giving to the church and to the poor, being kind to others, taking care of your family, being a great parent, and doing the best you can, *will not get you into Heaven.*

Elisha told this man something that didn't make sense. But Naaman had to take the step of faith, not Elisha. He could be saying, "How can washing myself seven times in the Jordan cure me; it is a dirty river? Just wave a magic wand over me."

"For it is by grace you have been saved, through faith and this not from yourselves, it is the gift of God, not by works, so that no one can boast" (Ephesians 2:8,9).

We have been saved by the grace of God when we ask Him to forgive our sins, acknowledge that He lived and died and rose from the dead to pay the penalty for our sins. We ask Jesus into our lives. We also ask Jesus to help us turn from the way we used to view life to love the things of the Lord and not the things of this world. If you can pray to Jesus and ask Him with a repentant heart, you will be saved for now and eternity.

You see a gift can't be bought, even with a penny because then it is no longer a gift. A gift is freely given, not earned. Jesus doesn't want us to boast by saying, "I went to church seventy times and you only went seven. I gave $1,000 dollars to the church and you only gave $10." God doesn't want us to boast, unless we boast about what God has done in our own lives.

I pray today that many of you would come to know Jesus. We have seen many tragedies this year as the world views them. People have been taken before we felt it was their time. If you think you can put off this decision, I would ask you to think again. Life is short, very short, and you are not even guaranteed this afternoon.

If this lesson teaches us anything, I would like it convey to each and every one of you to not feel guilty, but strong when trials come. Know that the Lord loves you enough to know that you can stand up under the pressure for God's glory. Just think of the faith the Lord has in you. Also what may be a preconceived notion about getting into Heaven by works is now put to rest. It is only by God's grace and your faith in Jesus that will open the doors to Heaven for you for eternity.

"Heal me!" Pray that you could get to the point in your life where it is all right to be healed or not, whatever brings glory to God. If you are hurting, please let us pray for you, as the Lord can give you His peace to get through the most difficult of circumstances.

Did You Open All Your Gifts?

Gold, incense, and myrrh were the first Christmas gifts ever given. Why? Because Christmas represents the birth of Jesus and the Wise Men were the first to offer presents. Thus a tradition was started. The older I get, the more the giving at Christmas bothers me. I think it bothers me because we forget why we are giving presents. I doubt that the story of Jesus is brought up or pondered most Christmas mornings. I doubt if Mary said to Joseph,

"Why don't you get gift receipts from those Wise Men so we can trade that incense in for diapers when they leave! We don't need myrrh, so let's take it back and get cash so we can get something we really need."

It seems that the holiday spirit has transformed itself into the holiday party. In America we are truly blessed. We are blessed with the freedom to worship where we want. We are able to make a good living to support our families and the opportunities are endless. The problem with this is that we can become lazy. In foreign countries, especially China, more Christians are coming to know the Lord than in the United States. This is because when people are persecuted, they have only one way to go—Jesus! When you have everything you need, you think you did it on your own and you can put off Jesus for another day. We are treading on very dangerous ground in this country because we are becoming too complacent.

I can remember getting a ton of presents as a child and being mad because I didn't get that go- cart I wanted. We had a lot of family members in town this year and the kids received so many presents that they lost interest in the ones they had just opened. In a perfect world, the best thing to do would be to get up Christmas morning, read the Christmas story in Luke 2:4-20, open one present to symbolize the joy of giving and receiving and spend the rest of the day enjoying family and friends. If something doesn't fit or it isn't the right color, then give it to Goodwill because someone probably needs it more than you or I do.

I am blessed to have a great family; mother, in-laws, grandmothers, and brother-in-law and sister-in-law, nephews, and nieces. There is another member of my family that I cannot reach—my brother. I am sad that I have not been able to have a relationship with him. I know God is working in his life, but my joy at Christmas would be for him to be with me. You are probably the same way. There is probably someone in your family whom you desire to be with, and that you would give anything to have them sit at the Christmas table with you.

I enjoyed getting some very thoughtful gifts this year, but I see all over the United States people missing the Spirit of Christmas. I say the "Spirit," because without the Holy Spirit there is no lasting joy. After all the presents are opened and if you don't know Jesus, then it is just another day. But if you do know Jesus, then the presents should be a reminder of the Wise Men who gave gifts to a baby who would change our world forever for all those who believe in Him. Do you believe and trust in Jesus as your Savior? Or do you believe Jesus just lived and died and that we have a fun day called "Christmas" to use as a reason to open presents?

Hopefully, this Christmas season you were able to set aside some time to reflect that the greatest gift to you is your salvation. Jesus gives it freely for all those who have believed that He is the Christ and that He died and rose from the dead to pay the penalty for our sins. Heaven is the best present we could ever get. This coming year let us all try to give much, much more than we could ever receive. We live in a material word where more is thought to be better. Just look in people's garages and attics to see where all that good stuff has gone. Instead of accumulating this year, start to give things away. Not only give away the material, but give of your time, your love, your compassion, and your tears to those who are in need.

You see, Christmas can be every day when we give and give freely. Without Christmas we would have no Savior. God gave his only Son to this world so that whoever believes in Him will not perish but have eternal life. That is the gift worth opening. Has that gift been sitting under your tree for many years and you have put off opening it? Now is the time to reflect on your life and realize that material things come and go, but the love of the Lord and His salvation last forever.

That is Christmas.

Jesus Will Save Me, or Will He?

John the Baptist came before Jesus to preach repentance. John could not baptize with the Holy Spirit, only Jesus could, but John prepared the way for Jesus. The Book of Isaiah in the Old Testament, talks about the coming of John the Baptist. Here is the problem. John was seemingly doing everything right. He lived in the desert, ate locusts and wild honey for food, and spent his life preparing the way for Jesus. His path was a narrow one, as Jesus calls us to follow the narrow way.

Now comes some palace politics. Herod, who was king, married his brother's wife, Herodias. John the Baptist told Herod straight out that this was unlawful. On Herod's birthday, Herodias's daughter danced before Herod and danced so well that Herod promised, with an oath, to give her whatever she asked. She went to her mother Herodias, and asked her what she should request. Herodias said that she wanted John the Baptist's head on a platter. King Herod couldn't go back on his word, so he had John beheaded.

John the Baptist was serving God, living a godly life, speaking the truth, living right, and what did he get? Beheaded! What does that say for you and me? You see, service for the kingdom of God does not come without trials, and maybe even death. Sometimes we fall into the trap that if we are kind to others, teach Sunday School, give to the poor, and do good works, God will be easier on us than the non-believer. This is not true. When we lose perspective that Heaven is a far greater place than living here on Earth, we will be shocked and surprised about the trials here on Earth. Heaven should be where we want to go now, if that is the Lord's will. What was John the Baptist thinking in prison? Without an eternal perspective, I would be thinking, "Okay, I just baptized Jesus. I know He has power, so I'm sure He will get me out of here." Even when the sword was at my neck, I would be thinking, "Lord, help me out here. I know You are performing miracles all over the place. Surely you can save me."

The key word here is "save." If you have accepted Jesus as your Savior and Lord, then you are saved. Not saved from an Earthly death *because we all have to die*. We are saved from hell and will live for eternity in Heaven. Once you are saved for eternity, what do you have to worry about? When you get to Heaven you may think, "Lord why did you keep me down there so long?"

We go to health clubs, some of us have cosmetic surgery, liposuction, and all sorts of treatments trying to prolong our lives. Let me tell you this:

The minute you were born, God had already determined when you would leave this Earth.

Working out can increase our quality of life, but not the quantity. If you are in a trial waiting for the other shoe to drop and fretting, rejoice, yes, rejoice if you are saved. Paul was in chains and singing. This life is not fair when we look at it with a worldly perspective. When we look at it with an eternal perspective nothing will compare to the glorious times we will experience in Heaven. If you have had a rough life, lost a child, a parent, or spouse, remember that God does not make mistakes and He is not out to get you. Satan would like you to think that, but God works all things out according to His will for those who love Him. If you are at death's door and are waiting for a miracle, remember that if you have accepted Jesus as Savior, then you have already experienced a miracle and will never die.

Oh, you will experience a part of life where you get rid of the tent you have been living in and substitute it for a new improved version, but you will not die.

Our focus here on Earth should be to share the gospel with as many people as we know. The Bible says the time is short and the workers are few. Jesus could come back tomorrow. Are you ready? Will Jesus save me? Of course He will if you have asked Him to be Savior and Lord of your life. Jesus is the King, Savior, Redeemer, Counselor and all you and I will ever need. This New Year throw off all that stuff that is slowing you down and focus on Jesus, the giver and sustainer of eternal life.

Why Should They Get In?

All around the country there are meeting places for temporary workers to be selected on a daily basis. These workers show up in a parking lot or a street corner and wait to be called to help build homes or pick produce in a field. To be called certainly brings a sense of relief. In the Gospel of Matthew, chapter 20, Jesus talks about men who were waiting for work. The master comes and picks out a few men and says to them in Verse two, "He agreed to pay them a denarius for the day and sent them into his vineyard." A few hours later, he did the same thing and told the workers, "I will pay you whatever is right." As the end of the day was approaching, he did the same thing. When it came time to be paid, he paid the men who worked one hour a denarius, just as he paid the men who worked all day.

"When they received it, they began to grumble against the landowner. 'These men who were hired last worked only one hour,' they said, 'and you have made them equal to us who have borne the burden of the work and the heat of the day.' But he answered one of them, 'Friend, I am not being unfair to you. Didn't you agree to work for a denarius? Take your pay and go. I want to give the man who was hired last the same as I gave you. Don't I have the right to do what I want with my own money? Or are you envious because I am generous?'" (Matthew 20:1-15).

Jesus tells us not to judge or we will be judged. Here is the whole heart of the matter. If you are a believer in Jesus Christ and have accepted Him by faith, then you will have eternal life. Jesus picked you, you didn't pick Jesus so be thankful that you have eternal life and will spend eternity with Him. Now why do we do good works? Is it to get in better with Jesus? No, we do good works as thanks for what God has done for us by sending His Son to die on a Cross to pay for the penalty of our sins, which we were helpless to do. If you get to the point in your life were you think of works as a burden, then you are serving for the wrong reason. If someone accepts Jesus on their death bed and you have served Jesus all your life, rejoice that another person has been accepted into the Kingdom of God.

It is a privilege to serve Jesus, not work.

Don't ever look down on unbelievers or think you are better than they are. I can tell you from experience that each of us could have ended up a beggar, but Jesus chose us for himself. That in itself, should be enough for us to lead a joyous spirit-filled life.

Why should they get in? If you and I get in, why shouldn't they? That is jealousy and jealousy has no place in the family of believers. Be thankful for your relationship with God and pray for all those who have yet to come to know the Lord. As the angels rejoice in Heaven when someone is saved, let us do the same.

Birth Pains

I remember when we had our first son, Bryce. Most pains come on gradually, but with a little Advil they go away. Not with birth pains. Whatever is causing this pain is not leaving until it shows itself. On that first big contraction, Julie grabbed me by the shirt and the look in her eyes said to me, "You've killed me!" She had to wait an hour for an epidural and then the pain eased up a bit. In the end, we were blessed with a miracle.

In the Gospel of Matthew, Jesus talks about the end of the age. The end of this Earth as we know it. Seems far-fetched doesn't it? But actually it isn't.

"You will hear of wars and rumors of wars, but see to it that you are not alarmed. Such things must happen, but the end is still to come. Nation will rise against nation, and kingdom against kingdom. There will be famines and earthquakes in various places. All these are the beginning of birth pains" (Matthew 24:6-8).

"Earthquakes in various places?" How about the Indian Ocean? The tsunami, which recently created unbelievable destruction in Indonesia, one would have thought to be impossible in this day and age. Imagine this: An earthquake in the Atlantic Ocean, 1000 miles off the coast of Florida at 8:00 A.M. The earthquake, a 9.0 on the Richter scale, creates a wall of water moving 500 mph, (as fast as a Boeing 737) heading toward the east coast of Florida. As sunbathers start to go out and find their best spot for the day, who would ever think what is coming? All of a sudden, everything from Ft. Lauderdale to Jacksonville and three miles inland is wiped out with over 1,000,000 causalities. Impossible? Not after what happened in Indonesia.

"… wars and rumors of wars …" Iraq, Afghanistan, Iran, Israel, Palestine, Somalia, and the Sudan. Power is being played out all around the world. Only one person knows the time, the place, and the outcome, and that is Jesus.

Have birth pains started for the end of the age? I would say they have, but we are not to know the time when Jesus comes back. We are just to be ready. What does being ready mean? First of all, we need to be saved. When Jesus comes back to take those in the Rapture who have accepted Him as Savior, you may be left behind for the period of time called the Tribulation. That will be a horrible time of wars, persecution, and satan's rule. Christians will be killed for their faith. If at the end of this time you have not accepted the Lord, or you have died before this happens, and you still have not made a decision for Jesus, it will be too late. If you were to die today and stand before Jesus and you were to say to Him, "I'm sorry that I didn't believe You. I believe You now as I see your glory," it *will be too late*. You would spend eternity in hell. I can tell you hell will not be a party, but "weeping and gnashing of teeth." A horrible existence.

You can prevent that by asking Jesus into your life, asking Him to forgive your sins, acknowledging that He died on the Cross and rose from the dead to pay the penalty for your sins. If you have done that, then you have nothing to worry about, even a 100-foot wave of water.

The birth pains have started and they won't end until Jesus comes back. If you think they are going away, think again! It could be this afternoon or 1,000 years from now when Jesus comes, but He is coming. Don't procrastinate on this one.

The last words Jesus says in the Bible are in Revelation 22:20: "… Yes, I am coming soon."

Start living your life as if Jesus were coming back today. Live your life with a sense of urgency and not complacency. Try to make the most of every opportunity. Have a great week and trust in the Lord for all things.

Blah, Blah, Blah, Blah

We are so overloaded with pleasures in this world that what once was valuable or fun now seems trivial. Most people come back from mission trips changed. This is because they see people literally with nothing (possessions-wise), but full of joy. How is this? Don't possessions bring joy? Yes, they bring joy for a moment, but then that moment passes. Think about the nicest thing you have ever received and then think now, "Where is it?" It's probably either sold or in the attic somewhere. When we have nothing, we want things, and when we have things we want more things. What is it about things?

You see, we use *things* to try to replace a void in our lives that should be filled with Jesus. The key to fulfillment, joy, passion, and contentment is knowing which goes where. Each of us has a void in our soul that can only be satisfied by the Holy Spirit. The farther we are away from God, the less we want to fill that void with Jesus. If we haven't prayed, gone to church, or have not been in the Word for awhile, then satan creeps in and tries to distract us and change our desires to things not of the Lord.

Let's look at the desires of this world.

"Put to death whatever belongs to your earthly nature, sexual immorality, impurity, lust, evil desires, and greed" (Colossians 3:5).

Then the things of Jesus,

" ... whatever is true, whatever is noble, whatever is right, whatever is pure, whatever is lovely, whatever is admirable—if anything is excellent or praiseworthy, think about such things" (Philippians 4:8).

What a contrast between the things of this world and the things of the Holy Spirit. We go to war with these desires everyday. When we become complacent, tired, have no purpose, no goals, lose hope, and just try to get through the day, we become an easy target for the evil one.

The World	The Holy Spirit
Sexual Immorality	Pure heart and mind
Impurity	Purity
Lust	Whatever is admirable, whatever is right
Evil Desires	Whatever is lovely
Greed	Whatever is true

We get the "blahs" when we get what we want and more. I brought a couple of toys home from my last trip and my oldest son said, "Do you have anything else, Daddy?" Whether you are eight or eighty-eight, our human nature will also struggle with our spirit. How do we become appreciative of even the small things when we have been given everything? A lot of times we may even take our salvation for granted. As any good coach would tell you when things start falling apart:

Get back to basics.

This means learning how to do things in their purest form. A football coach would teach professionals who know how to block exactly that, how to block. We as people of God need to get back to basics. Getting back to basics in the Christian faith is throwing off all things that hinder our walk. Each of us has different things that distract us from our walk with Jesus.

The basics are:

Having quiet time—Praying and asking the Lord to help rid you of all evil and create in you a pure heart.

Worship—We need to go to a Bible-believing church and not only praise God, but be filled with   truth in God's Word and be encouraged by other believers.

The Bible—God has written us a manual to live this life, a roadmap. Sometimes we take our own route, but in the end we get lost and still end up looking at the Bible. Wouldn't it be better to look at the Bible first?

There is nothing wrong with having nice things, so don't let the evil one take the joy out of giving and receiving. But be very careful that these things do not become more important than God. When they do, you will have a serious case of the "blahs," and you will be an ineffective witness for Jesus. Too much of a good thing is always bad, so do all things in moderation. If you have a desire for something really nice, rent it for a week and then make your decision. There is a price tag, whether tangible or intangible, for everything.

Let's all get back to the basics.

" ... Love the Lord with all your heart and with all your soul and with all your strength and with all your mind.... " (Luke 10:27).

This is your prescription for the "blahs."

Where is God?

People commit suicide, a baby pulls a deep fryer on top of her, terrorists kill innocent people, and a whole family dies in an auto accident. Where is God?

"Give thanks to the Lord, for he is good" (Psalm 107:1).

If God is so good, why doesn't He intervene? Let me try to explain what God does and does not do. God is the same yesterday, today, and forever. It is us who change. Here is a very important statement:

This world would make no sense if there were no Heaven.

Sometimes we live this life thinking that this is all there is. We store up possessions, trample over people to get what we want, and spend our time on useless projects that have no eternal value. If we were to view this world as a temporary place (which we should), our perspective of the trials, tragedies, and evil of this world would take on a whole new meaning.

When all those who have accepted Jesus into their lives get to Heaven, there will be an eternal peace and joy that we cannot even comprehend. The time spent on this Earth will be a blip on the radar. One of the purposes of trials and tragedies is for us to turn our focus to Jesus instead of putting our security in other people and possessions. There is tremendous evil in this world. We wonder why God doesn't get rid of it. He does in Heaven, and that is all we need to know. God's plan is God's plan and we will never understand it, and we aren't supposed to understand it. God created the Universe down to the atom. How can we comprehend, or even think we can comprehend, His plan? When tragedy strikes, we need to turn to Jesus, not man.

When my dad died at the age of thirty-four, I thought that was tragic. At the time I thought it made no sense; it was a stupid thing that God did. Now that I'm a believer, I see God working miracles through my dad. I share the gospel with a sense of urgency because I know life can be taken in an instant. I say things to people about how much I care for them because they or I may be gone tomorrow. So many good things came out of my dad's death because I have had over thirty-five years to reflect on it. Plus, my dad was a believer and I will get to see him in Heaven. For the last thirty-five years, my dad has been having the time of his life. What I once saw as pain, I now see as victory.

Right now God has everything under control—*everything*. He is working so that all would come to know Him as Savior and Lord. Since the fall of man, evil has crept into this world and evil will stay until Jesus throws satan into the Lake of Fire. The good news is Jesus wins. We already know how the story ends.

The next time a trial comes share the shock and pain with Jesus, as He is the only one who can truly understand and comfort. Things must happen in this world for many to come to Jesus. Where is God? God is still in control and on the throne. He loves you more than you could ever fathom. When I was younger, I thought God had it out for me. Yes, He was out for me, but to protect me and love me even when I pushed Him away. Thank the Lord for His forgiveness and mercy every day as He is God and we are not.

What Has Mastered You?

In other words, what have you mastered?

Mastered: "Learn something, to become highly skilled in something, or acquire a complete understanding of it."

Some people may have mastered their jobs, their sport, or exercise; maybe you have even mastered your hobby. But in reality the thing you have mastered has probably mastered you. Scary, isn't it!

" ... *for a man is a slave to whatever has mastered him*" (2 Peter 2:19).

In this life, the only thing we want to have mastered is our relationship with Jesus. Because when we do this, we are slaves to Jesus, not the to things of this world. The more I train for the Ironman coming up, the more I can see how this training can take on a life of its own. Back in the 1970's, the Lord had gifted me in running. Some thirty years later, I still have records that, to this day, have not been broken. I don't say this in an arrogant way, but to show you what is to come. Back then I took my health, my gift from the Lord, and those records for granted. I only ran because I wanted notoriety, not because I liked to run. I liked being number one. I liked the attention and the articles in the newspaper. I would have done anything to have mastered this sport, and did. I ran over 100 miles per week for many years without a week off. It became an obsession. When running twice a day wasn't enough, I had to run three times per day. I got to the point where I despised anyone who would stand on the starting line with me. In reality, I was on my way to self-destruction. My coach and friends didn't see it and I didn't see it until it was too late.

The thing I had mastered, finally mastered me.

It took control of my life, so that was my life. I was a runner, just as an alcoholic is an alcoholic. I had lettered my freshman year on the varsity cross-country team at the University of Maryland, and was now competing against those who were the best in the country. When I saw that I was reaching my goal, I quit and went off the deep end. I went from an athlete to a partying fool for over a ten-year period. You see, I was running for the wrong reasons. I couldn't understand why the runners who came in second through last kept running. If you couldn't win, why run? But in essence, they were the real runners—not me.

Some thirty years later, life has seasoned me by trials of many kinds. I no longer take my health for granted and it is finally a joy to run again. I don't take myself too seriously anymore. Even though I have to do a lot of training for this Ironman, I will not let it master me. If the Lord wants me to do this, He will keep me healthy enough to train and finish the race.

The only person that could have healed me from this obsession was Jesus, and He did. Don't get me wrong; I'm still competitive, but not obsessive. On most bike rides and runs, I talk to Jesus. Instead of worrying if I am going faster than the last workout, I am just happy to be able to work out.

Does something have you mastered where you are on the road to self-destruction? Is something other than Jesus your identity? Most of the time you know it's coming, but can't stop it. It has mastered you and you are a slave to either the high or security it gives you. So how do you jump off the treadmill of perfection and go with the unknown? Jesus is the only way.

When you gave up your life for Jesus, the Bible says you were bought with a price. Jesus snatched you from the grip of hell and gave you eternal life. You can only have one master in this world.

"You were bought at a price; do not become slaves of men" (1 Corinthians 7:23).

What was the price? It was the painful, humiliating death of Jesus on the Cross. Jesus had no sin, so He went to the Cross because we were dead in our sins. Jesus paid the ultimate price for you and me so that whoever believes in Him will inherit eternal and abundant life.

If you are mastered by anything other than Jesus, stop, and pray that the Lord will give you a fresh perspective on what really matters. It is not records, fame, fortune, or possessions; it is eternal life through Jesus Christ. Let Jesus reign in your life, and nothing will entangle or master you ever again.

Finishing Strong

The Bible speaks a lot about finishing the race of life strong in our faith.

"I consider my life worth nothing to me, if only I may finish the race and complete the task the Lord Jesus has given me—the task of testifying to the gospel of God's grace" (Acts 20:24).

Chase, our five-year-old who is autistic, has had an earache for the past four days. His autism and sensory issues make it difficult for him to take any medication orally, so he hasn't been able to keep down the antibiotics. I just got back from the emergency room where they finally gave Chase a couple of antibiotic shots. When I got to the emergency room, the nurses couldn't have been nicer. Then the doctor came in and I will have to tell you that he was one of the most offensive people I have ever met. Whatever good the staff had shown about the facility quickly diminished, and I was left with a tarnished opinion of the place. Finally, the doctor suggested a couple of courses of action, but I didn't trust him. I said okay to the antibiotic, but not the pain medicine, and we left.

What is your Christian walk like? Did it start out strong only to be tainted by the evil desires of this world or are you able to stand firm and joyful in your salvation? Once in a while, Julie and I go to a restaurant near our house. The meal is very good, but the dessert is awesome. The chocolate cake is actually at least eight inches high and about four inches wide. It's very smart that the last impression they leave is one of amazement. When I was an airline pilot I noticed most people remembered more about the flight by the landing than anything else, because that is the end of the trip.

I am giving you all these examples to say:

It's not how you start; it's how you finish!

My track coach trained us to run negative splits. This means that you would always run the last part of the race faster than the first. If someone started out like a rabbit, you would just let them go. He would always say, "They will come back to you, just run your own race."

How are you running your race? Are you pacing yourself to finish strong or have you started out too fast? I'm sure you can think of some similar analogies. These same types of experiences have happened to all of us. So how do we finish strong in the race of life?

1.   Pace yourself—Being a committed Christian, father, mother, son, or daughter is about the commitment and being consistent.

2.   Be joyful—No one likes to be around an angry person.

3.   Pray—We need the power of the Holy Spirit to help us in our Christian walk. The world is full of evil desires and we need to be able to put on the shield of the Lord to stop the attacks.

4.   Train—No one ever wins a race without at least first spending hours, months, and years in training. Don't think just being in the race guarantees victory. If you have made a decision to accept the Lord as your Savior, it is by His grace you are saved and you can't earn that. But the Apostle Paul says, "Should we go on sinning so that grace may increase?" If you are saved, then there should be fruit in your life. This fruit can be a kind, gentle spirit, encouraging one another in the faith, serving with a joyous heart, or being a prayer warrior with a joyful spirit. Remember that we do these

things out of love for what Jesus has done for us, not as a prerequisite to earning our salvation.

"Be joyful always, pray continually giving thanks in all circumstances for this is God's will for you in Christ Jesus" (1 Thessalonians 5:16-18).

Smile today, and no matter how bad your day gets, be kind to others. You never know who may be watching.

Does Being Distressed Bring Comfort?

If you were to ask me that question fifteen years ago, I would have said you were out of your mind. How can being distressed be good for anything? If I were distressed, I would find a good watering hole and stay awhile! Fortunately, that was then and this is now. I have tried to comprehend what God does, but it is not worth trying. It is only worth standing in awe of Him. Just think that God knows all the birds of the air, helps them find food, knows when all the animals give birth, knows every one of the hundreds of millions of people in the world and how they feel at any particular moment, keeps the oceans from going over their boundaries, and to top it off, He treats you and me as His own children. How can He do that? All we have to know is that there is only one God that we serve, and that is Jesus.

Comprehending God will never happen. We know that God can do all things and all things are under His control, so let's take a look at our lives here on Earth. Why are we here?

First of all, we are here to glorify God. The next two most important things for us to do in this world are:

1.   Come to a saving knowledge of Jesus as Savior and Lord of our lives.
2.   Share the gospel of Jesus with as many people as we know.

Other than these three things, *nothing else matters*.

This leads me to a question. What are you doing in your life that will matter for eternity? Each of us has different circumstances, but the same goal. Each of us comes from different backgrounds, but the same goal. Each of us has different problems and trials, but the same goal.

As we go through our Christian walk, we suffer trials of many kinds. Since we are children of God when we accept Him as Savior and Lord of our lives, shouldn't that make us immune to suffering? Why should we suffer?

" ... the Father of compassion and the God of all comfort who comforts us in all our troubles so that we can comfort those in any trouble with the comfort we ourselves have received from God. For just as the sufferings of Christ flow into our lives, so also through Christ our comfort overflows" (II Corinthians 1:3-5).

Before Julie and I had children, I used to have little tolerance for a child screaming on an airplane or anyplace else for that matter. Now that I have kids who have screamed all night with pain or tiredness, I now have compassion for those parents, instead of disdain. I have even gone up to them and said, "Can I help you with your child?" Before I had children, I would have asked the flight attendant to move me. God allows us to go through trials so that the comfort He gives us we can then pass on to others. I have seen parents who have lost a child be a comfort to those parents who have just lost a child. This is a pain that is beyond comprehension, but I have seen the grace and power of God comfort these families. To say, "I know how you feel," when you have not experienced this pain is not true. God allows trials sometimes in our lives so that the comfort we get from Jesus, we can then use to comfort those who are going through the same thing.

In this world we will suffer trials of many kinds. Being a Christian does not make you immune to life's tragedies. But being a Christian gives you a rock, a fortress, a deliverer, a redeemer to hold onto when the seas get rough. I don't know what I would do without Jesus. I would be stuck in an anxious worldly rut with no hope. I have not only the hope of eternal salvation, but I have the comfort of knowing that Jesus is there to get me through anything that comes my way. It is usually through the storms that I learn the most. Do I like the storms? Of course not! But after the storm has passed, the blue sky looks so much bluer.

"Consider it pure joy, my brothers, whenever you face trials of many kinds, because you know that the testing of your faith develops perseverance. Perseverance must finish its work so that you may be mature and complete, not lacking anything" (James 1:2-4).

I am grateful for the trials that the Lord has allowed me to go through. It's amazing how trials can break you down, but breaking you down to build you up in the Lord. Why should we suffer? We suffer so that we can have compassion for others and trust in Jesus. Suffering is good for our souls. Christ suffered on the Cross, even though He was not guilty. We were. But Christ took it upon himself to suffer and die a horrible death on the Cross so that all who believe in Him will have abundant and eternal life.

The next time trials come your way, and they will, turn to Jesus. He's the only one who can sustain and comfort you. Then and only then will you be able to comfort those with the same comfort and compassion that Jesus has given you.

Can I Be a Little Bit Bad?

This is a question that has been asked since Adam and Eve. When the devil tempted Eve with the fruit of knowledge, he was able to convince Eve that it wasn't as bad as God said. Once Adam and Eve ate the fruit, eternity was changed so that physical death became part of everyone's life. One choice, one result.

I take a bagful of pills each day because of a wrong decision that I made over thirty years ago. Someone said to try marijuana. I was an athlete who never smoked or drank and the temptation was at hand. Of course, I gave in to the temptation. I had a bad reaction to the marijuana, and spent days in coronary care at the age of twenty. One choice, one result.

"But among you there must not be even a hint of sexual immorality, or of any kind of impurity, or of greed, because these are improper for God's holy people. Nor should there be obscenity, foolish talk, or coarse joking, which are out of place, but rather thanksgiving" (Ephesians 5:3).

The definition of "hint"—a very small amount; an amount or trace of something that is so small that it can only just be noticed.

I have tried to be a little bit bad and it doesn't work. Before I was a believer, I could make a sailor blush. But by the power and grace of God, Jesus changed me and I am eternally grateful. Do I still struggle with my past and the things I used to do? I have to say yes, but each day it gets less and less. If I were to think about these things, and every once in a while indulge in acts of impurity, the next thing I know I would be drawn back into a life that Jesus died to get me out of.

The dictionary defines "hint," as a trace. "There must not even be a trace of sexual immorality, impurity, greed, obscenity, foolish talk, or coarse joking." Now, we are all sinners and at times we will say something we shouldn't, but the closer we are to the Lord the less likely any of these things will happen.

Nothing good comes after 10:00 P.M. I don't care how you try to justify it, but the night is full of evil. Why is it that bars aren't full during the day? It's not because we all work. It's because the evil forces comes out at night. This is not some hocus-pocus theory; this is reality. Satan is referred to as the prince of darkness.

Pornography is rampant in this country for a number of reasons. The Internet has made it more accessible, and most of the world has lost a healthy fear of the Lord. If you knew what Jesus was thinking when you look at these images, you would either throw the computer out the window or rip up any material that causes you to stumble in this area. Looking at pornography is a lack of respect for Jesus. This is the same with flirting. You may say, "How close can I get to the edge without really being bad?" I can tell you that even thinking about this is the first step to an affair. If you think you are immune to an affair or that you would never fall, then you are the one who is in danger. I say this not to convict you because only the Lord can do that. I say this is because I have lived this life and failed and because the Lord says it is so. You don't have to believe me, but you have to believe God.

Not too many people start out on their wedding night to destroy their marriages. But complacency, not being in God's Word, hanging out with unbelievers, or in nightclubs is very dangerous. Do you want to take a chance on something that will affect your spouse, your children, and their children's children because of selfishness on your part?

I had a wild past—and I say this from experience—if you want Jesus to save you from impure thoughts, from evil desires, and from addictions, He will. First of all, you have to ask Him with a repentant heart and you need to want to change. You can't say a prayer on Sunday morning after being out all night and then start the process over again the following week.

God will not be mocked!

The Lord's lessons are uplifting and encouraging. The Lord has laid upon my heart to preach His truth to keep you from stumbling. Satan would love nothing more than to see you spend eternity with him. If you say you are saved and continue to do the things of the world, then I have to question if you really made a decision for Jesus. When you make a decision for the Lord, the Apostle Paul says:

"Therefore, if anyone is in Christ, he is a new creation, the old has gone; the new has come!" (II Corinthians 5:17).

The "old has gone." Are you still doing things that you were doing in your younger days that are not appropriate, or are you a new creation?

Can I be a little bit bad? No! Since we are all sinners, we will never be perfect and we will have times that we stumble. The Apostle Paul says that we should not abuse the grace of God.

"What shall we say, then? Shall we go on sinning so that grace may increase? By no means! We died to sin; how can we live in it any longer?" (Romans 6:1).

God, by His grace, forgives us our sin when we come to Him with a repentant heart. But God will not continue to allow His grace to be used as a tool to keep on sinning.

I am speaking to you today out of love because I have seen personally what impurity can do. It will destroy everyone and everything in its path. Pray today that the Lord would give you the power and grace to lead a spirit-filled life.

I Think I'm Stupid

I thought that would get your attention. The dictionary defines "stupid" as "unintelligent; thought to show a lack of intelligence, perception, or common sense."

"Whoever loves discipline loves knowledge, but he who hates correction is stupid" (Proverbs 12:1).

I love to be in a disciplined atmosphere. Running and endurance sports give me a sense of commitment and structure. On the other hand, if someone corrects me, sometimes I find offense. That is an arrogant part of my nature. What I'm really thinking is that "I'm smarter than you, so don't tell me what to do; what do you know?" I'm this way especially with my wife Julie. She will say something that I may not be doing right and before she is finished, I'm shutting her down. The Lord has given Julie a unique gift of discernment. She is able to meet someone and usually know if they are on the up and up. I, on the other hand, am very gullible and can be taken in by the best of them.

When I sit still long enough to listen, I learn quite a bit from Julie. When I swallow my pride, I'm able to learn. Sometimes we are toughest on those we love the most. My dad used to quiz me after Sunday School. During Sunday School, all I could think about was how much time was left and what I would do when I got out. I remember my dad asked me, "Who is Mary?" Now we all know Mary was the mother of Jesus. I, on the other hand, was more aware of "Mary and her little lamb," than Mary the mother of Jesus. I can still remember my dad just shaking his head. The angrier he became, the more I shut down.

I remember coming home with a bad report card when I was in the seventh grade. I was walking home after the school bus dropped me off and a friend of the family asked me how I did on my report card. I told her, "I'm in trouble," then laughed and walked home. I had no fear of the consequences. When I say bad grades I mean mostly C's and D's. Not too good for a doctor's son. I did get a good grade in gym!

When I was in the seventh grade, my parents also had my IQ tested. Since I had ADD and was a daydreamer, my focus was non-existent. Was

I really stupid or just not interested? The verdict came back that I was just not interested in what I was being taught.

So many kids today are on Ritalin because we try to conform to a standard that is not normal. We have to get back to letting kids be kids. I remember my track coach telling me that the students who get C's are probably the ones who later will give money to build the new buildings on campus.

The Lord has made each one of us perfect. This is so because God does not make mistakes. Period!

The Lord puts people in our path to encourage, teach, and convict us. When we don't listen, we are thinking that we are better than others. When someone comes up to you and says things that may bristle the hair on the back of your neck, just take a deep breath and hear them out. God may be using them to keep you from falling or making a mistake that you will regret forever. The more I know, the more I realize how much I don't know. Pray today that the Lord will give each of us a calm, non-prideful spirit. Let us be open to any and all correction or criticism.

None of us is stupid, because God doesn't make stupid people.

Stupid in this sense means that we don't use the resources the Lord has given us. If you have been told in the past that you are stupid, don't believe it. You are an awesome, one-of-a-kind creation from the Lord. Think about how the Lord made you in His image and then build upon that.

Don't let anyone steal your peace.

The Possum Syndrome

A lot of us have a problem with sharing. Maybe it's not an outward problem, but rather an internal struggle that we face every day. It is certainly easier to share out of our abundance, than out of our need. Before I started training for the Ironman, I was eating cheesecake like it was a main course meal. I remember after one meal, I ordered dessert and Julie asked if she could have a bite. I had not tasted it yet, and became annoyed that she should get a bite before I did. Now if I had eaten almost all of my cheesecake, I probably wouldn't have had a problem giving her a bite.

Giving out of our abundance is not really sharing, it is just giving away. True sharing is giving what we need ourselves.

"All the believers were one in heart and mind. No one claimed that any of his possessions was his own, but they shared everything they had" (Acts 4:32).

They shared everything. Sharing not only includes our possessions, but our talents and our time. Our time—now that is something most of us have trouble sharing. It's easier to give money or things to an organization than spend time going to a soup kitchen, sharing the gospel with others, or going out with your kids.

In order to truly share, we have to first get to the point where we realize that all we have including possessions, our talents, and our time is a gift from the Lord.

We don't own anything we have. The Lord owns it all and has given it to us on loan until He calls us home. Someone gets a new car and has trouble if someone touches it. Then a couple of years later when the newness has worn off, they are a little more lenient. No one is asking you to give up your possessions as long as your possessions do not cause you to stumble. Are you holding onto something so tightly that it is affecting other parts of your life?

As quickly as the Lord gives, the Lord can take away. How can we get rid of the possession syndrome? First of all, we need to pray that whatever has a hold on us, the Lord would get rid of. We cannot beat satan unless we call upon the name of the Lord. The Lord will release us from this burden when we earnestly seek His face, but we have to want to get rid of this sin. Some people say I want to exercise, but it is only a statement, not a conviction. Are you willing to give up everything for Jesus? Jesus doesn't ask us to give up everything for Him, but He does ask us to give up those things that hinder our walk with Him.

Young children have a problem with sharing. This is not something learned; this is something in our sinful nature that we are born with. Since our sinful nature is always there, we need the Lord's strength to live a godly, selfless life. Pride is also an attitude that can destroy. When you think of yourself as better than others, pride of heart will eat away at you like a cancer. Pride will make you hold onto possessions and make you a very ineffective witness for Jesus.

Are you known by what house you live in, what job you have, or what car you drive? Or are you content with being known as a follower of Jesus? When you meet a new person is the first thing you say, "What do you do for a living?" Or is it "How can I help you?" and mean it. How many times do we ask someone how they are doing, really hoping they don't tell us?

If you are truly interested in living a life free of worry, strife, and accumulation, then pray today that the Lord would rid you of the evil desire for possessions. When you can learn to share out of what you need, instead of what you want to give away, those things that have had a hold on you will slowly slip away. The joy of truly giving will fill your soul. That is the medicine for the possession syndrome.

Be Still

Now here is something I will probably struggle with until the day the Lord calls me home. I remember my mom saying, "Grass doesn't grow under your feet." My nickname in college was "Hectic." Things haven't changed much, have they? I have been traveling for the past week to various cities and my quiet time has been minimal. Early meetings, long hours, and concerns about trying to fit round pegs in square holes. When I'm home, Julie and I usually get up early, pray and read the Word. When we started to pray today, I didn't have anything to say. Julie asked me what was wrong and I said, "I don't feel close to the Lord. I need to just be still for a moment to figure out where I am and where God is." Ever been there?

"Be still and know that I am God" (Psalm 46:10).

It doesn't say just to be still. This Psalm says to be still and then feel the Lord's presence. How many times do you and I pray and don't feel the Lord's presence? Probably more times than we would admit. When we are in a hurry, putting God maybe second, third, or fourth on the list doesn't get it done. What we are really saying when we do this is that God can't get it done and I'm in a hurry, so I will handle it myself. It is tough to be still when chaos seems to be all around us. Your family life, job, finances, or health may not be going as you had planned. I don't know who made this observation, but it goes like this.

"How do you make God laugh? Tell Him your plans."

We all have issues!

I don't care if you are the richest or the poorest person in the world— none of us has it all together. Maybe on the outside we portray confidence, but there are things in our lives that we all struggle with. It may be different for each person, but these things are there. You know what I'm talking about. What thing is causing you not to be still?

The more I know about God, the less I know. The more I try to comprehend who He is, the more I see how I will never understand the power, glory, and majesty of Jesus. But that is where Jesus wants us.

From the beginning of time Jesus didn't want us to try to figure out His plan. He wants us to trust Him and Him alone. Can you go through life content without knowing the plan? The more things we can give over to Jesus, the less hectic our lives will be. Wouldn't it be nice to be able to be still in body, mind, and spirit? No matter what you are struggling with, Jesus already knows the outcome. So why do we get in the way and try to speed things up? I don't think it's as much a lack of faith, as it is a lack of trust. You see, all of us are used to trusting man and man will always let you down. Somehow we have to get rid of that thought process and get to know God, *really* get to know God. Then and only then will we be able to trust, and once we trust, we can start to be still.

This life is not just aimed at the day Jesus calls you home. This life is made up of millions of events that mold our characters. When people see you and your actions, do they see Jesus or do they see a frantic lost soul? These past few weeks I may have exhibited strength on the outside, but on the inside I have felt lost because of my inability to completely trust in Jesus. Why has today been better? Because I had time to be still and know that God is God. Since God created everything and knows everything there is no excuse for not being still before the Lord.

No matter what is bothering you today, just be still until you know that God is God. When you can do that, then the Lord's peace will overwhelm you and those problems that seemed too big will quickly fade away. Don't let the evil things of this world creep into your life and destroy what is pure and good.

Be still because it is contagious. Those around you will start calming down also. Give it all over to Jesus.

Catch Me If You Can

It was a week ago today that I woke up around 4:30 A.M. with a very familiar pain. If you have ever had a kidney stone, you know what I am talking about. The pain normally starts in the lower back and continues to increase until you either pass out or run, and I mean run. They call it the stone dance because when you have one, you can't stand still. It actually looks like you are doing some type of weird dance. It's a cross between disco and the tango. The tango part is when the nurse is actually trying to catch you to give you an IV.

I live about a mile from the hospital and I didn't want to wake up the boys, so I got in my car and found myself going seventy-five mph in a thirty-five zone. I came to an intersection that was clogged with traffic. I ended up going on the grass and around telephone poles to cut the corner. I was hoping a policeman would see me so he could give me an escort. I slid into a parking space at the emergency room and crawled to the front desk. Luckily, I was the only one there, so they took me right in. The nurse gave me a painkiller and said that it should help. Ten minutes later the doctor came in and I was still dancing around the room. Another round of painkillers were called for and this time they worked. Of course, I didn't know what my name was or what zip code I was in, but at that point I didn't care. You know you are sick when you don't care if the hospital gown is open or not! Ever been there? The CAT scan showed that the stone was able to pass on its own, so that is what it did. Three days later, I was the proud papa of a one-ounce stone.

Then the fun part started. That afternoon, not only did I get the flu, but everyone else in the house. So, that week our house was more like a MASH unit than a home. The only one who wasn't sick was the dog, and he was sick the week before after eating a bowl full of bubbles.

As I was running around the room with the nurse trying to get an IV in me that day, I realized that that was the same way Jesus had pursued me. If you run long enough, you will get tired and, hopefully, give in. Where are you in your relationship with God? Are you still running? Or have you come to the point in your spiritual life where you know that Jesus is the only way? Sometimes the more pain we have, the more we run. Only after much reflection, do we realize that we need to run to Jesus, not away from him.

This life will never be perfect. That's why there is Heaven. Don't say, "I'll take another look at Jesus when I'm older, when I graduate, when I get out of this relationship, or when I feel better," because you are not guaranteed even today. Come to Jesus just as you are. We are all sinners and desperately need a Savior who is the ultimate Doctor. Are you still running away from Jesus not wanting Him to catch you? Or are you now ready for Jesus, but have been running so long you don't know how to get to Him? The good news is Jesus never left your side. You may have run all around the world trying to run from God and yourself, but Jesus knows. All you have to do is come to Him with a repentant heart, ask forgiveness for your sins, and acknowledge that He died on the Cross and rose from the dead to pay the penalty for your sins. If you ask Jesus into your life, He will never leave. Amen and amen to that.

Is today the day you are going to stop running? Stop right now and ask God for direction, hope, and restoration. He has always been there waiting for you.

Why Am I Here?

Have you ever questioned your existence? Have you ever wondered if you are making a difference? Are you just plain tired of life? (Sounds like I need more Zoloft, doesn't it?) Life is full of seasons. There are times of triumph and there are times of misery. Where does it say that life is full of roses every day? It doesn't! You see, Jesus was in agony in the Garden before He was crucified. Was it a good day for Him? No way. But Jesus was able to pray and get strength to make it through because He knew what He had to do. Do you know what you have to do?

One of the problems in our society is that we base our own worth on what other people have done. "They own hotels and motels, they own private jets, they gave a million dollars to the poor, but what have I done?" Here is what you have done. Some of you have spent a lifetime raising children for the Lord that He has entrusted to you. That is probably one of the most difficult and rewarding things God allows us to experience. Remember, our children are not ours. They are the Lord's, and He has given them to you to raise. This is an awesome task.

Some of you are heads of households and heads of companies. We can't be jealous in this life of what we think other people are doing. I know beyond a shadow of a doubt that everyone has issues!

All we are called to do is make sure our hearts are right before the Lord. If our hearts are right and pure, then we will be effective witnesses for Jesus. If our hearts are not pure, then we will be more of a hindrance than a help. Don't let other people steal your joy.

"We must obey God rather than man" (Acts 5:29).

This doesn't mean that we are not to obey our bosses or those in authority. This means that we can never impress man all the time. What we have to do is make sure that we are right with God. This means that at some point in our lives we have to acknowledge that Jesus died on the Cross and rose from the dead to pay the penalty for our sins. We acknowledge that we are sinners and ask Jesus to forgive us for our sins, and ask Him to come in and take control of our lives. If you have done that, then not only will you spend eternity in Heaven, but you will want to please Jesus more than man. When you can do that, then you actually please the one who created everyone in your life that you deal with. If you have a problem with your spouse, co–worker, or friend, take it to Jesus. When you ask Him for the wisdom and the words to say not only will He give you that wisdom, but He will also prepare the heart of the person you are going to speak with.

Why am I here? Two reasons:

1. To come to know Jesus as Savior and Lord.
2. To share the gospel with as many people as possible, and to encourage them in the faith.

Nothing else matters. Don't let the small things of this life distract you from your goal. Each day there will be small things that will turn into big things if you let them. God knows what is going on and God knows your heart. Open up to Him and He will let you know why you are here. Don't be too hard on yourself. Jesus died so we could live in freedom, not in bondage.

Why Am I Complacent?

This past week in our Sunday School class the teacher asked, "If you saw Jesus face to face, would it make any difference in the way you would live your life?" I would have to say that the more I thought about this the more intriguing it got. If I was in my room alone and all of a sudden Jesus appeared to me and started a conversation, I would be awe-struck. I would have so many questions. I would want to know so much more about Him. I would ask Him about my loved ones in Heaven. Of course, I know my encounter with Jesus would drastically transform me. If He appeared to everyone, would I have the same passion? I'm not sure. But I do know that if I spent a few moments seeing and touching Jesus, my life would probably change in several ways.

1. I would probably change professions and stand outside the Target store near my house and preach about what I had seen. I would know that nothing else is as important as coming to a saving knowledge of Jesus.

2. My prayer life would definitely be different because I have seen and talked to the one I'm praying to.

3. I have seen the miracle of Jesus appearing to me.

4. *I have seen Jesus!*

Do you know who I sound like? Yes, I sound like Thomas. When Jesus was crucified and died, the disciples ran like scared rabbits. Their faith was in jeopardy. It wasn't until they saw Jesus face to face that they believed and understood. Those who saw Him would never be the same and they were the people who started sharing the gospel of life and resurrection.

But Jesus said to Thomas:

"Because you have seen Me you have believed, blessed are those who have not seen and yet have believed" (John 20:29).

If I were to look back over my life I could write a book on all that Jesus has done for me. I have not seen Jesus in physical form, but I have seen the wonders and the results of Jesus' work, not only in my life, but the lives of so many others. So my life shouldn't be different if I see Jesus or not. As Jesus said, "Blessed are those who have not seen and yet have believed."

That is faith!

Am I waiting for Jesus to appear to me for me to give up the things that hold me back from really getting to work for the Lord? If I were to really think about it, I have seen Jesus. I see Jesus in creation, in the miracle of the birth of our two boys, the miracle of answered prayer, the miracle of everyday life. Why am I complacent? Even some of those who saw the miracles of Jesus, did not believe in Him. Since the evil one of this world does not want us to be effective witnesses for Jesus, he will try to distract us in many ways. He will try to get us to think that our jobs are more important than Jesus or our families. He will try to distract us with things. You know about things—the car, the boat, the vacation, the new home, whatever is most important to you. These things rob us of our time with our family and Jesus.

The real key to living a godly life is to simplify our lives. We all have too much stuff. Just look at our garages. If you were to get the news today that one of your family members were seriously ill none of that stuff would matter. By praying, reflecting on what God has done for us, and the things we have seen Him do we realize that we really have seen Jesus.

" ... *Let us throw off everything that hinders and the sin that so easily entangles, and let us run with perseverance the race marked out for us. Let us fix our eyes on Jesus, the author and perfecter of our faith.... "* (Hebrews 12:1,2).

The Book of Hebrews tells us to not only get rid of it, but to throw off everything that hinders our walk. What is hindering your walk with Jesus that you need to throw off? Complacency doesn't usually happen in a day. Complacency usually happens over a period of time. The good news is that Jesus can forgive and renew our spirits when we come to Him with repentant and open hearts. Let us live our lives as if we have seen Jesus. I am telling you that if we can, then the whole world will hear about Jesus.

Are Your Brakes On?

The more I train for the Ironman, the more I realize I don't know about bicycle maintenance or, for that matter, body maintenance. A pro rider I met in Orlando suggested I see a tech at a bike shop in North Carolina who has been fitting riders for over twenty years. When I got to the facility, he had me take all kinds of measurements. I would say he took over twenty different measurements of my body and bike. He had me get on the bike, ride, and stop, then ride some more; then he made adjustments to the bike. He raised my seat post quite a bit and did a couple of other drastic things to the bike. He said that all of this would give me more power and that in turn would compute to more speed. The bad part about this was that this man did a bike fitting only. I didn't know that in the process of the fitting, the back wheel had turned a few degrees, and was now rubbing against the back brake and the side of the frame.

Here's the interesting part. I went on what was to be a seventy-mile bike ride. It was raining off and on, and the wind was gusting to thirty-five mph. Not a great day! After about ten miles into the ride, I thought to myself, "I must be tired because I'm sure not going very fast." Well, most people wouldn't go very fast if the brake was always on! After three hours on the bike, I finally came to the turnaround. The ride which was to have taken four hours, turned into a six hour ride. I was going down a steep hill and started smelling rubber. I thought, "Boy, some truck needs to get its brakes fixed." Little did I know that it was me! At the end of the ride when I found out what the problem was, I was elated and mad. How could I start a ride without first checking everything?

Yesterday I was out on a bike ride and after about ten miles, I heard a huge bang—and I mean *bang*! I thought somebody had tried to shoot me. A few seconds later, I was riding on my rim. Yes, I had a flat tire. I got the wheel off and started checking the tire for any glass or thorns. What I found was a tear in the wheel. Apparently, I forget one important thing: Tires need to be changed on a bike like tires need to be changed on a car. I had ridden about 2,000 miles on this set of tires and they were only good for about 1,500 miles. Luckily I had a cell phone, so I called Julie. She came out with our support crew of Bryce and Chase, and we headed home.

How many times in life do we start things before we are ready? We think that we will figure it out once we get started. This is not only dangerous, but also unproductive. The Lord protected me yesterday in spite of my ignorance. Luckily, I had the blowout going up a hill instead of down one. I have never been one for detail, but I am starting to figure out that the details are what make an endeavor successful or not.

What are the details in our Christian walk? On the outside looking in, we could think, "I'll just go to church; that should be good enough." Like getting on a bike and just riding off, we find there is more to our Christian faith than that. We start by having and making a commitment to Jesus as Savior and Lord of our lives. We go to church to be around other believers and to worship the Lord. We study the Word, pray, and have quiet time to get to know the Lord better. Each day we try to refine our faith. When trials come, we are ready because we have put the time into getting to know God. Just going to church on Sunday is like getting on the bike without checking the equipment. It is shallow and dangerous.

Our culture is now considered obese. In Jesus' time, people walked from town to town. Probably only the people in palaces had a weight problem. Now we don't even have to get out of our cars to eat, go the cleaners, the bank, drug store, and a lot of other places. We need to take care of our bodies physically, as well as spiritually. Both go hand in hand. I had been on high blood pressure medicine for over twenty-five years, but with all the training I'm doing, I am now off of it completely. Of course, six-hour bike rides with the brakes on will do that!

"You were bought at a price. Therefore honor God with your body" (1 Corinthians 6:20).

We can honor God by doing the work the Lord has sent us to do. That is to share the gospel with as many people as we know and to be a light in a dark world. Honoring God with our bodies also includes not giving ourselves over to gluttony. Many times if we are angry, depressed, or feel a sense of hopelessness we will be lethargic and eat. This only makes matters worse. Young kids today are overweight because our generation has stopped exercising. When we do not take care of our bodies, our spiritual life suffers. We lose energy and develop a host of other health issues.

I have learned a lot training for this race. What started out as a goal to raise money for autism has turned into so much more. I underestimated the commitment and the preparedness necessary. Sometimes as Christians we underestimate the commitment, also. Here are a few things to consider:

1. Take one day and one step at a time.
2. Don't look too far down the road.
3. Before starting the journey, figure out what you will need.
4. Pray for wisdom.
5. Pray for discernment.
6. Pray that you would be able to finish the race of life strong, instead of crawling across the finish line. We can only do this by pacing ourselves.
7. Be very diligent in all that you do, and most of all pray, and then pray some more.

If you don't pray and ask for the Lord's wisdom, you may be living your life with the brakes on wondering why things are so difficult.

Your Past

Do those two words bring up joy or anguish? There are very few people I know who have had a great past. Some have wished they had taken a different fork in the road. Many have been victims of sexual, verbal, or physical abuse. Some have never had a chance to get a good start. I could list a hundred things that people have told me they have a hard time forgetting or forgiving. We are definitely "creatures of habit," so it is very interesting how people that have been in abusive relationships tend to end up in other abusive relationships. It isn't that they want to be in that situation, but it is what they know, and there is some comfort in the known rather than the unknown.

As I look back over my past, I see the Lord at work every day. Even though I did not believe in Jesus as my Savior until I was thirty-eight years old, Jesus was still watching out for me. Amen to that. But here is something very important that I want each of you to think about. A thorn that goes deep in your flesh, if left unattended, will work itself out. It may take days, weeks, months, or years, but it will come out. It is the same thing with events in our past. Something that you may have blocked, whether it is abuse or abandonment, and no matter how many years you try to block it, will eventually come out. At first it may show itself as depression, anxiety, or a host of other physical ailments. But in the end, you need to come face to face with the thing that you are most afraid of, that thing which has made you who you are today.

I don't like going back. I'm a person who says, "Let the past go; I can't change it, so why spend energy on something I can't change?" That may work for awhile, but unresolved issues will come up just like that thorn and probably when you least expect it. The good news is that our past does not have to dictate our future. But the only way that this can be true is by accepting Jesus into our lives. You see, we are sinful people and will be until God calls us home. Ever since Adam and Eve sinned, we have lived in a fallen world. Everything God has made good, we have corrupted. The Lord allows us to work to earn a living. At times we use lies and treachery to get ahead. Look at the scandals involving Enron and World Com. God made men and women to be one in marriage. Why are swingers' conferences all over the country? Why is it that females and males now lust after the same sex? (I should not say "now," because this was going on in Biblical times). God made sex to be a beautiful part of marriage between a husband and wife only. But we have corrupted every part of it that you can think of. There is perversion, adultery, incest, rape, rampant childhood sexual abuse, and addiction to pornography.

You may be crying out in your heart, "Help me," but you don't know where to turn. First of all, you need to turn to Jesus. He is the Creator, Sustainer, and Redeemer. When you put your faith and trust in man, man will always let you down because we are all sinners with selfish hearts. Jesus allows things to happen in our lives so we will learn to be dependent on Him instead of others or our circumstances. Pray that the Lord would direct you to a good Christian therapist. Please do not go to the world for help. You need to know how to treat problems from the Word of God.

I hate to say it, but the human heart is just as bad today as it was in the days of Sodom and Gomorrah. Nothing has changed in the human heart. Satan has been called the prince of this world and he will do whatever it takes to make your life miserable so you will not be an effective witness for Jesus. If satan can keep you down and depressed, he has won. But Jesus came to this world in the flesh, led a sinless life because He was God, died on the Cross and rose from the dead not only to conquer death, but to conquer sin forever and ever for all those who believe in Him.

Where do you stand? Do you want victory or do you want to stay in the comfort zone of past abuses? It may not be easy to go back, in fact it may be very painful, but Jesus will restore you and protect you. Have you ever wondered why you do the things you do? We are a product of our environment. But that doesn't always have to be the case. You can change, but this is a heart issue, not an issue of the will. Jesus is the only one who can change the heart. Out with the old and in with the new. But first of all you have to want to change.

Some people are paralyzed from events in their past. Are you one of those people who has given up, or are you ready to take the journey to victory? Don't let your past dictate your future. Live for the Lord and He will direct your path and your steps. Pray that if the thorn is finally coming to the surface, you would get help.

" ... *the truth will set you free"* (John 8:32).

Have a great week and don't let anyone steal your peace.

What's Your Problem?

We all have days, don't we? Sometimes we forget that other people have "those days" like we do. It is so easy to get aggravated by someone who either calls you a name, cuts you off in traffic, does a underhanded thing to you, or is just plain mad at you and the world. But let's get to a more important issue. When someone gets mad at you or does any of these things to you, it is not you who they are angry at. It is themselves; yes, themselves.

We are truly products of our environment. How can we expect a child who has been physically, emotionally, or sexually abused to be normal? How can we expect someone who has lost a loved one, been divorced, or lost a child to think clearly? Everyone has a past, everyone. Instead of firing back with something that may be hurtful, start giving people the benefit of the doubt. Isn't that what Jesus did for us? You see, even when we were deep in sin and didn't believe in God, Jesus died for us so that all those who believe in Him will have eternal life. Jesus didn't say, "If you are kind to me, I will think of saving you. You do this for Me and I may think of saving you."

No, Jesus saved us even though we were sinners.

So, when we start judging people, even though Jesus has forgiven all the bad we have done, we are discounting what Jesus did on the Cross. How can Jesus forgive us if we don't forgive others?

Matthew 18:23-35 talks about a servant who owed his master a lot of money. He fell to the master's feet and begged him to forgive the debt. The master forgave him. The servant went home and found someone who owed him money. Even though it was a small amount, he treated this man horribly and had him thrown in prison for not repaying the debt. When the master found out, he had the servant that he had forgiven put in jail.

"'You wicked servant,' he said, 'I cancelled all that debt of yours because you begged me to. Shouldn't you have had mercy on your fellow servant just as I had on you?'" (Matthew 18:32).

"This is how My Heavenly Father will treat each of you unless you forgive your brother from your heart" (Matthew 18:35).

You can't have it both ways. You can't ask Jesus for forgiveness and then not forgive others. Jesus will then not forgive you. The next time someone does something to you that you feel is demeaning or unjustified, try to understand. It probably isn't about you, but the pain of something this person has never dealt with. Insecurity, loss, pain, and abuse harden the heart and make it difficult to love and be kind. Pray each day that you would be able to take ridicule that may not be justified, so that you can share the love of Jesus with others. When we strike back with venom after someone has wronged us, how is that showing the love of the Lord in our lives?

Remember, Jesus forgave us when we were deep in sin. How much more should we forgive those who may be going through something so painful we can't even imagine?

Pray that all the words of your mouth and your actions would reflect Jesus in your life.

Missed Opportunities

I went on a long bike ride over the weekend training for the Ironman. I had gone approximately forty-two miles of an eighty-five mile ride and needed more to drink. Up to this point I had already used a half can of Halt on a nasty dog, been whistled at by two men in a pickup, and battled headwinds to the point where I wondered, "What am I doing?" I crested a hill and saw a man in his seventies picking up something by the side of the road. I stopped and asked him how far the next convenience store was. He said it was only a half-mile up the road. "Thank you Jesus." I told him I needed more fuel. He looked at me, looked at the bike, looked at me, and then looked at the bike again and said, "Does that thing take gas?" I said, "No *I* need fuel; I'm running out of gas."

He said, "What are you doing way out here?" I told him I was training for an Ironman and he had no clue as to what that was. He was too preoccupied with raking up little bits of insulation that someone had thrown on his property. He kept asking me questions and he really wanted to talk. I on the other hand was training for an Ironman. Training, training, training, and more training. You would think I was trying out for the Olympics. Right in front of me was a man who was more important than any Ironman or Olympics and I was worried that my legs might not hold up if I talked to him much longer. I needed to get back home. I was looking for a way to get out of the conversation and move on instead of listening to a man who wanted to talk. God had put him in my path. Was he a believer? I don't know and I didn't take the time to find out. Off I went down the road, found the convenience store, got refueled, and headed home all the while thinking of this man.

To be like Jesus is to be more "others"-centered instead of "self"-centered. Right then and there I was self-centered, thinking about me, not the eternal consequences for this man. You see, no matter how much training I do, if God wants me to complete this race I will; if He doesn't, I won't. It is ultimately up to the Lord. Since that is the case I put my faith in the wrong place—myself. I'm not saying I would have said, "Jesus loves you, you are a sinner and you need to repent." What I should have done was gotten off my bike, helped him clean up the yard, maybe had some ice tea with him, and then shared the gospel. Because of my being self-centered I missed an opportunity, not only to share the gospel, but also to get to know a man.

How many times when you are at work, home, or play do you feel in such a rush that you don't have time to get to know someone? Most of ask someone, "How are you doing?" hoping no one will really take the time to tell us! Why? Because we don't think we have time to listen. What we are really thinking is, "What I have to do is more important than what you have to tell me."

"Do nothing out of selfish ambition or vain conceit, but in humility consider others better than yourselves. Each of you should look not only to your own interests, but also to the interests of others. Your attitude should be the same as that of Christ Jesus" (Philippians 2:3-5).

I have a lot to learn. Don't let work, sports, or hobbies get in the way of what is eternally important: Share the gospel and love of Jesus with as many people as you know whenever the opportunity arises. It amazes me how quickly people forget about someone when they die. Oh, they are so important when they are alive, but life goes on just as easily without them. What matters is the soul. First of all, do you know for sure where you would go if you were to die today? If not, then you need to ask Jesus for forgiveness of your sins, acknowledge that He died on the Cross and rose from the dead to pay the penalty for your sins, ask Him to come in and take control of your life and help you lead a life that is pleasing to Him. If you say this and mean it from your heart, you will be saved for eternity. Once you are saved then you can minister to others with the power of the Holy Spirit who will give you the words to say and who will put people in your path to share with.

I'm going to need to take another can of Halt, spray those dogs, and try to find that man again. I'll pray that the Lord would give me another chance to stop and sit awhile with this man and be able to talk about Jesus. Whether you have a big deal on the table, cash flow problems, or are just frantic about life, there is nothing more important than sharing the gospel and loving the Lord.

God created the whole Universe with a spoken word. Don't you think He can turn on the faucet of deals and money, or take away all problems that we think are significant when we truly trust in Him?

Pray today that we would all "pray and believe" instead of "pray and doubt." Pray also that we would *stop* and minister to others instead of thinking that we are too busy and important. The Lord isn't interested so much in what you have to do, as how you do it. Are you a light in a dark world or are you in the world waiting to turn the light switch on? Stop waiting, the time is now.

Death, the Big Bad Wolf

W e all know the story " … I'll huff and puff and blow your house down." The big bad wolf in today's world is satan. When we build our foundation with straw, it won't take much to destroy it. The ones who build a solid foundation will not be moved.

Jesus was sleeping in a boat with His disciples in the middle of the Sea of Galilee when a big storm came up. The disciples became terrified and woke Jesus up. He said to them,

"Why are you so afraid? Do you still have no faith?" (Mark 4:40).

What were the disciples afraid of? They were afraid that they were going to die. Even before we were born, the Lord picked a date when we will leave this world. We cannot outrun an Earthly transformation. I don't ever like to say anyone "died," because no one will die. Listen to me very carefully. What makes you, you, is your soul and it will live for eternity. The body that temporarily houses your soul will one day be cast off and at that point, in an instant, you will be standing before God. If you have accepted Jesus as Savior and Lord of your life before you got there, you will enter Heaven and be with Jesus forever. If you thought that Jesus was a fake or that you would put this decision off to a later time, then you will be in for a very rude awakening. Jesus will look at you and see that your name is not in the Lamb's Book of Life and you will spend eternity in hell, forever separated from God.

So, if you have made the decision to accept Jesus as Savior and Lord of your life, you will spend eternity in Heaven. Your soul will live forever in Paradise. Jesus is saying, "Why are you afraid?" If you die an Earthly death, why be afraid; you will be in Paradise immediately. The more we cling to the things of this world, the more anxious we will be. We may even be clinging onto past hurts, past abuses, past failures, or things today like money, fame, and fortune.

A lifetime of service to God does not mean that bad things won't happen. John the Baptist came and preached repentance and prepared the way for Jesus. What did he get in return? He got beheaded. But after being beheaded, he was in Paradise. People that have plastic surgery are just prolonging the inevitable. Death will come to everyone's doorstep. The question is are you ready?

Is your house (body) built on the solid foundation of trusting in Jesus for everything, or are you trusting in your bank account, title, status, stocks, and anything else you think important? There have been so many prayer requests lately for people who are going through some tremendous trials. We pray that God would heal them and give them comfort. But one day we will be going home if we are believers.

A good friend of mine was going on a mission trip and I said, "Aren't you afraid to eat or drink something that may make you sick?" He said, "You have to die of something." Even though this was funny this was true. We all have to die of something.

Believers won't be dead; we will just be transformed.

So what does all this mean? It means not to worry about your life. Jesus is either in control or He isn't. Jesus does not want our faith to be like waves tossed back and forth. Jesus wants us to have a firm faith on a firm foundation. Jesus and Jesus alone. Where are you on that journey? Do you see this world as the big bad wolf around the corner, or do you lead a life that says, "Bring it on?" We cannot be truly effective witnesses when we are so consumed with ourselves that our "self-centeredness" blocks out our "others-centeredness." Jesus was all about others and being a servant.

Pray today that you would see this life in a different light. This life was meant to be lived with compassion, not fear and grumbling. Don't let the evil things of this world distract you from God's truth, love, faithfulness, and eternal protection.

Be strong and courageous today. There is a big bad wolf and his name is satan. But when our foundation is Jesus, he has no power over us. Let the trials come and blow and blow and blow. So what? The house will not come down.

Have a great day and don't worry.

Lost

Our six-year old son Chase and I were at a resort last week in the mountains. Chase was running in all directions, as always. As I was talking with the man at the front desk, I had to take my eyes off of Chase for just a few moments. I looked back and "no Chase!" I ran outside and he wasn't out front. I ran back behind the cabin and there was at least a 100-foot drop off into a deep lake. These are the types of lakes where the water is brown for a few feet, then black until it drops off to who knows where. There were waterfalls all around. I called and called for Chase, but no answer. I was terrified. How could I have turned my back on him? I called the police and they didn't seem too interested. I was running through the woods and open fields, but no one seemed to care. I could not bear to lose him and I started to weep, crying out his name. It was like I was in the worst nightmare ever. Then the alarm went off. It *was* a nightmare. Chase was in the other room fast asleep. Boy, did I give him a hug that morning.

I want to tell you something very important. Jesus searches for you the same way.

"What do you think? If a man owns a hundred sheep, and one of them wanders away, will he not leave the ninety-nine on the hills and go to look for the one that wandered off? And if he finds it, I tell you the truth, he is happier about that one sheep than about the ninety-nine that did not wander off. In the same way your Father in Heaven is not willing that any of these little ones should be lost" (Matthew 18:12-14)

This does not mean the man does not care for the other sheep. He knows the other sheep are secure, but hates to have one who is lost.

In the same way, Jesus is distraught over any of you who are lost, who have not accepted Him as Savior and Lord of their lives. Since the Lord has given each of us free will, it is up to us to take the final step. Jesus does not want us to love Him because we have to, like a robot. Jesus wants us to love Him because we desire to love Him.

Are you one of the lost? Has the Lord been tugging at your heart? Have you felt that something is missing, but you don't know what it is?

The Hound of Heaven, by Francis Thompson, talks about Jesus as the hound searching, running, going in every crevice to find you. If you have been running and don't know why you're running, make today the day you stop. Now you know who has been chasing you. Below is an excerpt from the poem, *The Hound of Heaven*:

> I fled Him, down the nights and down the days;
>> I fled Him, down the arches of the years;
> I fled Him, down the labyrinthine ways
>> Of my own mind; and in the midst of tears
> I hid from Him, and under running laughter.
>> Up vistaed hopes I sped;
>> And shot, precipitated,
> Adown Titanic glooms of chasmèd fears,
>> From those strong feet that followed, followed after.
>> But with unhurrying chase,
>> And unperturbed pace,
> Deliberate speed, majestic instancy,
>> They beat—and a Voice beat
>> More instant than the Feet—
> "All things betray thee, who betrayest Me."

Make today the day that you stop fleeing. The Lord desires that none of us should be lost. Where are you on this journey? If your life has been crumbling beneath you, if you have searched after worthless idols, if you have run the other way from God, God understands. Since God understands, don't feel guilty, but feel love for the only one who can save us from hell. If you will ask Jesus for forgiveness of your sins, acknowledge that He died on the Cross and rose from the dead to pay the penalty for your sins, ask Him into your life and turn from the things you used to do to the things of God, then you will be free to enjoy this life and life eternal.

Until then, the Lord will be tugging at your heart. As a fox has no rest when the hound approaches, you will have no rest until you turn your life over to Jesus. Jesus will find you. The key question is will you make that decision before it is too late?

Lost! None of us is lost. We may not know where we are, but Jesus does. Trust in Him and Him alone.

Running Away

As a child, did you ever think of running away from home? There were a of couple times that I was so tired of discipline that I just wanted to leave. But I knew that when I got back home, the discipline would probably be worse, so I stayed. Plus, where would I go? I remember movies about kids getting a stick and pillowcase and wrapping all their possessions in it and walking off into the woods. Seems so simple until you think of the consequences. What if it rains? What if I run out of food? Of course, when we do things in haste, most of us don't think far enough ahead to consider the consequences. If we did, the incidence of abortion, adultery and divorce would be much less.

The human heart is the same today as it was in the days of Sodom and Gomorrah. We are all sinners and we continue to be until the day we see Jesus. But by God's grace, when we come to Him with a repentant heart, He will forgive our sins and remember them no more. *Remember them no more!*

We are a lot like the Israelites. God brought them out of bondage from Egypt to the Promised Land and the Israelites grumbled. We could have everything we want and still grumble. Why is that?

"Do not run until your feet are bare and your throat is dry. But you said 'It is no use! I love foreign gods and I must go after them'" (Jeremiah 2:25).

Why do we run from God? Because most of the time we are looking for an easier way. A foreign god had no power, so the people could do what they wanted, and they did. They indulged in prostitution, human sacrifices, revelry, and all kinds of evil pleasures. Why? Because they were not convicted of their sin.

When things get tough at home or work, or when health issues arise, we sometimes just want to run away. We don't know where we want to go; we just know we want to run. God may be convicting you right now of not running away. You may know that you need to stay where you are right now. Obedience to God is much more important than the desires of the flesh. If we start running from the Lord, we will eventually tire and run out of gas. If you start running and say, "It's no use," or "I would love a better job, a better wife, a better body, a better whatever," it will never be enough. When you start running from God you will keep running until you are like the prodigal son. You will get to the point where the slop of this world will start to taste horrible, and you will see that God is not only good, but loving and forgiving.

Don't let the evil desires of the flesh start you on a path that God does not want you on. You know it in your heart when you are disobedient. But sometimes disobedience does take over, more out of pride than anything else. Many times in this life we feel that we deserve a raise, promotion, a bigger house, a nicer car, or a bigger financial cushion, but what we really deserve is hell. That's right, hell. Jesus came to set us free when He died a horrible death on the Cross and rose from the dead. So forget about what you think you deserve, and see how you can glorify God in your life instead of glorifying yourself.

Humility before the Lord is a heart issue and nothing more. The issue is not between you and your boss, spouse, girlfriend, boyfriend, or children. The issue is between you and Jesus. When was the last time you were honest with Jesus? Some of you reading this see Jesus as someone who doesn't understand or someone who you can't talk to. Jesus came to Earth and was tempted in every way but did not sin, so that He could feel your pain. He knows what you are going through and wants you to talk to Him.

We don't need eloquent words to talk with Jesus. Talk to the Lord as you would to your best friend. Because that's what He is, your best Friend. Start today by running to Jesus instead of running from Him. Ask Him, as you would a friend, for help, humility, brokenness, and His power to lead your life for Him—not lead your life for yourself. When we can start to think of others more than ourselves, our lives will take on a whole new, fresh, meaning.

All of us at times want a change. Sometimes when the fire is hot, we want to run. The Lord is the only one who can turn down the heat and get you through the fire.

The more you run away, the hotter the fire will get.

Stop! Call out to Jesus, voice your concerns, and trust in Him. He will *never* let you down. Jesus says in His Word and we know from experience this to be true: Don't be a slave to anything in this world.

Make this the day you break free.

Let's Be Kids

It was my turn to watch the three-year-olds this week at church. As I walked into the class, one of the girls came up and gave me a big hug. Sometimes I wish I could be in my own Sunday School class, but when I'm with these kids and experience their big hearts, I'm glad I spent the time. For example, in training for the Ironman I have decided to cut my own hair with electric clippers. I don't have much hair to begin with so not only is it easier to manage, but I don't have to pay for what was only a five-minute haircut in a salon. One of the three-year-old boys came over and said, "If you drank all your milk, your hair would grow!" Another boy chimed in and said, "I drink all my milk. See how long my hair is!"

The innocence and forgiveness of a child is wonderful. I could have told them a lot of things and they would have believed them. Why? Because their minds have not yet been tainted by the harsh realities of life, insecurity, status, and fame.

A child lives in the "here and now," not in yesterday or tomorrow.

"I tell you the truth, unless you change and become like little children, you will never enter the kingdom of heaven" (Matthew 18: 3).

Kids are all about trust and gullibility. They believe what we tell them. Do you believe all Jesus says to you in His Word or do you believe *some* of the things, but choose to leave other truths behind? Do you believe that Jesus can save you from hell by accepting Him as Savior, but then worry about your family, job, status, or money? Can you accept Jesus for who He is and live in the here and now, or do you need proof like Thomas?

Are you able to be a kid or are you too much of an adult? I will have to confess that I have a hard time being a kid. Training for this Ironman has gotten me back into more of a child-like state. Swimming, running, and riding a bike have brought me back to the simplicities of life. On a long bike ride I'm able to drift off and daydream, think about the cows; yes, I talk to the horses and cows when I pass them on the road. I even give a moo, moo and a neigh, neigh, now and then. I did this to a herd of goats the other day and boy, did they go scrambling!

We need to learn to live in the present, instead of the past or the future. The past is gone, and we are not even guaranteed this afternoon. Kids forgive so easily, so often. We may say a harsh word to our son and then when we ask him to forgive us, he says, "No problem," and goes on about his business. He has actually forgiven and moved on.

How many times do we say we forgive someone, but we don't move on?

That's why Jesus wants us to have the mind and heart of a child. If you are trusting in your own strength and not in Jesus, you will start to see the world full of stress, instead of grace. Jesus is much bigger than our circumstances. Are you too old in your mind to be a kid? You cannot be energetic and effective unless you have a little bit of "kid" in you. Jesus wants us to come to Him with a childlike heart; a heart that believes and doesn't doubt; one that is humble and forgiving. I know thirty-year-olds that are old and grumpy and seventy-year-olds that are like kids. One group has chosen to take life too seriously and depend upon themselves. The other group has not taken life too seriously and has trusted Jesus, not themselves, for the outcome of their lives.

As children trust their parents for all their necessities, can you get back to that frame of mind and trust God, the ultimate Father, to take care of your every need?

Maybe you just need to drink more milk!

Are You In The Race?

Thirteen years ago almost to the day, I attempted a Half-Ironman in Panama City, Florida. The race consisted of a 1.2 mile swim, a 56 mile bike ride and a 13.1 mile run. I got caught in a riptide during the swim, and twenty-six other people had to be rescued in the water that day. I was so happy to be back on land that I rode the fifty-six miles on my bike and totally burned out. I didn't have anything left for the run. Five miles into the run, I sat down on some guy's front lawn and called it quits. It was an easy decision since I was seeing three of everything, plus I was doing the race for me.

Yesterday, I attempted the race again. This time it was in White Lake, North Carolina. At least I didn't have to worry about a riptide. What I did have to worry about was the water temperature. It was sixty-seven degrees at the start and, even though I had a wetsuit on, I was *cold*. I got in the water and could hardly feel my hands. I had prayed and prayed beforehand, so I really did not feel anxious. For me that is a huge plus before the start of a race. I also kept looking at the wristband I carry to remind me of Chase's autism. There were probably sixty people in my age bracket. They had each group start off in five-minute intervals, with the Pros starting first. At 7:30 A.M., the countdown started at every ten seconds, and we were off. Of course, swimming in a pool is much different than swimming in a lake or an ocean. In a pool, all you see is twenty-five or fifty yards across. This lake was a mile wide, so we had to swim 600 yards out, 900 yards across, and 600 yards back in. Let's just say, all you could see was the next buoy out ahead.

As I started the swim, it was like putting your face in a bucket of ice water. Have you ever fed carp from the shore? They start a feeding frenzy and they climb over each other to get to the food. Well, in order to get in position, I was actually getting swum over. I went down a couple of times and tried to get out of the mess. Then all of a sudden, I felt *panic!* I couldn't get my breath and had to stop to get my bearings. That moment was one of the defining points in the race. I actually thought about giving up, when all of sudden the word "Chase" popped into my mind. I wasn't doing this race for me anymore; I was doing it for my son. Whatever obstacles lay ahead, they were nothing compared to what Chase goes through. I asked the Lord for help, took a deep breath, and started to get in a routine. I ended up passing most of the people who swam over me at the beginning, and got out of the water in pretty good shape. Now, fifty-six miles on the bike!

The swim was so cold that I actually had a cramp in my backside. Needless to say, during the first ten miles of the bike ride, I was trying to stand, sit, and do acrobatics trying to get the cramp out. One woman passed me who was about 4' 11," and weighed about 200 pounds; I thought, "What am I doing out here?" Since running is my strength, I decided before the race, first, to finish and second, to try to break six hours. After this woman on the bike passed me, just finishing started to become more of a priority. For some reason, I just didn't have the power in my legs on the bike. A good friend who I train with and who is an ER doctor, told me to only think about the next mile, the next aid station, instead of thinking about the whole course. So that is what I did. Breaking it up into segments was a little easier than thinking about what lay ahead. I would say thirty people passed me on the bike, but if I had tried to stay with them, my legs would have been shot. When I was younger my coach used to say, "Let them go; they will come back to you." I finally got off the bike, changed into my running shoes, and off I went to the running course.

There were 13.1 miles ahead of me to the finish line. When I started the run, there were already people walking. So far, so good. At least I passed a couple of people. After a while, I saw a sign and it read "Mile 1." I thought "Mile 1?" I have run further than that! "Okay, think only about the next mile and the next aid station, don't panic." All of a sudden, it was "Mile 3," and I started to get my running legs back. At six miles, I really started to feel good, but at "Mile 8" I stared to feel a little woozy. I had a thought for a minute that, "I don't know if I can make it." I said, "Lord, *I cannot* do this race without Your strength. Please help me to finish this race." I got to the next aid station and had more to drink and eat, and within five minutes I could feel the Lord's peace and strength. It was an awesome experience. At "Mile 10" I started to pick up the pace and after "Mile 11" I was able to really pick it up. Oh, by the way, I caught the woman on the bike who passed me at "Mile 3" of the run and congratulated her on an awesome bike!!

I got passed by at least thirty people on the bike, but on the run I passed over 100 people. All of a sudden I heard someone say, "You only have 400 yards to go." Finally, the emotion set in. I thought of all the time my family has sacrificed for my training. I looked down at my wristband and thought about Chase and realized that the *journey* is the reward—not just crossing the finish line. Most of all, I thought of the strength Jesus gave me at "Mile 8." I rounded the corner, and they called out my name as a finisher. I broke six hours and completed the race in five hours and forty-three minutes.

"... but those who hope in the Lord will renew their strength. They will soar on wings like eagles; they will run and not grow weary, they will walk and not be faint" (Isaiah 40:31).

That race yesterday parallels life. Too many times we become so overburdened with all that we have to do, that we just want to give up. Instead, we need to pray for the Lord's strength and peace, and break up our tasks into small amounts. Sometimes during the day when you can't take it anymore at work, or the kids are out of control, or you look over and see the bag of chemo going into your body, pray. Pray that the Lord will help you not to grow weary or faint. Pray that you would not be distracted by the evil one telling you, "You can't do it." I am here to tell you today that *you can do it, in the Lord's strength.*

After I prayed yesterday, the Lord did renew my strength. Instead of my legs getting tired, they felt stronger. I kept thanking Jesus throughout those last five miles. What an awesome experience. Did I win? Not as the number of people ahead of me would suggest, but yes, I did win. I finished the race. As a Christian, how are you doing in the race? Are you growing weary with all that has to be done? Or are you soaring on the wings of eagles? I saw some people yesterday that walked the last six miles. But you know what? They persevered and finished. Whether we walk or run, we need to get in and stay in the race. Are you in the race or are you thinking of dropping out? The only way not to drop out is to call upon the name of the Lord. *He will renew your strength.* Even if you have to walk, you are in the race. You may even have to lie down but don't grow weary or faint.

"Those who hope in the Lord will renew their strength."

Hope is a confident desire; it's a feeling that something desirable is likely to happen.

Jesus wants us to pray and not doubt, but have hope. Are you praying with hope, or are you praying with doubt? *Big difference.* Let our hope only be in the Lord who can sustain, protect, restore, and get us to the finish line.

Friendship in Pain

Most of us do not relish the idea of pain. There is pain in childbirth, body ailments, or the loss of a loved one, betrayal, or losing a job. Some of these are physical pain and some of these are mental anguish. But in all types of pain, there is a commonality among those with the pain. During the Half-Ironman, there didn't seem to be much interaction among the participants before the race. During the 1.2 mile swim and the fifty-six mile bike ride, there was mostly silence. But around mile six of the thirteen mile run, I started to hear people speaking to one another. You see, by this time the pain started to become apparent to all the participants and because of this pain, they started to feel a common bond. I heard words of encouragement between people who didn't know one another, but knew that they were suffering because they were in the *same race*. Some were faster and some were slower, but pain knows no boundaries. At the end of the race, all the participants were speaking to one another like long-lost friends.

If you were to talk with cancer patients receiving chemo, there is a certain bond between them that cannot be broken. A look can say it all. "I know how you feel." That's why support groups are so good. People come together and share the same painful things that someone else might be thinking, but be afraid to say. All of a sudden you realize that you aren't the only one on this horrible ride.

"Dear friends, do not be surprised at the painful trial you are suffering as though something strange were happening to you. But rejoice that you participate in the sufferings of Christ, so that you may be overjoyed when His glory is revealed" (1 Peter 4:12).

In any endurance race, one would be naive to think that they won't suffer. So to be surprised at the painful trial would indicate that you are not ready for the task. I'm sure most of the participants knew pain was coming, but with pain comes exhilaration when the trial is over.

If you go through life trying to avoid pain, you are missing a huge blessing.

Why? Because you are trying to stay in a comfort zone. It isn't until we are ready to face pain that we can come out on the other side and know what God can do. At "Mile 8" of the run, I felt God's presence in a huge way. If I had not run the race, if I had not pushed myself, I would have missed a huge blessing.

Are you willing as a Christian to get out of your comfort zone? Are you willing to pick up the pace into the unknown and rely upon the Lord's strength and not your own? The only way you will know is to try. There are many failed dreams because of a non-committal spirit. Make this the day you get in the race. Come to know Jesus as your Savior and Lord, ask Him into your life, and then start the race. There will be highs and lows and times of thinking that you can only crawl. But oh, the finish line when

Jesus says, "Well done good and faithful servant." Let's also encourage all believers to stand strong and keep running the race that the Lord has set out for us.

I guarantee you that there are people around you today who are hurting. They may not show it on the outside, but on the inside they are crumbling. We are all in this together. We have completed the swim and the bike ride. We are all on the "run" portion of this course.

" ... *the time is short"* (1 Corinthians 7:29).

The finish line is almost coming into view. Put that effort into finishing strong. Don't ever finish with something left undone. Give it all away to Jesus.

How are you holding up in the race? Do you need an aid station? Have you gone a long time without refreshment (e.g. fellowship, reading God's Word, etc.) or are you on course? Stand the test and keep on keepin' on. The finish line is right around the corner.

Power in Prayer

I believe that people truly know that there is power in prayer. I also believe that there are many people who view prayer, not only as a privilege, but also as a necessity. I would encourage you to read two powerful books on prayer written by E.M. Bounds. One is *The Power of Prayer* and the other is *The Weapon of Prayer*. In *The Weapon of Prayer*, E.M Bounds writes:

"Prayer must be broad in scope, it must plead for others. Intercession for others is the hallmark of all true prayer. When prayer is confined to self and to the sphere of one's personal needs, it dies by reason of its littleness, narrowness, and selfishness. Prayer must be broad and unselfish or it will perish."

I know that when a prayer request goes out and possibly hundreds of people pray, there is awesome power. That is not to diminish the power of one person praying. If God acts on one prayer, how much more so if a whole country is praying?

The family of believers is *one*.

When your prayers go to the heavens, in an instant, things begin to be put in motion. God does answer *all* prayers. Yes, God does change His mind, but since God's timetable and view of time is different than ours, we cannot comprehend this. We just have to trust. Abraham pleaded with God to change His mind when He was going to destroy all of Sodom and Gomorrah. Throughout the Bible, God has changed His mind in response to people praying. It's the same today as it was 4,000 years ago.

Prayer doesn't need to be flamboyant or ritualistic; prayer just needs to be from your heart. You can stutter and stop, but what the Lord desires is a humble heart intent on talking with Him.

"Do not be anxious about anything, but in everything by prayer and petition with thanksgiving present your request to God. And the peace of God which transcends all understanding will guard your hearts and minds in Christ Jesus" (Philippians 4:6-8).

God knows and does what is best for you and for me.

That is all we really need to know. When God says do not be anxious about anything, He means it. The question is, "Do you believe that God is in control and is looking out for your best interests?"

If not, then you need to pray that the Lord will give you peace in this world, a peace that seems to have no reason. You need to pray that you will get a glimpse of God's love and understanding instead of the world's understanding. *They are two complete opposites.*

This world will be full of trials, *full* of them; but the glory that awaits those that have accepted Jesus as Savior and Lord of their lives, will be unbelievable.

"I consider that our present sufferings are not worth comparing with the glory that will be revealed to us" (Romans 8:18).

Heaven will be an awesome place for the believer in Jesus. *Nothing* in this world will compare to what we will see and feel in Heaven. This time on Earth seems long, but at the end it will seem that we were only here a short time. If trials have you depressed and buried with an attitude of "I can't take much more," remember, Jesus knows what you are going through. He will give you the power and peace you need to get through any trial when you call upon His name. Look forward and look up to Jesus. All those things on Earth that seem to be so bad will slowly fade away.

Thank you all for praying as warriors in battle.

What Is Your "It?"

"I want *it* and I want *it* now! Everyone has an *it*. *It* can be a promotion, a new car, more money, an easier lifestyle, finding a spouse, having a child, or whatever dream is special to you.

"A man can receive only what is given him from Heaven" (John 3:27).

God is in control of *it*!

No matter how clever you are, no matter how many hours you work, how you scheme, or how you may lie awake at night, if God wants you to have *it,* you will. If God doesn't want you to have *it*, you won't.

So why do we still try to get *it*? There is an inherent desire for control in our hearts. The more we work and scheme and plan, the more we think we can get closer to *it*. Faith in Jesus can be difficult because what we are saying is, "Okay, God, You take control of my life." Now this is a daily decision, because one prayer usually isn't sufficient. It is a daily walk and requires humbleness of spirit for God to be in control. The world tells us to be selfish and get what we can get. The Word of God tells us that in order to lead, we need to learn to be a servant. Servants are not in control; *they are controlled by their masters.*

You can't have two masters. Either you are the master or Jesus is. What is your choice and are you living that choice?

"No one can serve two masters. Either he will hate the one and love the other, or he will be devoted to the one and despise the other" (Matthew 6:24).

122

It is either God who is in control of *it* or you. *It* is your decision. When I was in control of *it*, I failed miserably. Now, I still have issues with *it*, but by the grace of God, I'm getting better.

This is something very important to remember since we can only serve one master. Is *it* your master or is God? If you are spending countless hours trying to get that new house, car, or promotion at the expense of your relationship with God, then that is your master. Let your *it* be God and God alone. If you can do this in your heart, then everything you desire will be given to you. Why? Because your heart will be changed to desire the things of the Lord, not the things of this world.

Remember, let your *it* be the Lord.

I Want Respect

All of us from time to time desire to be respected. The more insecure we are, the more we desire to be respected. Respect really is a form of praise. We all want to be praised for what we do. But when we start to hunger for praise, then we are going down a path that has no end. When we don't get the praise we think we are due, then we become crushed.

"I do not accept praise from men" (John 5:41).

Jesus was confident in himself because He knew who He was.

How would your life be different if you did not expect praise? It would probably be a lot less stressful. Instead of working to try to impress and get praise, you would work to get the job done. Politics would be thrown out the window. Politics in the workplace takes so much energy that a person could probably get twice as much done if politics weren't a factor. Politics in the workplace actually means trying to keep, or advance, your job. A leader of any organization needs to make sure to cultivate an atmosphere where politics has no influence. It starts at the top. If a leader schemes and coerces, chances are the employees will do the same.

Jesus never schemed. He didn't have to; He was God in the flesh.

So let's look at respect another way. If you have accepted Jesus as Savior and Lord of your life then you are the child of a King!

So when you pull into the parking lot of work think this:

"I am the child of *the King*. I know the Creator, not only of the Universe, but the Creator of my boss and my co-workers. If the Lord wants me to advance, He will allow it to happen. If He wants me to stay in my present position, then that is where I will stay. If someone gives you praise, thank the Lord, because it isn't you, it's the Lord who gives you the gifts that are being praised.

Jesus came to this world and could have been a King. He could have had thousands of angels and thousands of men worshiping and catering to His every desire. Instead, Jesus came to serve and not be served. Jesus came to save us because we were dead in our sins. He gave up worldly comfort so that we may have eternal life through Him. He created the same people who mocked, spit on him, beat him, and crucified Him.

How did He do this without striking back? Someone does a little thing to us at work, in the grocery line, or on the interstate, and we either fly into a rage or think to ourselves, "How dare you?"

Look at the example of Jesus, and the praise that you crave will slowly fade away. Jesus needs to be your only portion, not anything in this world. How do we get to that point?

First of all, we need to be saved by the Lord and turn from the way we used to live to living for Jesus. We need to constantly be reading His Word and praying. We need to pray for the Lord's strength to feel and want His love more than the love of the world. We need to go to a Bible-believing church and worship God and be encouraged by other believers. We need to be immersed in the Christian faith, not just sit on the sidelines. There is something different about being in the game rather than just sitting on the bench. Are you in the game or are you cowering on the sidelines. Don't be afraid to get in the game and take a few hits. Jesus took the punishment *we deserved* so that through Him we would inherit eternal life.

Don't desire praise from man because man will always let you down. Seek to know Jesus and let His love overpower any praise that you desire from man. Remember to smile, because so often we go around with a frown when we should be joyful no matter what the world throws at us. Remember, *you know Jesus*. That is huge. Go with the power of the Holy Spirit today and make a difference for the Lord. Don't worry about making a difference for yourself.

Have a great day and *relax* in Jesus.

What Miracle Are You Missing?

D o you live life in freedom or are you under the hand of an overbearing spouse, buyer, boss, or co-worker? Jesus performed an awesome miracle when he raised Lazarus from the dead. Lazarus had been dead for four days when Jesus finally reached the tomb. There was no doubt he was dead. When Jesus said, "Lazarus, come out!" Lazarus awoke and came out. You see Jesus is life. Whether you are living on Earth, or are living in Heaven, you are of the same spirit. In Heaven, you will have no sin. Once you have accepted Jesus as Savior and Lord of your life, you already have eternal life. You don't have to die a bodily death to have this. Amen! The Jewish leaders could have experienced the same miracles, but they were afraid to lose worldly things.

"If we let Him go on like this, everyone will believe in Him, and the Romans will come and take away both our place and our nation" (John 11:48).

The Jewish leaders were more concerned about status and things, instead of salvation and eternal life. They were trusting in what was seen and not what was unseen. Their lack of faith would eventually lead to their demise, not only of themselves, but also of Jerusalem. The Jewish leaders felt that they could control their circumstances.

Have you come to the point in your life where you believe that you cannot control anything or are you still trusting in yourself? Since we cannot control anything, why do we still try? Sometimes our free will gets us into a lot of trouble. Taking a back seat to anyone or anything is a pride and a trust issue and can be very difficult to let go.

Are you willing to give up what you have in order to see a miracle?

Are you willing to take a stand for Jesus? Are you willing to put Jesus above your circumstances? Are you willing to put Jesus above what seems real and live on faith? Are you too secure in *things* and status to take a chance on letting the Savior take over? I don't care what your past has been. Sure, some of us have had a tough go of it, but don't blame your past for your future. Jesus came to this Earth and died a horrible death so that we could be free. When we are still in bondage, we are saying that Jesus has no power. If you can't get beyond your past, call upon Jesus. If you still blame others for mistakes you are making today, call upon Jesus.

No matter what life may throw your way, call upon Jesus.

Since Jesus is the only one who knows the past, present, and future don't you think it would be appropriate to call on Him? Have you ever come to the point in your spiritual life where you have called out to Jesus for forgiveness? Have you acknowledged that He died on the Cross and rose from the dead to pay the penalty for your sins? Do you believe that Jesus was God in the flesh and are you wiling to turn from the things you used to do, to do the things as a disciple of Jesus? If you truly have put not only your faith, but trust in Jesus, then *you now have eternal life.*

If you don't have these assurances, make this the day you call upon the name of the Lord.

Stop living in bondage, and expect miracles; they are all around you. Don't let anyone or anything in this world steal your peace. If you do allow these things to take over, what you are saying is that those things are bigger than Jesus.

Nothing is bigger than Jesus so please, please, please trust in Him, and Him alone, for everything.

Don't be like the Jewish leaders of long ago that put their status, possessions, and bosses ahead of the Savior.
Nothing should be more important than the Savior, nothing! Stop today and think if anything in your life is. If so, get rid of that and give it over to Jesus. He will handle it much better than you and I ever could.
Trust and rest in the Lord.

We All Need a Revival

When I think of a revival what comes to mind is a fire and brimstone preacher in a tent yelling and saying, "You're a sinner and going to hell." If someone today asked me to go to a revival I would be uncomfortable. Don't get me wrong. I love a preacher who, not only preaches the love of God, but also preaches the consequences of sin. Most of our churches today are more interested in attracting more members by not preaching about sin, than by preaching the total Word of God.

We cannot water down the gospel!

To do anything less is a travesty. There are some churches that have a Starbucks-like environment and there are some that are plain and simple. I don't think it matters what a church looks like, as long as the full Word of God is preached. It sickens me to go into a church and see the pastor waffle on certain issues. I'm sorry to say that in our world today, most pastors are more concerned about what people think than what God thinks. This is very dangerous territory. The Bible is explicit on who should be elders and deacons and who should be in church leadership. We cannot pick and choose what we want to take out of the Bible. Either we believe every word or we don't believe any of it. *We cannot pick and choose to suit our needs.*

"Revival"—A meeting or series of meetings for the purpose of re-awakening religious faith, often characterized by impassioned preaching and public testimony. "Revival" comes from the word "revive,"— to bring back to life.

"Revive"—To bring back to life or consciousness; resuscitate.

I used to work for an ambulance service when I was in college. I took CPR, but everyone I tried this on either died, or was dead already. If you were in an accident and saw me pulling up in an ambulance, you had better start praying. I did realize that even though I had the tools to do CPR, it was only the Lord who could revive. We got a call one time for a man who had a heart attack in a bookstore. We went to pick him up; he was not breathing, and didn't have a pulse. He was in his eighties, so after trying to revive him, I told the driver of the ambulance to slow down and I hopped up in the passenger seat for the ride to the hospital. We could do nothing more for him. When we got to the hospital, we put him in a room for the doctors to pronounce him dead. The doctor and nurses came in and pulled the sheet back. All of a sudden, the patient sat up and said, "What is going on?" Yikes! We all almost passed out. This man had a heart block, which is characterized by no respiration or heartbeat. Apparently the Lord wanted this man back. Like Lazarus, all of a sudden, the dead came back to life. Can you see a pattern here? I wasn't meant to be a doctor. You see none of us brought this man back; the Lord did.

In today's world we need revival. Not just the old-fashioned tent meetings with fire and brimstone preaching. We need a revival of the heart. No matter how many meetings or services we have, if the heart is not right, the fruit will not be there. Most of us today are spiritually dead and need to be resuscitated. Not resuscitated by a human like me, but resuscitated by Jesus, the Creator of life. I can preach to thousands, but if the Lord is not in it, nothing will happen. I can preach and not be very flashy, but if the Lord is there miracles will happen and people will be revived.

You see, when we have accepted Jesus into our lives, we are born again of the Spirit. I'm sorry to say that the things of this world—wealth, possessions, status, and worries—have numbed most of us into being spiritually dead, and now more than ever we need to be resuscitated back to life.

We need a revival in this country and it doesn't need to start in a stadium of 100,000 people. It needs to start in you, and then another and then another. Can you make a commitment today to let Jesus do the CPR, instead of someone or something else? If you are thinking that possessions, status, and wealth will give you the jumpstart you need, you are wrong. It is God, and God alone, who can only bring you back to life.

Let today be the day.

Find a quiet place and pray for a revival in your heart. One person can encourage many when the Lord is behind it. If the Lord is not behind it, *nothing will happen.*

Let the revival in this country start with you. You are not reading this by chance. God has sent this message to you to be a light in a dark world. Take a stand for Jesus, but first of all you need to be revived. Are you ready for a new life? Yes, you are. Get ready because the Lord desires to do a great work in you.

Who Is Your Boogey Man?

Nighttime can bring out a lot of anxiety. When I was camping in Pennsylvania when I was young, there was always that fear of something coming into the tent and dragging you away. (I have a wild imagination.) When it was daylight, there was no problem, but when the sun went down, look out! A bird chirping sounded like a lion; a stick breaking sounded like a mass murderer stalking us. Darkness seems to bring up all kinds of wild thoughts.

I was probably fourteen and my brother eleven and we had a friend sleeping over. Late at night, my mom dressed up in a sheet and threw something at the window to make us look out. All we saw in the back yard was a ghost running along the lawn. *Yikes*, that was bad! No wonder I shut the curtains at night. Why is it, that if you hide under the covers, nothing can harm you? Oh, the things we do in the darkness.

"You are going to have the light just a little while longer. Walk while you have the light before darkness overtakes you. The man who walks in the dark does not know where he is going. Put your trust in the light while you have it, so that you may become sons of the light" (John 12:35-36).

If you are walking in the woods in the daytime, not only can you walk fast, you could probably run. When nighttime falls, you have to slow down and at times you have to come to a complete stop. Those of you who do not have a personal relationship with Jesus are still walking in the darkness. Satan is called the prince of darkness. The darkness hides evil but the light exposes it. The bars around the world don't get going till 10:00 P.M., and close late at night. This is when the evil one is the most active. The darkness draws out those who feel more comfortable in the dark than they do in the light. Most people don't want to be exposed so they stay in the dark.

Jesus is the only one who can lead you from the dark to the light. But you have to be willing to reach out your hand and have Him lead the way. The darkness is full of envy, strife, arrogance, pride, idolatry, sexual immorality, and perversions of many kinds. The light is pure, honorable, trustworthy, and revealing. If you are in the dark you know what is holding you back. If you are tired and know you are in a dead end, then Jesus is there with His hands outstretched waiting for you to ask for His help in leading you to the light.

The choice is yours.

Are you ready for the light or are you still thinking that there is more to do in the darkness?

Who is your boogey man? Is it your boss, your spouse, your debt, your past, your future, your health, or is it something unknown. I am here to tell you today that *once the light shines, there is no more boogey man.*

Jesus created your boss, your spouse, your past, future, and what your health is to be. The darkness will stir your imagination, tell you that things are in a frenzy, and make you a nervous wreck. Why not go to the one who is in control of all things? Jesus is the light of the world. Jesus is freedom, not bondage. Are you ready to expose your fears for what they are? They are nothing when exposed to the light; they are everything when hidden in darkness.

Pray that today you would get a fresh start by bringing up all your fears into the hands of Jesus. Once you see things in the light for what they really are, you will worry no more. Jesus is Lord and Jesus is the Creator, Healer, Protector and Redeemer. Don't live in the dark anymore. Pray that the Lord will guide you out of the darkness into the light. Then and only then, will you be able to lead a spirit–filled, joyful life. Then you can say, "Boogey Man, bring it on!"

All Alone

Have you ever felt all alone in the middle of a huge crowd? Why is that? You would think that with so many people to talk to, you'd be able to talk with at least one? Being alone doesn't have to do with the number of people around you, as it has to do with what you feel you are worth.

This world tells us that we are worth a lot when we own things, when we acquire status, prestige, and power. As many of you know by now "things" are just a band-aid for something much deeper that we need. Things temporarily take our minds off the pain of emptiness, but inevitably we go back to the endless cycle of acquiring (whether possessions or status) and back again when the emptiness comes back.

In each of us, there is an empty place that only Jesus can fill.

No matter how we try to fill that hole, unless it is Jesus himself, it will never work. That is why we can feel empty with 1,000 people around.

"But a time is coming, and has come, when you will be scattered, each to his own home. You will leave Me all alone. Yet I am not alone, for my Father is with Me" (John 16:32).

Jesus was coming to the end of his Earthly ministry. He had spent over three years with His disciples. They saw many miracles and had preformed many miracles in Jesus' name. You would think that they understood. But, when the guards came to take Jesus away in the Garden, they all scattered. Peter trailed behind at a safe distance, but still denied Jesus three times. How would you like to spend three years with a band of brothers or sisters and when things got tough, they all packed up and went away? Emptiness and sorrow would probably be two strong emotions that you would feel.

Jesus knew that they would scatter, but Jesus also knew that He would never be alone. Why? Because His Father would always be with Him. The same thing applies to us today. Even though we may feel lonely, empty, persecuted, left out in the cold, or betrayed we can take solace in the fact that the Lord will never leave us or forsake us.

If your security is in family, friends, possessions, food, a job, children, or money you are building trust upon a foundation *that will always crumble.* The only security is Jesus and He is the only one who can fill the emptiness that you have been trying to fill with other things.

Jesus knows how you feel. He was left empty, but He knew where His strength was. He can sympathize with you because He has been there. The next time you feel lonely or about to give up remember, "Yet I am not alone because my Father is with me."

Don't let the evil one of this world tell you that you are nothing; that you cannot get the job done, that you will never amount to anything. God does not make junk and He does not make mistakes. You have been made perfect in His sight. Now it is up to you to find out your goal, passion, and purpose. Each of us has one and it is different for everyone. Don't try to be like the person across the street or the boss whose job you may want.

Your only role model and hero should be Jesus.

Stop today and reflect on your life. Who and what you are putting your faith and trust in? Anything other than Jesus is like trying to hold onto a hand full of oil. It will always slip through your fingers until there is nothing but residue left. Don't let the residue of past hurts and defeats get you down. When you trust in Jesus, you will *never be alone; never.*

Doubt

Doubt is uncertainty or mistrust: A feeling or state of uncertainty, especially as to whether something is true, likely, or genuine, or as to whether somebody is sincere or trustworthy.

How many times a day do we doubt the power of the Lord? For me, I would say far too often. Why is this? For all that Jesus has done for me and for me to still trust in me instead of Him is absolutely ridiculous. One of the key ingredients of doubt is being distracted. The evil one is very crafty in the way he twists things to make us doubt Jesus.

The doctor we take Chase to works on the assumption that autism is caused by metal poisoning. It is very interesting that Alzheimer research is now looking into the very same thing—metal poisoning. This doctor administers a form of chelation that takes the metals out of the body in order for the brain to function normally. This doctor also treats heart patients with chelation and has had great success. But this doctor has certain conditions (protocols) that you must follow. If he is treating you for coronary artery disease and you continue to smoke, drink, or eat poorly, then he will discontinue seeing you. His feeling is that either you want to be disciplined and have this work or you don't. You can't have it both ways.

Our society today is all about abundance. How many times have you heard, "I'll eat all I want this weekend because when Monday comes I will start on my diet?" Or, "I will start on a diet after the holidays."

We need to stop procrastinating!

I have been convicted of watching too much TV. I find it easy to just surf the channels at night instead of spending more time with Julie talking about our day. What a waste that is. I need to attack this addiction of television and make a note of what I want to watch for the week. Write it down and don't deviate from it.

We doubt because our faith may be weak but also we doubt because we have not had the time to focus on what is true and right. Distractions are one of the evil one's best devices. If he can keep you distracted, then you will always miss the miracles that Jesus does for you each and every day. I can tell you for a fact that if you concentrate on Jesus and what He has done and what He continues to do, you will start to see this world in a different light. You will slowly give up trusting in yourself to get things done, and trust in Jesus to make the right decisions for you. Getting ahead of Jesus is one of our main distractions. How often have you made a big decision first and *then* prayed, instead of praying first? Ouch!

"Stop doubting and believe" (John 20: 27).

If I were able to predict the weather correctly for ten years straight, you would probably start to believe me. How is it that Jesus:

1. Is always truthful
2. Never lies
3. Has the Universe in His control
4. Loves us more than anything …

and we still doubt?

It's because we have not taken the time to slow down. This world is fast-paced but this world is also not any different than when Jesus lived on the Earth. When I say the same, I mean the human heart is the same then as it is now. Stop doubting Jesus today and believe by:

1. Slowing down and taking time to reflect.
2. Write down or journal all the things Jesus has done, and continues to do for you.
3. Stop watching and doing things that are distracting.
4. Stop doing things that are not pleasing to the Lord.

5. Again, slow down your mind.

If satan can keep us in an ADD world, then he will have victory over those who work at a frantic uncontrolled pace. If I started the Ironman race at a frantic pace, I would burn out and not even make it to the second heat. Are you running at such a frantic pace that you are going to burn out and never make it to the finish line? Or is your pace controlled and you are able to trust and not doubt what the Lord can do? Remember, *the choice is yours.*

Stop doubting and believe.

Are You Powering or Cowering?

I was up in Lake Placid, New York, this weekend training and getting familiarized with the Ironman course. I knew I was in for a challenge when the road that took me to Lake Placid had 100-foot waterfalls and hills that only a mountain goat could climb! I will have to say it is one of the most beautiful places on Earth that the Lord has created. I had to put my bike back together since I took it apart for shipping it on the plane. When I was ten, I built a tree house for my brother Jeff and me. I forgot to nail a couple of boards down, and all of a sudden I heard, "Ugghhh!" and saw Jeff lying on the ground. Apparently I forgot to tell him that my workmanship was not quite up to par, and he fell on his back from about ten feet. Being my brother wasn't easy!

The bike course started off with a climb of about 400 feet and then went into a huge downhill. So when I approached this downhill (that on a bike you can reach speeds of over 50 m.p.h!) all I could think about was, "Do I have everything tightened?" All I can say is that is fast. I have a new saying, "What goes down must come up." In less than six miles, we dropped over 1,200 feet. For the next hour it was basically a lot of rolling hills. For the last sixteen miles, we had to go up those 1,200 feet that we had come down. It was a two-lane highway between a rock face on one side and a river waterfall on the other. If I were there to sight-see, it would be quite beautiful! Going up this long hill (all right—mountain) was very deceiving. You think you are getting close to the top and then around the bend it keeps going up again and again and again. Once at the top, there is a short downhill to the finish line and then you get to do this fifty-six mile loop *again*. Once the loop is finished, there is a marathon to run, and did I forget, the 2.4-mile swim?

I was telling Julie this morning that I am getting quite nervous about this event. But we have been praying about this and know that the Lord will enable me to do this. The key to this race, besides being mentally and physically prepared, is to just *be in the moment.*

In the water, I need to think about passing the next buoy, which is 200 yards ahead. When on the bike ride, I need to think about twenty-five mile segments. If I start the swim and start thinking about the mountains on the bike ride, then I am finished. If I'm on the bike ride and start thinking that I have to run a marathon, then I am defeating myself. When on the run I need to think about getting to the next aid station, which is every mile along the course. I can't let the thought of what's ahead defeat me mentally.

I can't let the thought of what's ahead defeat me.

Are you doing this in your life? Are you unable to live in the moment because you are too concerned about the future? Are you thinking about the mountains ahead, or is your life right now a nice long downhill? Life will always be full of ups and downs, so live in the moment because not only is tomorrow not guaranteed, but most of the things we worry about *never happen.*

"Who of you by worrying can add a single hour to his life?" (Matthew 6:27).

Worry can paralyze us into either making hasty decisions or not making any decisions at all. I have worked with some large corporations where each person is afraid of losing their job. Upper management has not fostered growth through trial and error. They have tried to foster growth through fear of making mistakes.

In order to grow, we cannot be afraid to make mistakes or fail.

I think that was a huge fear when I finally started to see the whole race before me. I thought, "Can I do this?" This is a negative emotion that has no place in my mind. If I were afraid to fail, I sure wouldn't be attempting this race. But for those who grasp life in the Lord's power and are not afraid to fail, then the satisfaction ahead will be so rewarding.

The Lord does not want us to lead a timid life. Where are you in the journey? Are you trying to coast into Heaven, are you powering up that mountain, or are you sitting at home waiting for the downhill to come? The downhill will never come without first transforming yourself to live outside of your comfort zone. The Lord wants us to live outside of our comfort zones because when we do, that is where we can sense the Lord's power and peace.

Start today by making some strides to get out of your comfort zone. You cannot be effective for the Lord without taking some risks. Pray that the Lord will help you overcome your fear and attempt things that you have been afraid to do for Him. In the Lord's strength, *anything* is possible.

Gifts

Everyone likes gifts. The bigger the box, the better, I say! We're told that it's better to give than to receive, but I beg to differ! However, as most gifts go, what was an exciting present over time turns dull and then it's put away.

Here are two important passages:

"We have different gifts, according to the grace given us. If a man's gift is prophesying, let him use it in proportion to his faith. If it is serving let him serve; if it is teaching let him teach; if it is encouraging let him encourage; if it is contributing to the needs of others, let him give generously; if it is leadership, let him govern diligently; if it is showing mercy, let him do it cheerfully" (Romans 6:12).

"Do not neglect your gift ... " (1 Timothy 4:14).

The Lord has given each of us a gift to use to further His kingdom. My question today is *what is your gift?*

Have you taken the gift of leadership and instead of encouraging others, employed it to persecute others? If it used to be the gift of encouraging, do you now put others down? If it used to be mercy, do you now scowl at someone instead of showing mercy? The key to living a Spirit-filled life is not only knowing what gift or gifts you have, but also using those gifts for good, instead of evil. Sometimes we make a big sale at work, our kids get an award, or we get an abundance of money. Don't think for one minute that you had anything to do with it. It was the Lord who decided to bless you in that area. The sooner you can come to the realization that the Lord controls and gives all things good, the sooner your life will be one of peace instead of turmoil.

So back to the question, "What is your gift and are you using it for the good of the Lord?"

Back in the 1970's, the Lord gave me the gift of being a long distance runner. That was my passion and it consumed me day and night. I didn't know the Lord then, so I ran for the following reasons: To get my picture and name in the papers and on TV, and to be a big man on campus. I did not use this gift for anyone but myself. How about you? Are you using your gift for you or for Jesus, the one who gave you this gift? I had a great platform to share the gospel back then, but my heart was not ready. I misused my gift and it was taken away.

Today as I train for the Ironman, my focus is not for personal fame. It took the Lord many years to get me (self) out of the picture. The trials and reality of life over time seem to do that, don't they? Others are my focus now and I enjoy my training because I know it is a gift that the Lord has given back to me. A year ago, I used to get migraine headaches at least once a week. I haven't had one in over a year. That is a miracle. Back when I was doing well in running, I hated it and did it for all the wrong reasons. Now I'm just glad to be without pain twenty-four hours a day.

I'm here to tell you that each of you has a unique God-given gift. Do you know what it is and are you using it for good instead of evil? When you use it for good, then your mindset is set on giving, rather than receiving. When we want to receive more than give, it will never be enough. Do you feel frustrated, overwhelmed, tired, and don't want to go on? If so, then chances are you are living for you instead of the Lord. Pray today that the Lord will give you a clear sense of your gifts and then pray again that He will give you opportunities to use those gifts.

When you get in the habit of using your gifts for furthering the kingdom of God and helping others, your energy is transformed. Why? Because when we spend all day and night trying to please ourselves, it *will never be enough*. As Solomon said, "… a chasing after the wind." I am here to tell you that chasing after the wind will tire you out. Start today by living in the Lord's strength and living to encourage others instead of living to encourage yourself. Not only will you feel and see the change, but it may be your only hope for happiness here on Earth.

Have You Robbed God Lately?

I'm sure your first thought would be, "Of course not!" Let me ask you this question, "Do you give at least 10 percent of what you make to your church or the needy or a mission group?" You may say, "My church is nothing but a bunch of hypocrites," or "They don't know how to manage money." It doesn't matter what your church or the needy do with the money you give them. Once you have given your money or first fruits, then you have done what God has asked. If the people you give to do not do what is required of them, then that is between them and God. You have fulfilled your duty.

You may also say, "I don't have 10 percent to give." Let me put it this way. God gives you *everything* in the first place, whether you realize it or not. So, when He gives you 100 percent and asks for 10 percent back to further His Kingdom, that is not a lot. In fact, when we don't give 10 percent back, we are stealing from God. Frightening, isn't it?

"When you receive from the Israelites the tithe that I give you as your inheritance, you must present a tenth of that tithe as the Lord's offering" (Numbers 18:26).

"Be sure to set aside a tenth of all that your fields produce each year" (Deuteronomy 4:22).

Money, at times, seems to be a real stumbling block in the Church. This is because sometimes from the pulpit, all you hear is, "We need more money." The churches I have been to that are following the Lord and are Spirit–filled, hardly ever have to ask for money. God provides. Sometimes to pay off debt more quickly, it takes some extra influence from the pulpit, but it is the congregation's responsibility to give a tenth of what they make.

So, let's get back to basics. Since everything we own comes from God, we need to give 10 percent back to whatever church or ministry the Lord puts into our hearts. *Do not hold back*. I have been so blessed when I didn't have the 10 percent and gave anyway because God provided money to support that which I gave. Julie and I saw miracles happen out of this 10 percent.

"But you ask 'how do we rob You?' 'In tithes and offerings. You are under a curse, the whole nation of you because you are robbing Me. Bring the whole tithe into the storehouse, that there may be food in My house. Test me in this,' says the Lord almighty, 'and see if I will not throw open the floodgates of Heaven and pour out so much blessing that you will not have enough room for it'" (Malachi 3:8-10).

Are you kidding me? God says that if we are faithful in this, then He will not only open, but *throw* open the floodgates of Heaven and pour out a blessing. That is the blessing I want. How about you?

Let me tell you something very important:

God can do just fine without our money.

God desires that we put Him first above our money and possessions. When we get paid and the first check we write is to God, then we are saying, "Okay, this is yours Lord." If we hold back until we have a cushion, then we are not trusting God and not believing that this is God's money. If you don't have 10 percent to give, my answer would be to cut back your expenses so that you can give 10 percent.

I can tell you from experience that when you do this, blessings will come in like a flood. Now blessings are not always money, but blessings can be so much more than money. Are you looking for peace from mental anguish? Are you tired of running the rat race of life? When you start to be faithful in the small things, then God will bless you in bigger things.

Robbing God sends chills up your spine, doesn't it? If it does not, then you need to take a closer look at you relationship with Jesus. Do you know and accept Him as Savior and Lord of your life? If so, then His Holy Spirit will guide and protect you in all the decisions you make when you are faithful to Him.

Start today by making some changes in the way you live financially. Pray first that God will give you clear direction on what route to take. There are not many things worse than being in debt, except for not knowing Jesus as Savior and not going to Heaven. Debt is a burden and will smother those who are burdened by it. But through the grace of God, He can deliver you when you call upon His name. Why don't you start today?

Shocked at Death

Why are we shocked at the inevitable?

"All the days ordained for me were written in Your book before one of them came to be" (Psalm 139:16).

This means that before we are born, God already has decided the day that we will leave this Earth and *nothing* we can do will change that. It is good we don't know the day, or we would probably worry to the point of exhaustion. So why are we shocked and distraught when someone dies?

Death is the unknown. We have not seen Heaven ourselves and we are content in this world, for the most part. If we were able to go to Heaven with our loved ones, we would not be shocked; we would be content, finally. The main reason for our sadness is not that our loved one has died or is dying, but that we are left behind. That is really the major part of our sadness.

In our hearts, we are saddened whether our loved one is seven or seventy-seven when they die. If our loved ones go to Heaven, we need not be saddened. Actually, we should be saddened to be left behind. Why?

Because this Earth is not our home.

If you were to be able to talk with a child in its mother's womb and told him that he was to be leaving that warm secure place, he would probably want to stay put, and then come out kicking and screaming. Hey, babies do come out kicking and screaming! They don't understand at the time that a new life awaits them, one that could never be explained in the womb. We get so comfortable in our daily routines that we fight change and we fight fate. Since our days our numbered, let us take a deep breath and make the most of every day instead of looking five, ten or twenty years down the road. As the Bible says, our life may be required of us tonight, so what did all that worry and planning accomplish?

The only thing we should be shocked about is when someone hears the gospel of Jesus and does not accept it. The gospel of Jesus says that He lived on the Earth, was sinless, died on the Cross, and rose from the dead to pay the penalty for your sins. If you ask Him for forgiveness and trust in Him, turn from the way you used to live and live for the Lord, then you will have eternal life in Heaven. This is something to rejoice about. When a son, daughter, mother, or father dies unexpectedly, we are all saddened. We are saddened because we will not get to see them again till Heaven, if we are all believers. You may have some unfinished business that you wanted to do or say. Let me tell you something very important:

None of us will die.

We will all live forever, but some of us will go to Heaven and some of us will go to hell. It doesn't have to do with being kind or giving to the poor. It has to do with a relationship with Jesus. If you have that relationship, your address for eternity will be Heaven. If you have not made that decision and your life is required of you, then you will spend eternity in torment. Make sure you know where you are going. There is great comfort in knowing you are going to Heaven.

The next time you stand in front of a casket, that person you used to know is no longer there. Our Earthly body is like a booster rocket that is used for a short time and then discarded. The spirit that makes you, you and me, me will live on forever. I'm not saying not to be sad, because even Jesus wept when Lazarus died. I think Jesus also wept because He saw the pain on His friends' faces. If your loved ones were to tell you where they have gone, you would be dancing instead of crying. I have been to some funerals that have actually been celebrations. The family and friends are so confident of Heaven that they are glad their friend made it there first.

If we view this world as our home and final resting place, we will always have pain and sorrow. When we can look to Jesus and Heaven as our real home, then not only will we not be saddened, but we can rejoice when a brother or sister in the Lord goes to be with Jesus. God knows what He is doing whether he takes a child, a mother, or a father. It may not make sense to us, but it is not supposed to. We are to trust in the Lord.

"Trust in the Lord with all you heart and lean not on your own understanding" (Proverbs 3:5).

The obvious may not always be so obvious. Don't look at the things of this world to make sense, but look to Jesus for everything.

Hating Life

Have you ever been in such pain that you wondered when it would end? This pain could have been physical or mental, each equally devastating. I don't care who you are and what you may view as security, but trials will come. Let me give you the analogy of a barrel overflowing. Let's say we have a fifty-gallon barrel to put water in. Let's view this water as trials in your life. When you start, you can put a lot of water in this barrel. Eventually over the years, if you don't let any water out, it will get to the point of overflowing. It's interesting that you could put a gallon or maybe even two gallons of water in this barrel at one time, but when the barrel is full, *all it takes is a drop of water to make it overflow.*

Are you there now? Will one more drop send you over the edge? If so don't despair. The Lord knows exactly where your water level is.

" ... we were under great pressure, far beyond our ability to endure, so that we despaired even of life. Indeed, in our hearts we felt the sentence of death. But this happened that we might not rely on ourselves but on God" (2 Corinthians 1:8,9).

Let's say you are a parent and your child is not obeying you on a crowded street. All it would take is for them to run out in traffic and they could easily be hit and killed by a car. They don't understand what is beyond the crowd, but you do. So you may strap them in a stroller or use a harness to make sure they don't get hurt.

The Lord knows what is beyond the crowd. What you may view as something you want to do and are stifled at every turn may be the Lord's protection. Please listen and meditate on this.

God is always in control.

We may have health, money, business, or personal issues that are heavy burdens. Have you ever wondered why the pressure keeps on? Have you felt like you just can't go on, and when the day starts you already want to go back to bed?

"But this happened that we might not rely on ourselves, but on God."

What is holding you back from relying on God, instead of yourself? What are you afraid to give up or give over? The Lord wants to show you His power, mercy, and grace, but you have to be the one to start the process by giving up.

Many times we think the apostles had it all together. They saw Jesus and all His miracles and should have been happy and strong all the time. Well, apparently not, because they were human. They were depressed at times. "They despaired even of life." If that isn't depression, I don't know what is. They had lost hope, but with prayer they got it back.

When I was running competitively back in the 1970s, I ran because I did well, not because I liked it. As a matter of fact, I hated running, but I did it because that was all I had; that was my security. I call it the "Alberto Salazar Syndrome." Alberto won the New York City marathon many times and was one of the great distance runners of all times. Now he is heading the Oregon Project, which trains elite runners in the Northwest. He has said that he hated running, but he was driven to succeed. He said in the *Runners World,* August 2005, issue:

"I hated running with a passion. I used to wish for a cataclysmic injury in which I would lose one of my legs. Then I wouldn't have to torture myself anymore."

I thought and felt the same thing. My coach used to see that I was nervous and say that there are a million Chinese who don't care about this race today. I couldn't comprehend this, because it didn't matter. I had put more pressure on myself than anyone else could imagine. I didn't care if a million Chinese didn't care I cared, and I cared too much. My identity was in my running and I was willing to experience pain way beyond my ability to endure in order to succeed. I used to run over bridges and wondered if I fell off, would I have to run again? Eventually, the pressure became too much and I opted out of the life. I went off the deep end into all sorts of other things.

But the Lord wanted me to have my strength and trust in Him, not me. It took over twenty years for me to go out and run and enjoy it, instead of thinking I was going for a root canal. But first of all I needed to come to a saving knowledge of Jesus. I needed to put my faith and trust in Him *instead* of me. I needed to grow through many hardships *way beyond my ability to endure—even despising of life* in order for me to give it up to Jesus. You see whatever you are holding onto is wrong. The only thing we need to hold onto is Jesus and His Word. That's it! It is simple, but we make it hard. The things of this world creep in and before we know it, we are trapped. The good news is that when we pray and ask the Lord to deliver us, He will. We just need to be the one to let go. Whatever is holding you back, whatever is making you depressed, angry, or afraid, God wants you to give it to Him and worry no more.

"But this happened that we might not rely on ourselves but on God."

When we can do this peace will finally come. I know you are ready for some peace in your life. Stop right now and pray that the Lord would help you give it over to Him and finally get some rest.

Spiritual Glasses

Back in 1979, I was the fourth person to have RK (Radial Keratotomy) in the United States. Since then, it has been renamed "laser surgery." I was trying to get hired by the airlines as a pilot, but at that time, you could not get hired if you wore glasses. The first operation on my left eye went great. I had to wait a month for the right eye. When they did the second eye, they cut too deep and fluid started running out of my eye. The next thing they did was unbelievable, and it was done while I was awake! They needed to suture my eye and all I could see was a hook coming into my eye bringing the thread through to tie a knot. This happened six times for six wire stitches. For twenty weeks I was in unbelievable pain and all to try to get hired by an airline.

Why did I risk my sight to get a job? You see, ever since I was a young boy I loved airplanes. My focus was to be an airline pilot and nothing was going to stop me. Eventually I became a captain for an airline. Now when I look back, the Lord *allowed* me to be a captain, not in my will, but His at the time. I lost my job as a pilot due to some heath issues, but that was only to bring me into a relationship with Jesus. You see, my focus was on other things instead of God. I didn't know what I wanted, but it certainly wasn't Jesus. It wasn't until I had tried and experienced just about everything and failed, that I came to the end of my rope. On November 29, 1992, my new prescription came in. For thirty-eight years, I was looking through worldly glasses, not spiritual glasses. My focus was on myself, not the things of the Lord.

Where is your focus and are you even able to focus?

There are times that you may be trying to do your best to focus, but if you have the wrong prescription, you will never see clearly. Do things in your life seem blurred and out of control? Chances are you are not focusing on what is important. "Multi–tasking" has become a new term in the field of business. All I can say, from someone who has ADD, is that this is just wrong.

Forget multi-tasking and focus on one thing at a time.

145

What good is it to have ten projects going at once and not get any of those projects done? It is useless, totally useless. When was the last time you sat in a quiet place and asked the Lord to help you focus? Asked the Lord to give you the right prescription for spiritual glasses? Only one pair of glasses will do. They are not the glasses of this world, but they are the Lord's glasses.

To do anything well in this life you need to focus.

Each of us has a different prescription.

What is good for one may not be good for another. Have you tried looking through the glasses of another person? Sometimes you can't even see you own hand it is so out of focus. In order for the business I'm in to do well, I need to focus on the plan, *and not be distracted by anything.*

Certain projects come across our desks with which other people are doing well, but we turn them down. Why turn them down when you could make money at it? Because they would dilute our focus. Not only would it take time to switch gears, but also it would not be fair to those who I work with. Either I'm committed to the plan or I am not. Each person needs to be passionate about what they are doing in order for them to succeed. You have to love what you are doing and I am lucky because I love what I do. There are many other professions out there where people are successful because they have focus and love what they do. You cannot dilute your efforts in order to succeed.

Have you ever used a magnifying glass to start a fire with a piece of paper? You hold that glass and let the sun go through until the paper gets hot enough to burn. One slight turn to the right or the left and you end up having to start all over again. In life, how many times are you on the right course only to be distracted by something else that takes away your focus.

Do you need a check-up from the Doctor of All Ages to see from a spiritual perspective instead of a worldly one? Has your life been out of focus and have you been stumbling over things? Get your prescription renewed from the Lord and things will come into focus like never before. Wouldn't it be nice to experience life from the Lord's perspective, instead of the world's? Set up an appointment today by prayer. Find a quiet place and ask the Lord for a new prescription. Ask Him to help you focus and see what can be done when it's done for the glory of the Lord.

Don't let anyone distract you and steal your peace.

Will I Make It?

Last Sunday morning I got to the transition area for the Ironman at 5:00 A.M. to get my race number marked on my arms and legs. After doing a once-over to check my bike, I got into my wetsuit and headed to the swim start. Two thousand athletes in an area of less than an acre was quite an amazing sight! When the cannon went off, I stayed out of the madness in the middle and after about a mile of swimming, it started to thin out. It took me approximately one hour and fifteen minutes to complete the swim. After getting out of the water, people were there helping us get our wetsuits off. After I finally got mine off, there was a 400-yard run to the bike transition area where we got our bike clothes on and headed off into the mountains for the 112-mile bike race.

The bike race was two loops of fifty-six miles. The last fourteen miles of each loop is a climb of about 2000 feet. Needless to say, the first loop was much easier than the second. The first loop I completed in three hours and fifteen minutes and the second I finished in three hours and thirty-eight minutes. Total time for the bike phase was close to seven hours.

When I finally got off my bike after being on it for seven hours, walking was a little difficult. I got into the tent to change into my running clothes and now I thought, "I have to run a marathon!" I finally made my way out onto the course and when I got to "Mile 2," I thought, "Twenty-four miles to go—yikes!" There were many personal signs posted along the bike and run routes. One particular sign caught my attention. It said, "Pain lasts but for a moment, quitting lasts forever." Who wrote that sign? Pain was lasting for more than a moment here! I can't tell you how many times I thought about that sign. I was praying for strength around "Mile 14" when I came upon a girl with a shirt that read:

"Those who hope in the Lord will renew their strength, they will soar on wings like eagles, they will run and not grow weary, they will walk and not be faint" (Isaiah 40:31).

Right at the moment I needed strength, the Lord answered. At "Mile 16," my hamstrings started to cramp up. A young man offered me water and sprinkled salt into it. It didn't taste good, but it did the trick. At "Mile 17," we were headed back into town with nine miles left. I now had to walk into every aid station for Gatorade, water, or whatever else would stay down. All of a sudden in the distance, I could see the stadium where we were to finish. I knew Julie, Bryce, and Chase would be waiting for me at the finish line. As soon as I came into the stadium, they were there and they ran the last 100 yards with me. All four of us broke the tape together. My time for the marathon was about four hours and twenty-five minutes. My total time was twelve hours, fifty-six minutes, and twenty-five seconds.

There must have been fifty times that I thought, "Will I make it?" Doubt crept in, but the prayers of my friends and family overshadowed that doubt. Whether it was a sign, an encouraging word, or that feeling only the Lord can give always came at the right moment.

I couldn't have done this without prayer.

I could feel the power of the Holy Spirit lift me up and strengthen me when it seemed hopeless. Life is the same way, isn't it? At times the finish line seems so far off that we either want to give up, or just put our heads down and tread onward without joy. Maybe you are there right now. You see, the journey is the reward, as much as crossing the finish line when Jesus will say, "Well done, good and faithful servant." But in the meantime, can you enjoy the moment, no matter how painful? That is the key to life. There is nothing worse than a Christian without joy. Non-believers are looking at us because they are searching. If we don't have joy, what hope do they have? Why would they want what we have when we act the same as they do—without hope? Actually, I have seen some non-believers who have more joy than believers.

No matter how long the climb, no matter how long the race, no matter how far off the finish line seems, pray that we would smile along the way. Pray that we would not be faint or grow weary.

The Lord is our strength, our hope, our joy, and our salvation.

Let us start today by living a life that is joyful, *no matter what our circumstances are.*

We can only do this in the Lord's strength, but we must do it. We must be joyful and thankful because Jesus paid a horrible price to set us free. Let us live like the finish line is in sight. Let us be strong and joyful in all that we do.

How Will You Be Remembered?

All I can say to those of you who think you have done too many wrong things is *it is never too late to change.*

A lot of people don't start something because either they don't think they can do it, or they are so far behind, they think they will never catch up. What we have to realize in this life is that we should not judge ourselves against the accomplishment of others. The Lord has given each of us unique gifts. To try to be like someone else is telling God He made a mistake in creating us the way we are. The only hero or role model we should have is Jesus. Man will *always* let you down, because man is human and sinful. Jesus lived on this Earth, but was without sin. He could have come and been a king, but He chose to serve. He could have lived in luxury, but during His ministry, He never had a home.

Jesus is all about change. Jesus doesn't change, as He is the same since the world began and will be the same forever. But Jesus is in the "changing" business. I hear some people say, "If I went to church, the walls would fall down." If that were the case, when I started going back to church after my rebellion, there would have been an earthquake. You don't need to change to come to Jesus. Once you ask Jesus into your life, accept that He died on the Cross, and rose from the dead to pay the penalty for your sins, then you are forever a child of God. Up until then, *you are not.* Since the Lord has given us a free will, we can choose to keep Jesus at arm's length or surrender to Him and let Him in. Where are you on the journey? Are you still keeping Jesus at arm's length?

If your life is full of turmoil, strife, bouts of anger, frustration, and loss of hope, then chances are you have not given your *whole* life over to Jesus. Trusting in ourselves is a huge sin. Jesus created all of us and created everything in this world and beyond. Don't you think He can handle your problems better than you can? Most of the time, pride keeps us from surrendering. We think we are weak if we have to give up and give things over. But I tell you that unless you give it all to Jesus, you will not only be in trouble here on Earth, but you will be in trouble for eternity.

There is a restaurant in North Carolina that has the biggest chocolate cake for dessert I have ever seen. It actually fills a whole plate and is about seven inches high. The owners are smart because they know most people leave a restaurant thinking about the end of the meal. People leave that restaurant happy because of such a great finish to the meal. Just like a trip on an airplane, if the whole flight was smooth but the landing was rough, most of the people will say that the flight was bad.

No matter what you have done in your past, no matter how you feel you have failed with your kids, family, or co-workers, *it is never too late to change.*

When you turn your life over to the Lord, He is the only one who can restore and make things new. If you have finished the main course and the meal has been bad, you can make it up by having a great dessert. Ask the Lord today to forgive you for what you have done in your past, to help you finish strong, and to bear fruit in keeping with repentance. We are remembered by the fruit we bear.

We aren't remembered for how much money we had, the homes we built, the material things, or the trophies we won. We are remembered for our kindness, service to others, humility, grace, forgiveness, and dedication to the Lord, as an example to serve others more than ourselves. It is never too late to leave a legacy of service behind.

"Thus by their fruit you will recognize them" (Matthew 7:20).

You cannot be a Christian and not have fruit. If you say you are a Christian, but are not kind and you are prideful, boastful, selfish, don't serve, and think of yourself more than others, chances are you are not a believer. People who say they are Christians and are angry all the time and all out for themselves are not producing fruit. Of course, Jesus is the only one who knows who is saved. That is between you and Jesus. How will you be remembered? Will it be how you served or will it be how you wanted to be served yourself? The main course is over and all that is left is the dessert. What will you bring out?

Will Your Faith Stand the Test?

I heard a story yesterday that rocked my soul to the core. This story was about a man who was sharing the gospel just recently in a country that still persecutes Christians. The authorities arrested him and stripped him naked. It was wintertime, with sub-zero temperatures, and snow on the ground. They bound his hands and feet and anchored him face down in the snow to die. The next morning the guards came back expecting to find him dead, but he was still alive. The guards looked at each other and said, "This must be a man of God; we need to let him go." Now, if you were that man, what would you do next? I would probably run to the hills or get on the next plane or train out of this country. Instead this man went back to the people who originally captured him and started to preach the gospel to them, *again*.

I had tears in my eyes as I heard this because as Christians, we are one in the same Spirit. What touches this man's heart touches you and me also. But I was also humbled and saddened at my lack of faith. This man was not afraid to die for the Lord; on the other hand, I guess I still am. Jesus died for me, why am I afraid to die for Him?

You see, faith is truly tested in the persecuted church where people are put in jail and tortured. They also can see the *power* of God firsthand. There are stores of miracles every day where the Lord sustains people, even though death is at the door. But as Christians, death is never at our door since the minute we accept Jesus into our lives we will never experience death. Yes, a bodily death, but not death of our souls. In America, we live in luxury compared to most nations. We don't have to hide to go to church and we start taking the gospel and our freedom for granted.

Let me tell you something about freedom. I was speaking to a veteran who just got back from Iraq. We were talking about the Lord and he wondered if God would ever forgive him for killing others. Most of us have no clue what is going on over in Iraq. We sit in our comfortable homes and here is a man who will probably remember the horrors of war until the day Jesus calls him home. This is one man who was laying it all on the line so we could go to church and live a life of freedom. Since he laid his life on the line, now he is suffering in ways we cannot even comprehend. Now multiply that by thousands of men and women who are fighting, not only for our freedom, but the world's freedom.

We need to pray for our troops and the persecuted church every day.

This life we live is too comfortable. If you were to poll people who live in homes with dirt floors and those who live in homes bigger than 10,000 square feet, you would probably find those in poverty having more joy. Something is terribly wrong here. We all need to be shaken to the core if that's what it takes for us to experience the power and forgiveness of our Lord Jesus.

In chapter 16 of the Book of Acts, it tells how Paul and Silas were beaten, thrown into prison, and put in stocks. Instead of fretting, they were signing hymns. A violent earthquake came and the doors of the cells flew open. Instead of running away, Paul and Silas stayed. The jailer thought they escaped and was about to kill himself because he knew he would be executed for letting them go. When the jailer saw that Paul and Silas were still there and observed the power of their faith, he said:

"Sirs, what must I do to be saved?" (Acts 16:30).

I have to say that my faith needs to be strengthened. I can talk a good game, but when it comes to a real test, will I stand up when the end is near? Will I stand up if something tragic happens to my loved ones? Will you and I stand up if the worst happens? I want that faith that stands up proudly in the face of death. Until you and I are not afraid to die, we will never be free to live. Being afraid to die means that we want to hold onto the things of this world more than being with Jesus. From my conversation with this courageous soldier and hearing of the persecuted church, a couple of things came to mind.

First, I need to quit taking our freedom for granted. Secondly, I need to pray for our troops every day. I need to immerse myself in God's Word and pray that the Holy Spirit will be free to do a good work in me. I know you want the same thing. You see, persecuted people have nowhere to run, but to God. We, on the other hand, can turn any way we want. Pray that we would all live with the mindset of a persecuted Christian. Pray that the Lord would help us not take *anything* for granted. Too many people, including Jesus, have sacrificed their lives so we could worship freely and encourage others in the faith.

Let's stop today trying to gain pleasure for ourselves and try to encourage others in the faith. In the end, this is all that will be left. Let us pray that we can stay in the fire of trials and hold up, not in our strength, but in the power of the Lord. Let us wage battle against evil in the power of the Holy Spirit and never take our salvation for granted again.

I Feel Like Swearing

Many years ago before the Lord saved me, swearing was just a normal part of my vocabulary. There were times that a swear word was the only appropriate response. But on November 29, 1992, Jesus came into my life through His Holy Spirit and I was forever changed. The old was on its way out, the new me was to come. I didn't get a verbal word from Jesus telling me not to swear. It was just that now I was convicted of my sinful nature and I realized that Jesus had forgiven all my sins. Since Jesus paid such a high price to make me free, why should I keep on sinning? I stopped doing a lot of things I used to do a not only because of conviction, but out of love for Jesus. Jesus died for me when I was still a sinner, and He still saved me. I now have eternal life in Heaven as a reward for my faith. That should be all I need on this Earth to be joyful.

I say, "should be all I need," but sometimes pride gets in the way. I think our pride has a lot to do with our not being joyful. Yesterday I received a call that a client of ours had done something that was just plain wrong. I confronted them and they ended up apologizing for what they did, but the damage had been done. I said, "It isn't about the money, it is about our integrity. I don't want to get paid for something that we don't do. I don't want it to look like we are freeloaders." I was ready to send out a scathing email, but the Lord held me back. I was so close to saying a swear word to this person that I could taste it, but the Lord held my tongue. I think that I got upset because of my pride. I could have avoided getting upset and still handled the problem without getting mad. I would have accomplished the same thing.

"If it is possible, as far as it depends on you, live at peace with everyone" (Romans 12:18).

This life is not about getting even; this life is about coming to know Jesus and then leading others to Him. If I build up a barrier with anyone, then I have lost that opportunity to share the gospel. Satan would love for me to lash out at someone who needs the Lord. Satan would also love for me to fall and lose my testimony. You and I need to be very careful as to how we live and not only *what* we say but *how* we say it. There is more at stake than job security; there is life and death eternally. What good is it for me to win a battle and end up seeing someone live forever in hell because of my pride? Let me say this: It is the Lord who saves, not you and me; but God uses us as His vessels to share His Word. We need to be godly examples—*no matter how we are treated.*

Jesus was on the Cross being ridiculed, unjustly persecuted, and accused and humiliated beyond belief; not only to those around Him, but to those He created. Jesus chose to not strike back, so that by His death those same people might receive eternal life. Jesus could have called a legion of angels to come at any moment and wipe out the Earth. This would have saved Him from pain and humiliation, but it would have left *no chance* for us to be saved. The next time someone does you wrong and you want to lash back, think of the bigger picture. Think of them standing before God, which they will do eventually. You have Heaven in your future and they do not. How horrible it would be to think that you had a chance to show them the way to Jesus and you chose to turn out back. Jesus didn't turn His back on us; let us not turn our back on others. To see someone be eternally separated from God would be horrible, no matter how bad an enemy.

Pray today that you and I would be able to hold our tongues, not be prideful, and let the Holy Spirit reign in our lives. When God can have free reign in our lives, then the evil one will be prevented from doing evil through us.

If it gets bad, which it will at times, take a deep breath, pray and then wait five minutes, then, make your response. I guarantee it will be a different response than the one you would have made out of pride and anger.

Why Can't We Get Things Done

How do we become one? How does our family become closer? How do we grow our business? How do we become a better team?

After the Lord sent a flood over all the Earth, all that was left was Noah, his family, and the animals in the ark. As the population started to increase again, all the people were speaking the same language. They said, "Come, let us build ourselves a city, with a tower that reaches to the heavens, so that we may make a name for ourselves and not be scattered over the face of the whole Earth" (Genesis 11:4).

The Lord said, "If as one people speaking the same language they have begun to do this, then nothing they plan to do will be impossible for them" (Genesis 11:6).

There are so many great lessons from these two passages. First of all, the people came together as one to build a city that would reach to the heavens. The Lord saw this and said that "nothing they plan to do will be impossible for them."

How can we do things where *"nothing will be impossible?"*

First of all, we have to do things for the Lord instead of doing things for ourselves. If our ultimate goal is selfish ambition, we will ultimately fail. The Lord made these people speak different languages and what they were trying to build was eventually called the Tower of Babel—confusion. Things may start out great and the future may look bright, but God's will, *will* be done. Let me say this; prosperity doesn't always mean material riches!

Peace of mind is more beneficial and to be desired than riches and fortune. So, back to our story: God said His people were "working as one," but *they were working for the wrong ideals*. They were working to build a name for themselves, instead of working to build a name for the Lord. When we look at these two passages, one thing we know for certain is that *nothing is impossible when the Lord is involved*.

So how can we be successful in the Lord's eyes?

1. We can begin to pray that the Lord would give us a pure heart that desires to please Him and not ourselves. When our desire to please God

overrides our desire to please ourselves, then the things we do will change. Our perceptions of this world will change and change for the better.

2. We can stop working for our selfish desires and work as a team. This is the case in everything from our families to corporate America. The reason families and companies don't succeed is that we aren't working together and we each have different agendas. Different agendas will always fail. The key to this is:

3. Talk with your family members or your company about your plans, your goals, and your dreams. People can't read your mind, so talking about these things will help everyone get on the same page.

4. We can all have different dreams, but we need to have the same goal. Quit being selfish.

5. Don't think of yourself better than others, ever!

6. Pray that criticism would be taken as from the Lord instead of in the flesh. If you are in the Lord's will and you get criticized, then when people are criticizing you, they are actually criticizing the Lord. Now we can see that we can pray for those who persecute us because the wrath of the Lord is *the wrath of the Lord.*

7. Pray, read God's Word, pray some more, go to worship with a family of believers, and then pray some more. Being successful in the Lord's eyes is doing things for others more than for ourselves, not only in outward appearances, but in our hearts. Many times we can do things for others either with a jealous heart or by thinking, "Okay, I have done something good; what is the Lord going to do for me?"

8. *Do good things for others without expecting anything in return.*

9. As time passes on, so do people's dreams and goals. That is why we need to have family and corporate meetings more often. We need to get everyone's input on how they feel about *everything.* Let no stone be unturned. God *will bless your efforts when the good of others is sought more than your own good.* Remember peace. We all want peace in our hearts in the long run.

Money and riches do not give us peace.

The Lord is the only one who can give us peace. He will give us that peace when we are doing things that further *His* kingdom instead of furthering our own. So here is the heart of the matter. We can do tremendous things when the Lord is consulted first in our plans. When the Lord approves our plans, then we can get great things done and those things will take off like a rocket. If you have been on the launch pad for some time, and no matter how hard you try, the fuse never lights, regroup and look at your heart and your desires. Are they for the things of this world or the things of the Lord?

Let It Go

What are you holding onto that is detrimental to your soul? Is it resentment, guilt, an addiction, hatred, a proud heart or whatever is *your* besetting sin? Each of us has something that is keeping us from not only living a godly life, but a joyful life as well. We cannot lead a joyful life when have put something ahead of God. You cannot reap the rewards that Christ has to give when you are harboring hatred toward another. You cannot experience peace when you are prideful. You cannot experience joy when accumulation of wealth and things is your master. So how do we let things go?

First of all we need to have Jesus not only in our lives, but also in *control* of our lives. This means acknowledging that Jesus came to this Earth, led a sinless life, died on the Cross and rose from the dead to pay the penalty for our sins. If you believe that in your heart and confess this to Jesus, then you have Heaven in your future and the Holy Spirit will now live within you. If you have not done this yet, no matter what good you have done on this Earth, hell is in your future. We don't get to Heaven by good works; we get to Heaven by faith in Jesus Christ alone.

Now some people have put their faith in Jesus, but still hold onto *things*. This is called accepting Jesus as Christ, but not as Lord of your life. Accepting Jesus as Lord means that Jesus is in control. You can't have it both ways. You can't experience forgiveness on one hand and then go out in your own strength. This doesn't have to do with salvation; this has to do with joy and being an effective witness for Jesus.

If I am a believer in Jesus, but fret over everything, what am I really saying? I am saying, "Okay, Lord, I believe who you say you are, but I really don't think You can help me on this one." People, the Lord created you and me, the Universe, and all creation—don't you think He can handle your personal and business issues?

Of course the Lord can. Actually He is the only one who can.

Now this does not mean we can just sit on a street corner and expect money to fall out of the sky. We need to work hard with the talents the Lord has given us, but at the end of the day, we need not fret. You may have gotten bad news from the doctor, business may be taking a turn for the worse, your children aren't behaving as they should, and life isn't going as planned. What are you going to do? I struggled with this more when I first got saved than I do now because *I have seen the Lord work and He is powerful.* When I do things in my own strength I might get lucky and get it done. In the past I thought that was skill. Now I know that I cannot do anything good unless Jesus is behind it. I say anything good, because the evil one would love for us to go our whole lifetime trusting in "self" instead of God. Whatever burden you have, no matter what past wrongs you have done, or have had done to you, *it's never to late to call upon the name of the Lord.*

Right now, stop what you are doing and ask the Lord for help. Pray for forgiveness of past sins. Pray that the Lord will set you free form the treadmill of life, which you can't seem to get off. Pray that the Lord will help you see His power and grace and to really trust that He can do it better than you. When you can turn it all over to Jesus, you will be so joyful that you will be shouting it from the rooftops. Why? Because whether you know it or not, most of you have been robbed of the joy that the Lord wants you to have. Break free today from the shackles of the evil one and put out your hand and heart to Jesus.

What Have I Done Wrong?

I think if anyone in the Bible could say this, it would have been Joseph. Of course, there are others like Job who could ask the same thing, but let's concentrate on Joseph today. Joseph was born to Jacob and Rachel. But Joseph had other brothers born to Jacob's other wives and concubines. It was like *The Brady Bunch* with as many parents as there were kids. Talk about dysfunctional! Jacob had children with Leah and Rachel and then he also had children to their maidservants. Raising kids is tough enough, especially blended marriages with four different mothers. I'm sure each mother was trying to get her children noticed and put ahead of the rest, so there would be animosity between them, to be sure. So here comes Joseph into the mix.

"Now Israel (Jacob) loved Joseph more than any of his other sons because he had been born to him in his old age...." (Genesis 37:3).

I'm sure the others brothers knew this. When a parent shows more love for one child over another, there will always be animosity. To make matters worse, Jacob made Joseph a richly ornamented robe to wear. His brothers were probably thinking, "What is this? I get a smelly sheepherders robe and this little boy gets the best of the best." Well, Joseph had a good heart and was a little naive because he told his brothers a dream he had:

We were binding sheaves of grain out in the field when suddenly my sheaf rose and stood upright, while your sheaves gathered around mine and bowed down to it" (Genesis 37:7)

Now if Joseph had not put his brothers over the edge wearing the robe, he really put them over the edge now. One day Jacob sent Joseph out to check on his brothers to see how they were doing with the sheep. When his brothers saw him coming in the distance, (because of that bright robe) they plotted to kill him. Instead, they put him in a cistern and then sold him to some slave traders on their way to Egypt. His brothers also tore Joseph's robe and put goat's blood on it so it would look like an animal devoured him. When his brothers showed this to Jacob, Jacob was so distressed, "that he refused to be comforted."

Joseph was sold into slavery to Potiphar, one of Pharaoh's officials. However, the Bible says, "the Lord was with Joseph in all that he did." Because of this, the Lord also blessed Potiphar's household. But Potiphar's wife tried to seduce Joseph and even though he refused her, she made it look like Joseph tried to seduce her and he was thrown in jail. While in jail, the Lord was with Joseph and all the guards felt this, so Joseph was again put in a leadership position. Soon, some of Pharaoh's staff was put in jail and Joseph interpreted their dreams. He asked them to get him released. Joseph had told them the correct interpretation of their dreams, but they forget about him and did not tell Pharaoh. Later when Pharaoh had a dream and nobody could interpret it, they brought Joseph to Pharaoh and he interpreted Pharaoh's dream and was made second in command in all of Egypt.

You and I go through the same types of trials in our lives. Sometimes it seems that the better we act, the more honest and loving we are the more we get kicked in the teeth. Ever been there? But one of the great verses in this book is "The Lord was with Joseph and he prospered...." (Genesis 39:2).

So if the Lord was with Joseph, why didn't he set him free and get him out of Egypt? Because the Lord had a much better plan for Joseph than Joseph could have ever imagined. While Joseph was sitting in that well, would he ever have imagined that he would be second in command in Egypt and eventually save his father and the rest of the country from famine?

But in all that Joseph did (no matter how he was treated) he was faithful to the Lord. In the end the Lord gave Joseph victory.

You may be in the middle of something you don't understand right now. You may be doing all the right things. You may be praying every day, putting the Lord first, going to church, giving to others, and being kind but you are still getting kicked in the teeth and wondering *why*? As we see from the story of Joseph, I'm sure he wondered at times "Why?" but he knew that God has a perfect plan that we cannot see. We have to trust and have faith that the Lord is working at keeping us protected. The Lord will deliver us, whether it is today, tomorrow, ten years from now, or it may not be until we reach heaven.

But He will deliver us.

The key is to be joyful in the trial. If we are not joyful, we are really saying, "Lord, I'm not sure if You can get me out of here. I didn't want to go through this." Our faith grows by leaps and bounds in trials and when we come out of the other side, we see the Lord's grace and power. We all go through trials and we can choose to be joyful or we can choose to filled with doom and gloom. You know what? No matter how we feel, the Lord's will, *will* be done, so we might as well try to have joy, no matter what the trial.

"Consider it pure joy, my brothers when you face trials of many kinds because you know that the testing of your faith develops perseverance. Perseverance must finish its work so that you may be mature and complete, not lacking anything" (James 1:2-4).

We need to be joyful in the trial because when we do, our faith will be stronger and we will be better able to persevere in the face of *any* trial. Today you may be in the bottom of the well, not knowing when you will be lifted out and even if you do get lifted out, if you will be rescued.

No matter where you go or what trial you are in, the Lord will be with you.

We need to pray and see how good, powerful, loving, and caring Jesus is. Trials strengthen us when we trust. Trials break us down when we become bitter. Some of us look at a trial as another way that God hates us. But God loves us enough that He wants us to grow in faith and to see His power, love, and grace. No matter where you are on your journey, pray that you would be able to be joyful in the face of adversity. Instead of feeling like you have done something wrong, you will start to see that God is molding you to be an effective witness for Him.

Remember, this is not our real home. We are here for a very short period of time. Let us live with an eternal perspective, not a worldy one.

God, Where Are You?

Iwas reading a verse today that I had questions about. When Joseph and that generation died in Egypt, the new ruler had no recollection of Joseph and what he had done. The Israelites at this time started to multiply in great numbers. Pharaoh was concerned that the Israelites might gather an army with other countries and rise up against the Egyptians. Pharaoh put slave masters over the Israelites and forced them into slave labor to keep them under oppression.

"The Israelites groaned in their slavery and cried out, and their cry for help because of their slavery went up to God. God heard their groaning and He remembered His covenant with Abraham, with Isaac and with Jacob. So God looked on the Israelites and was concerned about them" (Exodus 2:23-25).

My first question was if God knew their hearts and their pain, why didn't He help the Israelites in the beginning? Why did He have to wait until the groaning came up to Him?

" ... You do not have because you do not ask God" (James 4:2).

God wants us to cry out to Him and Him alone.

The Lord does not want us to handle things in our own strength, and He desires the glory. The Lord is not prideful or boastful, but He did create the Universe and us. He is the all-in-all. If the Lord had released the Israelites from their persecution right away, they might have forgotten the oppression. Things had to get so tough that they would be able to handle forty years in the desert. And God wanted the Israelites as He wants you and me to call out to Him. We are not to wallow in self-pity and hopelessness, but we are to cry out to God and *He will deliver us.*

Now let me say something about asking and receiving:

"When you ask you do not receive, because you ask with wrong motives, that you may spend what you get on your pleasures" (James 4:3).

162

We all need to think when we ask God, "Why are we asking for this? Is it for pleasure or is it for need?" Asking for money for provisions is not the same as asking for money for a yacht. I say all this to get a glimpse of how God responds. First of all, God wants us to call or cry out to Him in prayer. "You do not have because you do not ask." When was the last time you truly talked with Jesus? I'm not saying a rote prayer, but a prayer as if you were sitting down talking to your best friend. You wouldn't spend only ten seconds talking to your best friend. You have a best friend because you spend time with them, talking to them, and sharing your innermost feelings. Why can't we do that with God? Believe it or not, the Lord desires to become your best friend. The phone lines are open; all we have to do is make the call. Why do we wait? Maybe it's a lack of faith, impatience, or arrogance. Whatever the reason, when we ask God with the right motives, He will move mountains for us.

Where is God? He is waiting for your call. He is waiting for you to come to Him *and spend some time*. He desires to hear what is on your mind and to reveal His power and compassion to you. If the storm is brewing today or it is on the horizon, call out to God and He will hear your prayers. If you are in a season of calm water, call upon the Lord in thankfulness and as a friend who keeps in touch. Our Lord is the beginning and the end, forever and ever. He knows what's ahead, *we don't*. Start today by trying to make the Lord your best friend. Cry out to Him in humbleness of spirit and watch the mountains move for His glory and honor. You might be surprised at the peace you will have.

Slow down!

Why Are Things Getting Worse?

Have you ever prayed for the Lord to deliver you from a trial and things seem to get worse? Moses was sent by God to deliver the Israelites from the hand of the Egyptians. When Moses first went to Pharaoh, Pharaoh got mad at Moses and the Israelites. The Israelites had to make bricks for building and they needed straw and mud to make the bricks. Originally, the Egyptians gave the Israelites the straw, but when Pharaoh got mad he told the Egyptian slave drivers to tell the Israelites, "Go and get your own straw wherever you can find it but your work will not be reduced at all" (Exodus 5:11).

From God's perspective, things were getting better because He knew the process of deliverance had started and that He was going to free them. But for the Israelites, the perspective was much different. They probably thought, "You were here to deliver us, Moses, and not only have you messed up, but now things are worse for us. Thanks, but no thanks!"

Ever been there? If you are in a trial right now and have prayed for the Lord to deliver you, He will. But the Lord will deliver you in His time and according to His plan. His plan is perfect, ours is not. His timing is perfect, ours is not. We get upset at God at times because of our lack of patience.

Lack of patience is really lack of faith. In order for our faith to be strengthened in trials, we need to slow our lives down and pray. We need to get to know God. Listen to this very carefully. We need to not just know of God, we need to know God personally. We can only do this through a relationship with Jesus Christ, a strong prayer life, and being in worship and fellowship with other believers.

You may have to learn to wait and wait some more. If you feel like you are in a lifeboat stranded in the middle of the ocean, remember this: Jesus is bringing all of His resources to rescue you. You may not see the army coming, but it is.

You will be rescued at the right time and at the right place. Hang onto the promises of Jesus, not the promises of man. Have joy in the storm and when the light finally comes, you will not only have unspeakable joy, but that joy will be contagious. Jesus wants us to be light in the world, not darkness. Have a great day and if you are frowning, smile! If you are smiling, keep it up in the Lord.

Smile :)

Stand Back, God; I've Got It Covered

How many times in our lives do we get out in front of the Lord? The Lord is powerful beyond comprehension. He can do any and all things. So why do we attempt to get out ahead and say to the Lord, "Follow me," instead of praying and following the Lord?

The Israelites had been in slavery in Egypt for hundreds of years. The Lord brought up Moses to deliver them from the persecution of Pharaoh. After numerous plagues, Pharaoh still did not let the people go. It wasn't until the Lord killed all the firstborn of both men and animals that he had enough. The Israelites were to put the blood of a lamb on their doorposts, so when the angel of the Lord came to destroy the firstborn, the angel would see the blood and pass over the house. This is how the term "Passover" came to be.

That night when children started dying, Pharaoh summoned Moses and told him to take the Israelites and go, so more people wouldn't die. The angel of the Lord kept a cloud by day and a pillar of fire by night for the Israelites to follow. Then the Lord hardened Pharaoh's heart and he said, "What have we done? We have let the Israelites go and have lost their services."

Then Pharaoh sent over 600 of his best chariots, along with all the other chariots of Egypt, to find the Israelites and bring them back.

The Israelites were camped by the side of the Red Sea. They were penned in by the sea on one side, and by the Egyptians on the other side. What separated them was the pillar of cloud of the Lord. The Israelites were filled with doom and gloom. They told Moses, "Was it because there were no graves in Egypt that you brought us out in the desert to die?" Moses said, "The Lord will fight for you; you need only to be still" (Exodus 14:14).

We live in a performance–based, "get it done" world. Get up and get going, do something! The Israelites are told to be still. Are you in the midst of a trial and feel the need to be still, when everything around you says to forget what God wants, and go out on your own?

"Be still and know that I am God" (Psalm 46:10).

We cannot be running and be in chaos and see the hand of God at work. Be still!

Telling me to be still is just the opposite of what I am about. I'm running even when I don't have anything to do! There have been a few times that, in the Lord's strength, I have been still and something miraculous has happened. The quietness first made me uneasy, but then became peaceful. The sounds of the world started to fade away and Jesus became more real. We all strive for peace, but we usually try to get peace through having a better job, house, car, or other things. This will never give you and me lasting peace. What gives us lasting peace is being still before God and trusting in Him.

So how do we learn to let God be God? Pray! First, we need to get to a quiet place. Slow down, try not to think about anything else, and be still before the Lord. The first couple of times I tried this for about five seconds I was doing really well, then all of a sudden, I found myself thinking of everything other than the Lord. To be still takes practice, commitment, and wanting to know who Jesus is more than what the world is. You have to make a choice; you can't have both. When you pray for discipline, guidance, and wisdom to know God, He will give you that wisdom and peace. I know, because the Lord has delivered me and He can deliver you.

My nickname in college was "Hectic." Some would say, "Brad, you still are hectic." All I can say is I was really bad in my twenties. So if I can be still, and at times it's very tough, you can be still also. So often the reason we aren't still is because of a lack of faith. It might sting to hear this, but I'm talking as much to me as I am to you.

Right now you may have the armies of aggression, guilt, shame, and persecution at your doorstep. You may want to run or fight back with whatever resources you have. But God is telling you to *"be still and know that I am God."*

We have missed many opportunities to see God's miracles because our lives are too hectic. You may already be in the throws of chaos today like a hamster on a treadmill. You need to pray right now that the Lord will get you off the treadmill called "life," and help you to be still.

God wants the victory; God wants the glory.

Let God be God. Not only can He heal your heart and save you, but He can also change the hearts of those who are persecuting you. Don't ever discount the power of the Lord. Jesus is asking you to be still at heart. Can you start today by letting God be God? Pray right now that the Lord would come into your life and clean house, especially the garage and the attic. Get rid of all the old things that have kept your life cluttered. God can change you, but you have to be wiling to be changed. Are you willing to give up self and be still? I know you are. Let this be the day and don't let *anyone* steal your peace.

Joy In The Storm

The Book of Acts, Chapter 27, talks about the Apostle Paul sailing from a port near Jerusalem on the Mediterranean Sea. He was on his way to Rome to appear in a trial before Caesar. As soon as the ship started sailing, it was buffeted by the winds. The trip was approximately 800 miles. In a ship without a motor that is a long way. They were trying to land on the island of Crete, but a northeaster came in and swept them south, so they had no way to get to land. They were at the mercy of the storm.

Some of you right now are at the mercy of a storm. You may be thinking that there is no way out. You may be thinking that all is lost and it is just a matter of time until the Lord takes your life, the life of your loved one, or friend. " … we finally gave up all hope of being saved" (Acts 27:20). The last thing you are thinking about is joy.

"Just before dawn Paul urged them all to eat. For the last fourteen days, he said, 'You have been in constant suspense and have gone without food; you haven't eaten anything. Now I urge you to take some food. You need it to survive. Not one of you will lose a single hair from his head.' After he said this he gave thanks to God in front of them all. Then he broke it and began to eat. They were all encouraged and ate some food themselves. Altogether there were 276 of us on board" (Acts 27:33-37).

If you want to lose twenty pounds, get through a bad relationship or divorce, or have a loved one in the hospital for an extended period of time, we seem to put ourselves in survival mode. I have been there, and what am I saying? I am saying that I was focusing on my pain, instead of being strong for those around me. I might even be feeling sorry for myself because someone dumped me! The pain of rejection and fear can be overwhelming. It can be as overwhelming as being lost at sea in a storm.

What did Paul do? Paul prayed and gave thanks. Now what type of person does it take to give thanks in the storms of life? I finally know the answer to one of my questions. We can never give thanks in the storms of life unless we have the supernatural power of Jesus living in us. That is the first step. The next step is that we need to stop quenching the power of the Holy Spirit and then let God be God in our lives. Many Christians are living defeated lives because even though they believe in Jesus, they still don't understand the power of the Cross!! Jesus didn't come just to give eternal life to all those who believe in Him. He came so we could also live an *abundant life*. Paul knew the power of Jesus. He saw it first-hand on the road to Damascus when he was blinded by Jesus. Jesus lifted the scales from his eyes and spoke to Paul and told him that he must suffer for His name.

You see, Paul was not focusing on the storm; he was focusing on the goal. The goal is to win souls for Jesus, to be a voice for truth where truth is not found. To have joy when others are paralyzed by fear. If you and I act just like those who are paralyzed by fear, then why would they want what we have?

We have to be different.

We need to show others that there is power, hope, love, and joy in knowing Jesus and having the Holy Spirit in us. We cannot do this when we have fallen captive to this world. We cannot do this when our possessions mean more than the souls of others; we cannot do that when our time is more important than stopping to help someone in need.

Let me talk about how we can stop this cycle. One day without joy is one day too many. One day without joy means satan 1, Jesus 0. Let's say you have thirty years left on this Earth. That is about 10,000 days. Now when a day is gone, *it is gone forever*. Trials are part of life and they will come. Some will come like a freight train and some will creep up on you, *but they will come*. Are you and I going to cower down when they come or are we going to face difficulties in the power of the Holy Spirit? I don't know about you, but I have already given too many days over to satan. I have robbed the joy from my family and friends when problems arise that

I can't overcome. But God is forgiving and can restore. He is supernatural; we are not without Him.

There are no problems or storms that Jesus can't conquer. Again, *there are no problems or storms that Jesus can't conquer.*

"Consider it pure joy my brothers when you face trials of many kinds" (James 1:2). Storms will come and storms will go. If we hunker down in a storm and act like everyone else then *we have been ineffective witnesses for Jesus,* we have robbed the joy we could have given to others, and we have given another day over to the evil one. I am tried of giving a day over to satan. I am going to do everything in the power of Jesus to give all I have.

What about you?

Yes, we have a choice. We are in a battle and souls are at stake. We need to pray, read God's Word, have fellowship with other believers, and pray again that the Lord would sustain us in His power. Let us look at the goal: Heaven, with no suffering, living in glory. Let us not look at our problems, let us look to Jesus for our strength, hope, and deliverance.

Let us all go out today in the power of the Cross and not ever cower again in the face of adversity.

Get ready!

Defeat

I participated in another Ironman last week. The race day forecast was for sixty-degree temperatures with light rain in the afternoon. In my race bag for the run I had rain gear, but just warm weather gear for the bike ride. As I got to the race site at 5:00 A.M. Sunday morning, the weather forecast was a little off. The weather was around fifty-two degrees with twenty mph. winds and light rain. The wind that morning was already whipping the water with three foot swells. On top of that, the biggest Ironman start for the swim race was about to begin with 2,600 athletes. I was able to get on the far outside and miss most of the kicking and elbows for the first 1,000 yards. The next 1,000 yards were facing right into the current and wind. We had to actually roll on our backs to breathe as the waves were breaking over us. On the 4,200-yard swim, it took about 2,000 yards for the pack to even out. I finished the swim in one hour and twenty-eight minutes, which was about fifteen minutes slower than it should have been.

Then the fun began. I got all my layers of clothes on and started out on the 112-mile bike ride. This race consisted of a thirteen-mile leg out to the town of Verona, Wisconsin, where we would do two forty-three mile loops and then thirteen miles back into town. Who said Wisconsin was flat? About ten minutes into the bike race, it started to pour and didn't let up until Monday, Yes, Monday! By Mile 20, I was soaked through all the layers of clothes and by Mile 60, I had started to develop hypothermia. On top of the rain, the wind was steady at fifteen mph with gusts to twenty-five mph. At "Mile 90" of the bike race, it was all I could do to get back to the starting line. Instead of being on the bike for six hours, I was on for seven hours and twenty-three minutes. I have never been that cold in my life. It is now the "Coldest Ironman on Record!" There were many people who had horrendous bike accidents on the sharp curves; many people went to the hospital with hypothermia; and many people had flat tires. I was not one of them thanks to the power of the Lord.

When I finished the bike race, I had been out on the course for over nine hours with twenty-six miles still to run. I was too cold to take my bike clothes off, so a volunteer helped me undress and get into my running clothes. He then wrapped me in seven layers of clothes and a blanket. I was still shivering so badly that I couldn't stop. I had lost a lot of fluids on the run and was actually dehydrated, even though the weather was cold. All the energy it took to try to keep me warm took its toll. I went outside to attempt the run. It was still pouring rain and I know at that point that if I were to go, I would be risking my life. I had to swallow the bitter pill of defeat. I gave the volunteer my name, number, timing chip, and quit. I hate to use the word quit. Some call it a DNF (Did Not Finish), but in reality, I quit. I don't feel bad about the decision because I knew that I could not go on.

I called my wife Julie, and she was very supportive. I called my coach in San Diego and was expecting disappointment, but he said that he tried to finish a race when he had hypothermia and was injured for six months. When I got up the next morning to get coffee at the hotel, I saw a number of people that had their "Ironman FINISHER" T shirts on, and I was embarrassed. I didn't get coffee at the hotel. I walked out to get coffee elsewhere. A defeat is tough to take, but defeat can either get you down or make you better. I talked with Julie for over four hours that night about the race.

Just remember, *all of us suffer defeats.*

It is what we do after a defeat that shows the quality of a person. It isn't how many times you get knocked down, it's how many times you get up that counts. All you have to do is get up one more time than you were knocked down, and you are victorious. This can be because of a bad relationship, a health problem, death of a loved one, troubles with your children, or all of the above. The taste of defeat should be bitter enough to make us better, not *more* bitter. A lot of us live a life where we just exist. Jesus wants us to live a life where we truly live and give it our all.

I prayed most of that day and I know many people were praying for me. So why didn't I finish? I believe prayer sustained and protected me from serious harm. I felt the Lord's peace and presence, and the ability to retreat and get better to fight another day.

There are a number of us who feel that quitting is bad. Yes and no. It depends on the circumstances. How many people attempt to climb Mt. Everest, but the conditions get so bad they have to turn around, sometimes with the summit in sight. Mark Allen, a multiple winner of the Ironman, suffered some DNF's and some horrendous defeats in the Hawaii Ironman before he became victorious. This year I had a calf injury, two bad bike accidents, and a bad race in Hawaii. Some have said, "Is the Lord trying to tell you something?" I don't believe the Lord is trying to tell me something, I believe the Lord is trying to teach me something. Perseverance builds character and character builds hope. We can't feel the effects of perseverance without pain and suffering.

" ... *we also rejoice in our sufferings; because we know that suffering produces perseverance, perseverance, character, and character, hope. And hope does not disappoint us"* (Romans 5:3-5).

Many of us have lost hope because we have lost our dreams. Some may say I am too old to dream or have hope. *No, you are not too old to have dreams and hope.*

When we have none of the above, we just exist in life and slowly wither away. Don't let defeat linger! Don't let defeat get you down! Don't let defeat keep you from trying again! We allow the Lord to be victorious when we get back up after falling. Get back up in the Lord's power and I can tell you from the Word of God and from experience, great things will happen to you—*great things.*

Let us all go out in the power of the Lord with dreams and hope for a great future.

Why Did You Make Me Like This?

" ... 'Why did you make me like this?'" (Romans 9:20).

When you first read this, most of you probably thought of a time when you faced difficulty, sickness, the loss of a job, insecurity, an addiction, or some other form of pain. It is easy to question God when things are going wrong. It is easy to put the blame on someone else.

But when things are going great, we sometimes forget about God.

Isn't God the one who is the potter and we are the clay? Doesn't He have the right to do what He wishes with His creation? In our own minds, we freely accept the good, but have a very hard time accepting the bad (what we think is bad).

"But who are you O man, to talk back to God? Shall what is formed say to Him who formed it, 'Why did you make me like this?' Does not the potter have the right to use out of the same lump of clay some pottery for noble purposes and some for common use?'" (Romans 9:20,21).

I think most of the time we forget that we were formed by God, and He knew us long before we were ever born. If we had a chance not to be born and experience pain, we would not experience Heaven either. With life we get the potter who formed the clay and that is God. Most of us would want life. But with life comes God's plan, not our plan. We have to learn to accept the good with the bad.

" ... Shall we accept good from God, and not trouble?" (Job 2:10).

172

Job certainly knew a lot about pain. But he also knew that God is sovereign. What does this mean? Sovereign means that God has a *perfect plan*. Perfect. When a two-year-old dies of cancer, or a man rises to the top of his field, it is for a purpose that we cannot fathom nor should we, because we are not God. *With life comes pain, but also with life comes joy.*

We cannot have one without the other in this life. The next time something great happens to you, and it will, thank God and say, "Why did you make me like this? Why am I so lucky to have this opportunity? Why am I so lucky to have this family, these friends and, most of all, my salvation?"

For once, let us turn the tables on self-pity in our minds and be in awe that God has made us perfect. Some of us, at times, feel unworthy, but I want to tell you that Jesus doesn't make mistakes. He tells us we were perfectly made. Since that is the case, let us start believing it today and go out into the world with joy, instead of cowering in fear. Remember, God is in control and when all else fails, remember God is in control. You were made for a purpose—yes, you. If you have been on the bench for a while, dust yourself off and tell God you want to get back in the game. You may get a few bumps and bruises, but that pain will be far outweighed by the joy of a spirit-filled life.

I'm Too Far Gone

Many people don't start a task because they feel too tired, too insecure, or too overwhelmed by what's currently going on in their lives. This is of the devil. The devil will do everything in his power to make you an ineffective witness for Jesus. The more he can distract you and keep you down, the less effective you will become. How many times have you started a project only to get overwhelmed, and say, "What's the use? Let someone else do it."

As you start the day today you can start fresh, but you need to come before the Lord in prayer. We get so busy in our lives that we sometimes forget the power Jesus has.

Let us look at some of His power. He:

1. Died and rose from the dead to conquer death.
2. Holds back the waves of the oceans.
3. Forgives sins and remembers them no more.
4. Knows when each bird needs to eat and finds food for them.
5. Knows when we need to eat and finds food for us.
6. Knows our hearts and prayers even before we ask.

You and I know we could write a million other things that Jesus can do, but this is a good start. If you think that you are too far gone, then you don't know Jesus. If you think you have been too bad, have fallen too many times, have done some pretty horrible things, then *listen*. You are not here on this Earth to impress man. You are here to have a relationship with Jesus. What you do on this Earth is between you and the Lord. When you take your last breath, none of your family members, friends, or people in the church will be sitting beside you. It will be you and God. So if your whole life has been spent acquiring possessions, impressing people, or climbing the corporate ladder, that ladder has been leaning against the wrong building. It will be too late then to change.

With God's grace and infinite wisdom we can come to Him today and ask forgiveness for our sins, any sin! But we need to come to the Lord with a repentant heart and believe that Jesus died on the Cross and rose from the dead to pay the penalty for our sins. By God's grace we are forgiven, but that should not give us a license to sin and take advantage of God's grace.

"Flee from sexual immorality. All other sins a man commits are outside his body, but he who sins sexually sins against his own body. Do you not know that your body is a temple of the Holy Spirit, who is in you, whom you have received from God? You are not your own; you were bought at a price. Therefore honor God with your body" (1 Corinthians 6:18-20).

Since the Bible speaks of sexual immorality frequently, what exactly is sexual immorality?

"Do you not know that the wicked will not inherit the kingdom of God? Do not be deceived. Neither the sexually immoral, nor idolaters, nor adulterers nor male prostitutes, nor homosexual offenders, nor thieves

nor the greedy nor drunkards nor slanderers nor swindlers will inherit the kingdom of God" (1 Corinthians 6:9,10).

I am here to bring you God's Word; these are not *my* words. I used to be among the sexually immoral, the drunkard, and the slanderer. If it weren't for the grace of God, I would be on the fast track to hell. But with God's grace and mercy, He pulled me from the pit of destruction and saved me from hell. When I was deep in sin, I did not know it. I was a slave to evil; I was not a slave to God. The more I sinned, the unhappier I became. I talk to you as one who has been through the fire and can see what destruction can bring, not only to myself, but to many, many others.

Are you unhappy today? It may be because you are not right with Jesus. Maybe you have not asked Him to come into your life, to take control, and to save you. You may have done this, but have some area of sin in your life that you need to repent of and change. Are you living with someone outside of marriage and have that feeling that things just aren't right? That's the Lord prompting you to leave. Are you in an adulterous or homosexual affair and don't know how to get out of it? Are you addicted to pornography on the Internet? Do you feel so far gone that the Lord can't forgive and restore you?

You are never too far gone for God to save; never too far gone.

Some may say I don't want to give up control. All right then, here are two options. Whether you know it or not, if you are not a slave to Jesus, then you are a slave to the devil and are on your way to hell, with no turning back. Really! Jesus could have come to this Earth as a king and had a lavish lifestyle, but He came as a servant. He came to serve, be spit upon, to be nailed to a Cross, naked, humiliated, and to die an agonizing death so that He could conquer death once and for all. This was not for Him, but for you and me.

Now think about that. Jesus conquered death for you and for me and for those who believe in Him by faith. Going to church, being baptized, confirmed, giving tons of money to the poor, and serving in a soup kitchen will not get you into Heaven. If it could, then that is "works," and Jesus died for nothing. The perfect example of being too far gone was the thief on the cross. Here was a man who was a criminal and was being crucified just like Jesus on a cross. He saw and believed in Jesus, and what did Jesus say to him? Jesus did *not* say, "I didn't see you in church," or "I need to baptize you first."

"Then he said. 'Jesus remember me when you come into your kingdom.' Jesus answered him, 'I tell you the truth, today you will be with me in paradise'" (Luke 23:42,44).

The thief didn't have to do anything but believe.

Where are you today? Are you overwhelmed with some type of sin? Burdened by debt, overcome by grief? Jesus is here waiting for you to call out to Him. Jesus gave us free will, but He can only do so much. It is up to us to repent, call out to Him, and be saved and restored. We have no good power in this world, unless it is from Jesus. Remember, it is never too late to start fresh. Jesus is in the restoration business. Don't let the evil one make you think that life has passed you by, because it has not. Eternity is a long time and if you are reading this lesson, then God has a plan for you. Cry out today to Jesus and ask for forgiveness, restoration, direction, and confidence in Him and Him alone.

Isn't Heaven Enough of a Reward?

Why worry? Because it gives me something to do in the face of a crisis. Now, if I were to remember all the times that the Lord has pulled me through I should not worry, should I? Julie, the boys, and I had to take a plane ride during Christmas. A year ago this would have been impossible because our seven–year-old son Chase is autistic. But the Lord has done miracles in his life and we felt it was time. I had booked the flight five months early so I could make sure we all sat together. I wanted everything perfect to make our plans succeed. What was I thinking? Do things ever go as planned?

The night before the flight, I went to check in online, but the system would not let me do it. I called the airline's reservations desk and was told that for some reason our seat assignments had been kicked out of the system.

Our seats were spread out all over the plane. Time to worry and worry I did. I told Julie about it and she said, "Wait till we get to the airport and I am sure things will wok out." Now, how could things work out when things were not working out?

Our flight was to take off at 9:00 A.M., so we got to the airport at 5:30. Was I stressed or what? I walked into the reservation area and asked the agent if she could help us out. I don't know what reservation agents do on that computer, but they type and type and type away some more. Chase was starting to get a little antsy, so I told her that our seven-year-old was autistic and that whatever she could do to help would be greatly appreciated. All of a sudden she looked down and tapped the woman beside her on the shoulder. She looked up at me with tears in her eyes and said that her son had Asperger's Syndrome, which is a form of autism. She said, "I will make sure that you all sit together." She also said that her friend was working the gate and they would take care of everything. I gave this woman a book, *Whoever Gets To Heaven First Wins*, and we went on our way to the gate. Julie, the boys, and I got to the gate still without seat assignments and had not waited more than thirty seconds when the gate agent called out, "Henry family party of four." We got to the desk and the man said, "Here you go." We actually had better seats than the ones I had picked.

Now the question was who were we going to sit next to? Worry again. A younger woman sat next to Chase and me. Julie and Bryce were in the seats in front of us. I asked her what she did and she said that she worked with handicapped children. Not only that, but she was going to see one of her friends who was opening a center for autistic children. Why, why did I ever doubt the Lord's power, love for us, and plan to get things done?

This was a miracle that happened right in front of us. This could have never happened by chance. Of course, I don't believe anything happens by chance. God has shown me time and time again that He can provide.

I was reading the story of Joseph in Genesis. He had tremendous struggles for someone who didn't do anything wrong. He was put in a cistern and his brothers sold him into slavery. They took him to Egypt and he became the head of Potiphar's household until Potiphar's wife falsely accused him of improper sexual conduct. Joseph was put in prison and ended up running the prison and then was later made second in command over all of Egypt. No one was more powerful than Joseph, except for Pharaoh. Joseph succeeded because "The warden paid no attention to anything under Joseph's care because the Lord was with Joseph and gave him success in whatever he did" (Genesis 39:23).

But Joseph upheld his part of the bargain.

" ... How then could I do such a wicked thing and sin against God?"
(Genesis 39:9).

This was Joseph's response to Potiphar's wife when she tried to seduce him. It would be well for all of us to live and breathe this passage. You may be thinking that someone you are with now is better than your wife or husband. You may think that a little cheating on your expense account or proposal will not get noticed. You may think that looking at pornography on the Internet is not hurting anyone. Or you may think that whatever sin you can get by with will continue to go unnoticed. All I have to say is *God is watching, everything.*

I will tell you now that you will not get away with anything in the long run. If you want to suffer the consequences, keep living in the sin of deception. Here is the whole heart of the matter, and I mean your physical heart, too. God has done as much for us as He did for Joseph. To be sure, Joseph experienced some severe pain and trials. But in the end, God raised him to the highest level imaginable to save Egypt and ultimately his family, who had also tried to hurt him. Even if you do not get the justice you think you deserve in this life, *isn't Heaven enough of a reward?*

Let us all quit kidding ourselves. If you keep on sinning then you will suffer consequences. If you repent today, ask the Lord for forgiveness, and ask Him for a pure heart, He will give you one. *But you have to want to change.* When you look back and see all the good and wonderful things that God has done for you, you will look upon only God as your Savior, King, and friend. Then when temptation comes, you will say,

"How could I do such a wicked thing and sin against God?"

Let us all wake up, be aware of the devil's schemes, and lead a life that pleases God. Lord, help us to be more like You each and every day.

God Has Allowed

"I never expected to see your face again, and now God has allowed me to see your children too" (Genesis 48:11).

Most of you know the story in the Book of Genesis about how Joseph's brothers sold him into slavery in Egypt, but God made Joseph second in command after Pharaoh. All the time that Joseph was gone, his father Isaac thought he was dead. But he not only sees Joseph again, but Joseph's children, too. Now because of all this heartache Isaac could have said, "I never expected to see your face again. I am glad I was strong enough to see your children too." No, he gave the credit to God when he said, "God has allowed."

How often do we give credit to ourselves instead of to God? How often do we give credit to God with our mouths, but in our hearts we give credit to ourselves? Probably far too often. We all need a heart transplant each and every day.

"The heart is deceitful above all things and beyond cure. Who can understand it?" (Jeremiah 17:9).

Our hearts are beyond curing, at least in this world. Each day we have to consciously pray to the Lord that He would bind our tongues, forgive our sins, help us to think pure thoughts, and let God reign in our lives. When we reign, we quench the Holy Spirit's power in our lives and evil things start to happen. We speak and then later wonder, "Where did that come from?"

In order to live a life where, for better or for worse, we can joyfully say, "God has allowed," we need to constantly be in God's Word. We need to be constantly praying and giving thanks in all circumstances.

"I am not saying this because I am in need, for I have learned to be content whatever the circumstances. I know what it is to be in need, and I know what it is to have plenty. I have learned the secret of being content in any and every situation; whether well fed or hungry, whether living in plenty or in want. I can do everything through him who gives me strength" (Philippians 4:11-13).

You may be asking now, "Why has God allowed this cancer, why has God allowed financial hardship, why has God allowed death to take my mother away, why won't God allow the pressure to stop building, why, why, why?"

From the above passage, we know that we serve a loving God who is just. We need to give credit in all things, not with just our mouths but with our hearts. Philippians 4:13 says to us that we *cannot do anything good in our own strength.* But we can do all good things and survive all things when we can say like Paul, "I can do everything through Him who gives me strength." The evil one does not give power for good. He taints everything that God has made good. If you allow satan to get a foothold in your life, then the Holy Sprit will be quenched and will not be as effective as He can be in your life. If you allow anger, sexual immorality, worry, impatience, and greed to stay in your life, then you will have a very difficult time fighting the arrows of the evil one. When you can let go and let God be in control, then amazing things will start to happen.

When you can start giving credit to God for everything, then you will start to feel the freedom and power that is in God.

Let us pray today that no matter what the circumstances are in our lives, we will be able to sing praises. I want to leave you with a diagram of our lives.

When we look at worry and we look at eternity, the worry we have is insignificant compared to what God has planned for you and me. We will all live forever. The only difference between the believer and the non-believer is the address when you leave this Earth. The riches in Heaven will be far surpassing anything we have experienced on this Earth. Pray that we would have the strength to look ahead, instead of focusing on our circumstances whether good or bad. We are on this Earth only a short time, a very short time.

Let us make the most of every opportunity with a joyful spirit and give all the credit to Jesus.

Have You Ever Been Shot?

I was having some knee problems this past week so I had to get a couple of X-rays. While I was waiting for the film to be developed, the technician asked, "Have you ever been shot?" I said, "Yes, about thirty-five years ago when I was rabbit hunting." The doctor had gotten most of the buckshot out of my legs, except for one pellet. There it was, clear as day, on the screen. It is amazing what the human eye cannot see, but modern technology can. This got me thinking about the human heart. No matter what technology we use, no one can see us like God can.

"The Lord does not look at the things man looks at. Man looks at the outward appearance, but the Lord looks at the heart" (1 Samuel 16:7).

Rich or poor, it would be great if we could see the heart instead of the outward appearance. But in reality that would probably keep us away from most people. If we saw people's hearts and the resentment they held toward us or others, we might feel they are too far gone to share the gospel with. That is why we must let God be God because He can handle it. *We cannot!* In the movie *A Few Good Men,* Jack Nicholson said to Tom Cruise, "You can't handle the truth!" In our lives today, most of us would be very offended if we could see the truth about ourselves.

"The heart is deceitful above all things and beyond cure. Who can understand it?" (Jeremiah 17:9).

Here are two verses that have the power to change us forever. Sometimes we think the Lord is not watching, the Lord is too busy, or we just plain forget about the Lord in the things we say and do, *but God sees all things, including all of our thoughts.* Our thoughts come from our hearts and 1 Samuel says, " ... the heart is deceitful above all things." I believe the reason people respond to money so strongly is that a lot of people use money to hide behind. Money shows power and success, at least to the world. But who are you trying to impress, the Lord or man? God doesn't need our money.

Since the Lord looks at the heart and the heart is deceitful, what hope do we have? The only hope we have is in Jesus. He is the only one who can give us the heart transplant we need. If you have never accepted Jesus into your life by asking Him to forgive your sins, acknowledging that He died on the Cross and rose from the dead to pay the penalty for your sins, then you have no hope of recovery. You will spend eternity in the hospital called hell. Once you are in the hospital of hell, you are there forever.

But since God can see the heart He can also heal the heart through repentance, forgiveness, and restoration. What heart do you have? Your life may be demanded of you today, so you better make sure. It will be too late when you stand before God and you have put this off. Just as I saw that pellet in my leg through the X-ray, the Lord clearly sees your heart. *We can't hide.* Are you hiding anything today that you need to get right with God? Are you harboring resentment for the past, pride, sexual immorality, addictions, or anger? Whatever it is, God is the only one who is on this insurance plan. Make sure today that you have the right medical plan. There is only one that will last for eternity in Heaven.

Stop today and quit hiding or running away from God. He knows your pain and your weakness. Call out to Him and you will be restored, lifted up, set apart, and live in glory. That is a lot better than running away from the invisible enemy of pride and selfishness.

Lord, Where Are You?

In life we all go through seasons of triumph, pain, and waiting. I think waiting is the most difficult part of life. There are many passages in the Book of Psalms about David waiting upon the Lord. I can relate to David. He had it all when he was young. The Lord showed him great favor and made him king and what did he do? He had an affair and caused great grief for himself and those around him. Plus the Lord took his firstborn son. Many times the Lord gives us great things and then we sabotage them. Ever been there?

Each day the Lord is refining us. Gold is a very precious metal, but to get out all the impurities, it needs to go through fire. We could be considered gold before we were saved, because each one of us has been created by God. But when we become believers, God refines us. If He didn't love us, He

just leave us alone to self-destruct. So often,
out and we want out now! If you look back
seem as long now as when you were going
eaven all this *stuff* we have experienced and
he only thing that will matter is our salvation
ared the love of Jesus with. That's it!
ay, the Lord is still refining you. You may have
iness, or personal problem. You may have had
ay doubt God's goodness and power. You may
portant things to do or you may be thinking,
be thinking, "I can't take another day."

ll you forget me forever? How long will you
w long must I wrestle with my thoughts and
y heart? How long will my enemy triumph
nswer, O Lord my God. Give light to my eyes
enemy will say, "I have overcome him," and
all. But I trust in your unfailing love, my heat
will sing to the Lord, for He has been good to

questions in the first five sentences. Impatient,
to the point where he thinks God has forgotten
r passages say that he will trust God and rejoice
ease the pain of waiting.
ession for over thirty years. About three months
to come back violently. A few weeks ago, the
ion and things really went downhill. It seems
ication to work, I need to wean myself off the
my system, which may take two to six weeks.
a feeling of dread and helplessness. I have not
ars. But this is one of the side effects when first
am tired. I am tired of waiting to feel good. I
of life. I am tired of being tired. But after Julie
y heart felt better, the anxious thoughts started
once again taken me out of a dark, deep pit.
ng depression that the Lord has allowed me to
ister to so many people. Why? Because I have

seen time and time again how the Lord has delivered m

I know, beyond a shadow of a doubt, He can deliver you

I would rather have the depression and write about
than to not have it and not be able to write to you about

The Lord has been good to me and I know that. I ha

and I thank the Lord for the refiner's fire. I don't like t

I like a root canal. But after getting a root canal, finally

and the tooth is saved. Each of you today has somethin

always full of joy. Satan wants to be the victor of our

do anything to make us ineffective witnesses for Jesus.

defeated satan and the one who will throw satan into th

our only hope. Amen!

In this life we will not escape pain, but we have a ro

hang onto and that is Jesus. When Jesus said in Matthe

"easier for a camel to go through the eye of a needle than a

the kingdom of Heaven," He did not mean the rich will no

I know a number of very wealthy, godly people. But th

where their wealth comes from. People who are wealthy a

it themselves by their own craftiness have problems. They

think, "Why do I need Jesus when I have all the things I

more I will work more?" Fortunately for the rich in hea

saved by God's grace, there is an inheritance in Heaven

will far outweigh, *far outweigh,* all the treasures here on

Let us today lift each other up in prayer for a numbe

1. Pray that even though we have to wait, that we c
upon the Lord.

2. Pray that we can wait in joyous anticipation, as G

3. Pray that we would not let the evil one keep us d
mission.

4. Pray that we would have joy, even when we fee
die.

5. Pray that no matter how hard the pain, no matt

suffering, no matter how long the wait, and no matte

outlook, we will rejoice in our salvation. That we will sing

remember and remember again that He has been good to

Amen!

would not refine us, He would just leave us alone to self-destruct. So often, in the midst of a trial, we want out and we want out now! If you look back on your worst trial it doesn't seem as long now as when you were going through it. When we get to Heaven all this *stuff* we have experienced and left behind will not matter. The only thing that will matter is our salvation and how many people we shared the love of Jesus with. That's it!

If you are reading this today, the Lord is still refining you. You may have a health, financial, family, business, or personal problem. You may have had it for quite some time. You may doubt God's goodness and power. You may be thinking God has more important things to do or you may be thinking, "I deserved this." You may be thinking, "I can't take another day."

How long, O Lord? Will you forget me forever? How long will you hide your face from me? How long must I wrestle with my thoughts and every day have sorrow in my heart? How long will my enemy triumph over me? Look on me and answer, O Lord my God. Give light to my eyes or I will sleep in death; my enemy will say, "I have overcome him," and my foes will rejoice when I fall. But I trust in your unfailing love, my heat rejoices in your salvation. I will sing to the Lord, for He has been good to me (Psalm 13).

David asks the Lord five questions in the first five sentences. Impatient, yes! David has been waiting to the point where he thinks God has forgotten about him. Of course, the later passages say that he will trust God and rejoice in salvation, but that doesn't ease the pain of waiting.

I have suffered from depression for over thirty years. About three months ago, the depression started to come back violently. A few weeks ago, the doctor changed my medication and things really went downhill. It seems that in order for the new medication to work, I need to wean myself off the old and get the new drug into my system, which may take two to six weeks. I woke up this morning with a feeling of dread and helplessness. I have not experienced this in twenty years. But this is one of the side effects when first starting the new medicine. I am tired. I am tired of waiting to feel good. I am tired of autism. I am tired of life. I am tired of being tired. But after Julie and I prayed this morning, my heart felt better, the anxious thoughts started to subside, and the Lord has once again taken me out of a dark, deep pit. I also realize that this lifelong depression that the Lord has allowed me to have, has enabled me to minister to so many people. Why? Because I have seen time and time again how the Lord has delivered me from the pit and I know, beyond a shadow of a doubt, He can deliver you, too.

I would rather have the depression and write about Jesus to all of you, than to not have it and not be able to write to you about Jesus!

The Lord has been good to me and I know that. I hang on to His truths and I thank the Lord for the refiner's fire. I don't like this any more than I like a root canal. But after getting a root canal, finally the pain is gone and the tooth is saved. Each of you today has something. This life is not always full of joy. Satan wants to be the victor of our lives and he will do anything to make us ineffective witnesses for Jesus. The one who has defeated satan and the one who will throw satan into the Lake of Fire is our only hope. Amen!

In this life we will not escape pain, but we have a rock and fortress to hang onto and that is Jesus. When Jesus said in Matthew 19:24, that it is "easier for a camel to go through the eye of a needle than a rich man to enter the kingdom of Heaven," He did not mean the rich will not get into Heaven. I know a number of very wealthy, godly people. But these people know where their wealth comes from. People who are wealthy and think they did it themselves by their own craftiness have problems. They are the ones who think, "Why do I need Jesus when I have all the things I need and if I need more I will work more?" Fortunately for the rich in heart who have been saved by God's grace, there is an inheritance in Heaven. This inheritance will far outweigh, *far outweigh,* all the treasures here on Earth.

Let us today lift each other up in prayer for a number of things:

1. Pray that even though we have to wait, that we can wait patiently upon the Lord.

2. Pray that we can wait in joyous anticipation, as God's love is pure.

3. Pray that we would not let the evil one keep us down and stop our mission.

4. Pray that we would have joy, even when we feel like we want to die.

5. Pray that no matter how hard the pain, no matter how long the suffering, no matter how long the wait, and no matter how bleak the outlook, we will rejoice in our salvation. That we will sing unto the Lord and remember and remember again that He has been good to you and to me.

Amen!

Have You Ever Been Shot?

I was having some knee problems this past week so I had to get a couple of X-rays. While I was waiting for the film to be developed, the technician asked, "Have you ever been shot?" I said, "Yes, about thirty-five years ago when I was rabbit hunting." The doctor had gotten most of the buckshot out of my legs, except for one pellet. There it was, clear as day, on the screen. It is amazing what the human eye cannot see, but modern technology can. This got me thinking about the human heart. No matter what technology we use, no one can see us like God can.

"The Lord does not look at the things man looks at. Man looks at the outward appearance, but the Lord looks at the heart" (1 Samuel 16:7).

Rich or poor, it would be great if we could see the heart instead of the outward appearance. But in reality that would probably keep us away from most people. If we saw people's hearts and the resentment they held toward us or others, we might feel they are too far gone to share the gospel with. That is why we must let God be God because He can handle it. *We cannot!* In the movie *A Few Good Men,* Jack Nicholson said to Tom Cruise, "You can't handle the truth!" In our lives today, most of us would be very offended if we could see the truth about ourselves.

"The heart is deceitful above all things and beyond cure. Who can understand it?" (Jeremiah 17:9).

Here are two verses that have the power to change us forever. Sometimes we think the Lord is not watching, the Lord is too busy, or we just plain forget about the Lord in the things we say and do, *but God sees all things, including all of our thoughts*. Our thoughts come from our hearts and 1 Samuel says, " … the heart is deceitful above all things." I believe the reason people respond to money so strongly is that a lot of people use money to hide behind. Money shows power and success, at least to the world. But who are you trying to impress, the Lord or man? God doesn't need our money.

Since the Lord looks at the heart and the heart is deceitful, what hope do we have? The only hope we have is in Jesus. He is the only one who can give us the heart transplant we need. If you have never accepted Jesus into your life by asking Him to forgive your sins, acknowledging that He died on the Cross and rose from the dead to pay the penalty for your sins, then you have no hope of recovery. You will spend eternity in the hospital called hell. Once you are in the hospital of hell, you are there forever.

But since God can see the heart He can also heal the heart through repentance, forgiveness, and restoration. What heart do you have? Your life may be demanded of you today, so you better make sure. It will be too late when you stand before God and you have put this off. Just as I saw that pellet in my leg through the X-ray, the Lord clearly sees your heart. *We can't hide*. Are you hiding anything today that you need to get right with God? Are you harboring resentment for the past, pride, sexual immorality, addictions, or anger? Whatever it is, God is the only one who is on this insurance plan. Make sure today that you have the right medical plan. There is only one that will last for eternity in Heaven.

Stop today and quit hiding or running away from God. He knows your pain and your weakness. Call out to Him and you will be restored, lifted up, set apart, and live in glory. That is a lot better than running away from the invisible enemy of pride and selfishness.

Lord, Where Are You?

In life we all go through seasons of triumph, pain, and waiting. I think waiting is the most difficult part of life. There are many passages in the Book of Psalms about David waiting upon the Lord. I can relate to David. He had it all when he was young. The Lord showed him great favor and made him king and what did he do? He had an affair and caused great grief for himself and those around him. Plus the Lord took his firstborn son. Many times the Lord gives us great things and then we sabotage them. Ever been there?

Each day the Lord is refining us. Gold is a very precious metal, but to get out all the impurities, it needs to go through fire. We could be considered gold before we were saved, because each one of us has been created by God. But when we become believers, God refines us. If He didn't love us, He

Jesus, the Criminal

Most of us get mad, try to get even, and get downright ugly when we are accused of something. Sometimes we get mad when we are accused and we're actually at fault. The main reason we get mad when we are accused and it isn't our fault is because of pride and insecurity. We may think, "How dare they say that; don't they know how hard I work or how nice I have been to them?" In this life, you will never please everyone no matter how hard you try. But your pride can dictate a lot about what you say and do. Wouldn't it be nice if you could truly live in a way that you did not worry about what others thought about you? You may think that it is not an issue for you, but I would beg to differ. We all want a pat on the back. We all want to be acknowledged. But sometimes instead of what we think we deserve, we get a slap in the face.

Some of you have fallen into an arrogant, prideful pit. I say pit because once you are in it, the pit is very difficult to climb out. Why? Because you have an unhealthy view of yourself and the only way out of the pit is to repent. You can't get out of this pit by having more arrogance. You have to confess to the Lord that you have sinned and need His help to overcome this evil. The only way out of the pit is to realize that you need to be a servant instead of being the one served. Money, power, and pride can get you in a pit that has very steep, slippery walls.

"He committed no sin and no deceit was found in His mouth. When they hurled their insults at Him, He did not retaliate, when He suffered, He made no threats. Instead, He entrusted Himself to Him who judges justly" (1 Peter 2:22, 23).

So here was a perfect, sinless man. Jesus was God in the flesh. The King of kings and Lord of lords was being nailed to a Cross between two criminals. Jesus came to this world to be the ultimate sacrifice for you and me. We would no longer have to slaughter animals on the altar to pay for our sins. Jesus was to die on the Cross to pay for our sins so that whoever believes in Him would not perish, but have everlasting life. But what we all seem to forget is that Jesus, who was God in the flesh, who created you, me, and everything on Earth was put on the Cross *unjustly*. He was insulted and spit upon; His clothes were sold beneath Him. He had a crown of thorns, as sharp as needles, put on His head. He bled and the people mocked Him. In an instant, Jesus could have called 72,000 angels to His rescue, *but He did not.* Jesus knew that we had no way to Heaven without Him. He had to stay and pay that price for you and me, when we were the ones who deserved to be on the Cross.

When you are mocked and you poor pride is hurt, *remember Jesus.* When you have worked hard and someone else gets the credit, don't try to justify yourself—*remember Jesus.* When you start to think that you are better than the person next to you, think of the Cross and *remember Jesus.*

I hate arrogance. Maybe because in my heart I used to see how destructive it was. No believer who has the power of the Holy Spirit has any excuse to be arrogant. If you are, then you may not be saved! Yes, you and I need to be frightened to realize the fear of the Lord. God will not share His glory.

Jesus did not get on the Cross and say, "You got the wrong man. The two men beside Me are criminals and I am not. I came to save you. Don't you know who I am? Can you please get help to get Me off of here?" No, no, no. Jesus kept silent. Jesus kept silent because He knew the one He served was God, who has the power and mercy to do good in all things. When we take matters into our own hands, we are really saying to God that we do not trust His timing.

Stop right now and pray that the Lord will forgive your sins of pride and arrogance. Pray that He will help you see what you are doing and find a way out of this evil snare. Pride comes before every fall. Jesus could have come back to Earth to explain His actions and to say He wasn't a criminal, but He did not. Jesus was secure in himself. Jesus knew where He was going and pride had no place in His work or plan. Don't try to justify your actions to people.

Do your best with a pure heart and pure motives and leave the rest to God.

If people come against you, they are actually coming against God. God can handle retribution better than you and I. Live an honorable life as a servant and quit trying to be the one served. When you can do this, peace will flood your heart and you will see people in a whole different light. "Jesus, the criminal," of course not! He did not spend good time trying to explain why He was not. Be productive in the Lord; don't try to please man.

Why Me, God?

Have you ever wondered what your purpose is? Have you ever started out going one direction only to end up somewhere else? Have your dreams been shattered? At times we fall into the trap of thinking that the life we are living now is supposed to be like Heaven. We want everything right; healthy kids, healthy marriages, no debt, a great job, and no problems with anyone. I could probably add one hundred other things to this. But when you look at these desires, this is what Heaven will be like, *not life on Earth.*

"Dear friends, do not be surprised at the painful trial you are suffering, as though something strange were happening to you. But rejoice that you participate in the sufferings of Christ so that you may be overjoyed when his glory is revealed" (1 Peter 4:12).

Why is it that we are shocked when bad things happen? Sometimes I think when we become believers in Jesus Christ, we feel we are protected from the tragedies of life. Let me give you an example of a great man who had some hardships even when following Jesus. John the Baptist came before Jesus and he preached in the desert, calling everyone to repentance for their sins. John prepared the way for Jesus. John even baptized Jesus in the Jordan River. You would think that John was in the *in* crowd with Jesus. So what did he get for being obedient? John got beheaded!

Following Jesus does not mean that we will not face trials. Being a believer does mean that Jesus will be with us in our times of trial, *every step* of the way. Jesus will never leave us, but He will allow things to happen in our lives that will make us stronger believers and give us a platform in which to proclaim the glory of the Lord.

In the Book of Job, it was God who focused the attention on Job, not satan. If I was in that meeting with God and satan, I would be hiding under a chair praying to God, "No, not me, not me! I have been good! Why me, God?" Have you ever said, "Why me, God?" Job passed the test. He stayed true to the test, gave glory to God, witnessed to others, and then was given twice what he had before.

Our son Chase was diagnosed with autism over five years ago. When we first found out, our hopes and dreams for him were shattered. Not God's plans, but ours! But after five years, we have been given more by this child of God than we would have had with a "normal" boy, whatever "normal" is. We have learned a deeper love than one could imagine, we have learned patience, we have learned to slow down, and we have learned that God is *forever* faithful. The "why me?" turned into the "thank You" for a wonderful boy who has probably taught us more than we have taught him. We are elated at his small steps because there are no huge leaps. If you are distraught that your child has not made the varsity traveling team, does not get straight A's, does not fit in with his peer group, and gives you fits, quit worrying right now. God knows what He is doing and you and I aren't God. He has given you the perfect child, prefect spouse, perfect job, and perfect life.

Nothing in this life will ever be perfect. So why do we except it to be? Maybe it's too much television, where in the end, the good guy always wins. Maybe it's too little being in the Word of God. All of God's people suffered, from Abraham to Peter, and yes, even Jesus. Why should we be any different?

Do not start to feel guilty that you have done something wrong when the trials come. Sometimes our sins create trials, but for the most part they do not. Don't over analyze the situation, just turn to God. Just turn to God and ask for His help. If you have a child in the hospital, you might come into contact with people who would never have crossed your path. If you have a tough boss, you can be an example to co-workers who will see how you act as a Christian. God does not make mistakes.

The next time you are asking yourself, "Why me?" rejoice that you are in good company. God saw fit to use you in many ways. Some of the ways are to strengthen your character, minister to others outside your core group of friends, and to be a light in a dark world. This life is not all about us! We are on this Earth for two reasons:

1. To come to know Jesus as Savior and Lord of your life. (I pray all reading this have made this decision)
2. To minister to others about the gospel of Jesus.

Other than these two things, nothing else matters or will last.

In this life each day is a trial. Some days are tougher than others, but we are all in a battle. Let us put on the armor of God and fight the battle with a joyous spirit instead of one of defeat. Hold your head up, not down. Don't pity yourself; pity others for not knowing Jesus. Start living like the child of a King with an inheritance in Heaven, instead of thinking you are a pauper. That is evil, satanic thinking. We are forgiven, restored, and set apart for eternity. That should be enough, along with the Lord's presence, to get us through until we reach Heaven and leave the trials of this Earth behind. One second, one minute, one day, one year at a time. Don't look too far down the road as you may miss the glorious opportunities right in front of you. Stop concentrating on yourself and focus on the needs of others.

Can't You Sit Still?

How often do we tell our children this? Let's take this one step further. How often does the Lord tell you this? "Still," to us means to do nothing. In this world today, if we do nothing we get run over. We lose position, preference, we look weak, and certainly we will not get ahead. The Israelites were just like us. They were happy for a time when they came out of Egypt, but after a while of the same old thing, they started grumbling. Sound familiar? Sitting still can breed complacency when we are trusting in our own strength and wit.

The Lord brought severe plagues upon the Egyptians so Pharaoh would let His people go. Pharaoh would not have let the Israelites go if he just had one or two calamities happen to him, but to get Pharaoh's attention the Lord brought:

The Plague of Blood
The Plague of Frogs
The Plague of Gnats
The Plague of Flies
The Plague of Livestock
The Plague of Boils
The Plague of Hail
The Plague of Locusts
The Plague of Darkness
The Plague of the Firstborn

The Plague of the Firstborn was more than Pharaoh could handle. His firstborn son died in the night along with all the other Egyptian firstborn sons and animals. Finally, Pharaoh said after his son had died, "Take your flocks and herds, as you have said, and go. And also bless me" (Exodus 12:32).

Pharaoh is asking Moses to bless him! That's quite a change. But Pharaoh was not a believer and he turned back to his wicked ways. Sometimes in trials if we are not believers, we can ask the Lord to bless us. But unless we ask forgiveness of our sins, trust in the Lord, and call out to Him then and only then will we be saved. Asking for a blessing or forgiveness as a temporary fix will not cut it. Our hearts need to be changed, not just our words.

Pharaoh let the Israelites go while he was in a state of fear and shock. After awhile, he came to his senses and realized that he had no one to do his labor for him. He got all his chariots ready and his army and started out into the desert to bring the Israelites back. At this point, the Red Sea was on one side of the Israelites and the Egyptian army was coming upon them from behind. The Israelites has nowhere to go.

"Moses answered the people, 'Do not be afraid. Stand firm and you will see the deliverance that the Lord will bring you today. The Egyptians you see today you will never see again. The Lord will fight for you, you need only to be still'" (Exodus 14:13,14).

"Be still, Moses? Are you kidding me? We have the sea on one side and this maniac army on the other." I think most of the Israelites were ready to grab some sort of weapon and get ready to fight. We have to do something to protect ourselves, right? Today you may be getting ready to go into battle with a boss, co-worker, social worker, ex-spouse, or a disease that just doesn't seem to ever go away. All I can tell you is that you are in good company. Good company meaning that being afraid to stand still before the Lord is a common situation. Don't beat yourself up because you have a hard time standing still and waiting for the Lord to deliver you. The Lord did a miracle when He parted the Red Sea and the Israelites went through on dry land. After they went through, the Egyptians tried the same thing and were starting to catch up to the Israelites. But the Lord knocked off the wheels of the chariots and caused confusion in the army. Then the Red Sea covered them and they all drowned. Could the Israelites have planned this any better? No way!

The Lord defeated the Egyptian army—*not the Israelites*. The Lord will defeat your foes too, if only you will pray and stand still. Maybe it is just holding your tongue, but whatever it is, the Lord needs to be the one who fights the battle and gets the glory, not us. If the Israelites had become impatient and started to fight the Egyptians, they would have suffered many casualties. When the Lord handled it, they did not suffer one casualty out of a million people.

Can you quit squirming around wanting to get even, get back, get mad, and get revenge? Can you *just sit still* before the Lord? This accomplishes two things. It shows the great power the Lord has and it also proves your faith, which is refined when you wait upon the Lord.

Sitting still can be seen by the world as a sign of weakness. Forget about the world and all the false pleasures it has to offer. Focus on Jesus, our *only* deliverer. Let God do battle for you; trust in Him by praying, reading His Word, trusting completely in Him and praying some more. Things will work out when you let God be God. Amen.

Are You Really Saved?

I have suffered depression for over thirty years. For some reason, the past four months have been brutal. There have been some very, very dark days. It seems that the world we live in today is more understanding if you were to do something bad against your neighbor than it is about mental illness. Mental illness still holds that stigma that "He is insane," "Stay away from him," or "He is weird." This year, six million men will be diagnosed with depression. I am sure there are countless more that are afraid to come forward because of the stigma that this brings. When men are boys, we are taught to not cry, just get up, and dust yourselves off, and get back in the game.

Depression leaves you unable to function, unable to find hope and joy in the smallest of things. This may sound strange, but I do thank the Lord for allowing me to experience this trial. This trial has enabled me to have more compassion for others than I would have ever thought possible. If your life is great and you have not suffered many defeats, you could become a little arrogant. You could think that *you* accomplished it all yourself, instead of knowing that only God allowed it. Trials are not fun at the time, but they do refine and enable us to see things in this life for what they really are. We are able to cut through the clutter of what satan would like us to see and we see more of what the Lord wants us to see.

So what are some of the things that trials leave us with?

Brokenness—You cannot come to the Lord unless you are broken. You cannot be saved when you are the one commanding your ship, your destiny and your future.

Hopelessness—Jesus wants our hope to be in Him and *not in anything or anyone else*. Our hope is not in our job, spouse, family, talents, or our bank account.

Weakness—We need to get to the point to where we are too tired to go it alone any more. Jesus loves the weak, because He can work with them. He has a tough time with the stiff and proud at heart.

"Come to me, all you who are weary and burdened, and I will give you rest" (Matthew 11:28).

This does not say some of you, but *all of you*. The ones who come to Jesus are the ones who have come to the point in their lives where they are overburdened with life, overburdened with pain, suffering, hopelessness, loss of direction, and loss of purpose. Thank the Lord; yes, thank the Lord for the trials that He has allowed you to experience because this is the beginning of being saved. This is not being saved, but the beginning of it. Let me explain that.

In this world today, the polls say that 90 percent of Americans believe in God. Now there is a difference between believing that Jesus was someone who lived on this Earth like Abraham Lincoln or Thomas Jefferson, and *believing* that Jesus came to this Earth, died on a Cross over 2,000 years ago, and then rose from the dead so that all who believe in Him will not perish but have everlasting life. So what does "believing" mean? Before I tell you what believing is, let me explain what believing isn't.

It isn't going to church, putting money in the offering plate, being baptized, confirmed, being kind to others, or teaching God's Word as a way to get you into Heaven. This is works and works do not make you a believer.

"For it is by grace you have been saved, through faith, and this not from yourselves, it is the gift of God, not by works, so that no one can boast" (Ephesians 2:8,9).

So what good are works? Our works are thanks for what God has done for us, period. If God cannot love you any more than He loves you today, then why do you do good works? Search your heart because it should *only* be for thankfulness for what God has done for you, not to get in better with God or to earn a place in Heaven.

Back to belief and what it is not: Faith is not a temporary thing where you are in a hospital bed crying out to the Lord for help and then when the crisis is over, you go back to your own ways. Faith in Jesus is called "saving faith." Saving faith is trusting in Jesus alone for salvation. You have to come to the point in your life where you realize that nothing you have tried will work, except Jesus. Nothing you have secured, possessed, or have guaranteed to you will give you hope, except Jesus. Your own strength, craftiness, and frugality are not what Jesus wants. Jesus desires all you have and the less you have, the better. Why? Because the less you have, the less you have to give up. That is why Jesus says that it is " ... harder for a rich man to enter the kingdom of Heaven than it is for a camel to go through the eye of a needle." This is because they have to give up so much.

The more trials you have experienced in life, the more you realize what is important. Now some people have experienced a lot of trials and have become bitter instead of better. To those I say, "God is still working in you." But to those who have come to the end of your rope with only the abyss below and God with His outstretched arms above, I say, "Hallelujah!" Take hold of the Lord's hand and never look back. But once you do, *never* forget who saved you. Do not go back to your worldly ways and think that Heaven is here on Earth. Don't ever think you are the master of your ship and in control of your destiny.

Over 2,000 years ago, Jesus paid a horrible, painful, humiliating price through death on a Cross for you and for me. It was the only way for us to be saved. God needed the perfect sacrifice for our sins and Jesus was that sacrifice. If Jesus is in your head and not in your heart, pray today for Him to come and take over your life. Quit running away. You know what I mean, as it is different for each one of you.

There are serious problems in this world with wars and rumors of wars. Jesus said that this must happen before He comes back. But Jesus also says that He desires that none should perish. We have much work to do in evangelism. No amount of evangelism will work unless we focus on the Cross. That is where our real power, comfort, strength, and hope come from. It is through, not only the death of Jesus, but His resurrection that we have all the hope, power, and security we need. Are you really saved? You are if you have put all your faith, trust, hope, glory, and future in the Lord. And, most importantly, that you have asked Jesus into your life and asked Him to forgive your sins. If you have, then you are a child of God with a place already picked out for you in Heaven. That is what Easter is all about. His power and resurrection to conquer death is what all of us have our hope and future set on. Think on those things and no matter what the trial, Jesus will get you through.

Lord, Why the Pain?

Pain is a universal language, isn't it? You could go into any hospital in the world filled with people speaking different languages and *understand.* For the Christian, the faces of pain bring out in us the compassion, love, and mercy we have received from Jesus. We want to jump in and help. Why is this? Because even as believers in Jesus Christ, we also suffer in the flesh. But we suffer with a new perspective instead of an old one. The old flesh sees pain as temporary, with no purpose. The believer sees pain as something allowed by God to refine us to be more like Him.

I am thankful for the depression that the Lord has allowed me to have. To be sure, some days and years have been very dark, but nothing compared to the glorious riches that await all who believe in Jesus. So what has this depression brought about? Patience! My nickname in college was "Hectic." Some might say that hasn't changed! But it has. I used to be all over the place in my personal and business lives. I was not content to sit still. I was persecuted in every direction by the evil one. He thought he had me for eternity in hell, but in reality, the evil one was pushing me to the Lord.

Depression has allowed me to take away most of the clutter in my life and to only hold on to those things that are important and worth keeping in my mind. What does this mean? When there seems to be no way out, when the darkness covers the light, when you can't seem to put one foot in front of the other, and when God seems distant, there are only a few things that matter:

Getting closer to God through prayer and fellowship with other believers.

Getting to know and get closer to your family and friends.

Praying for peace, strength and hope.

Loss of life in this world is loss of hope, so how do we get our hope back?

" ... but we also rejoice in our sufferings because we know that suffering produces perseverance; perseverance, character, and character hope and hope does not disappoint us" (Romans 5:3-5).

Without hope in our lives, we will wither away. If you would make a study of most retired people, you would find some very disturbing results. If those retired people do not keep active both physically and mentally, then they will soon die. There has to be something to live for.

Do you have something to live for that is of the Lord, instead of man?

Living for a better job, better home, better car, better bank account, and better retirement plan will only get you so far. Once you achieve some of those things, you will start to get a little frightened because the job that you thought would bring happiness did not bring any lasting joy. The only lasting joy in this life is coming to know Jesus as your Savior and Lord and then sharing that good news with as many people as possible. Do not think like the world thinks; think like Jesus thinks. How do we do that? Through prayer, which is not just talking to Jesus, but letting His Holy Spirit talk to you and direct your life. Jesus has a plan for each of us. Do you know what your plan is?

Again, back to pain. Have you ever seen a woman in childbirth? Once those contractions start, the party is over for the time being. I remember Julie's first big contraction that she had with Bryce. She grabbed my shirt and had a look of terror in her eyes. I thought, "What did I do? I was partly responsible for this pain." But pain allows you to focus. If I had asked Julie if the house payment had gone out or where she wanted to go on vacation, she would have looked at me with a worse look than the one I was getting. Why? Because this pain was for a reason. This pain was to bring a new life into the world. She was focused on the task and not the clutter of daily living. Since Julie persevered through the suffering for a time, there was a glorious baby and hope at the end. The pain was forgotten after a time, but the glorious riches of the new birth remained.

That is what the Lord is talking about in our suffering. In order to be a believer in Jesus Christ we must be refined. I do not know of anyone in this life who can be refined by sitting on the beach in Hawaii. Being refined comes through trials, tragedies, loss of direction, and loss of hope. Then hope is restored. Most of you will attest that when things looked the worst, the Lord eventually shined the most. The next time you are in pain or in a trial, look to the one who is unmovable, unshakable, the Creator and Sustainer, the only one with all the everlasting hope we will ever need. That is Jesus. Do you know Him or do you just know about Him? There is a big difference.

If you are worried and concerned today it may be because you have no hope. The hope you thought you had was fleeting and you are left with a pile of sand that is quickly slipping through your fingers. Jesus is the rock, the one who will never let you slip away. If you have never asked Jesus into your life by faith, do it right now. Ask the Lord to forgive your sins. Tell Him that you believe He died on the Cross and rose from the dead to pay the penalty for your sins and that you want Him to come in and take control of your life. If you do that from your heart, then you will spend eternity in Heaven with Jesus and you will be able to lead a Spirit-filled, purposeful life here on Earth.

Why the pain? Sometimes we will never know, but we do know that God's plan is always perfect. *Always!* It doesn't matter how many times we get knocked down, it matters how many times we get up.

Have a great week, stand strong, and have compassion for all those around you who are in pain.

"DNF"

In Sunday School this past week, I talked a little bit about depression and then spoke about suicide. I said that it is usually the people you would never expect, who take their own lives. A great friend in the class emailed me that he was concerned for my welfare. The Lord showed me the love this man had for me and for my walk with the Him. He had also suffered depression and knew the depths of this horrible disease. He could have easily gone home and not said anything, but he chose to step up and give me godly encouragement.

In this life we are not meant to go it alone. I think sometimes we get into a rut where we just put our heads down and go. Hunker down, get the job down at all costs, and never give up. While this may be a good strategy for a moment, it isn't for the long run. This way of thinking can easily get us off course. The only way is to have help, someone to look out and see if we are going off course. Jesus could have easily gone it alone. He created everyone and everything on Earth, keeps all the stars in place, holds the oceans back, and a billion other things He does every day. Why did He need to associate with other men? Because since the beginning of creation, God wanted to converse with us. God made man in His image, as it says in Genesis 1:26.

Jesus could have easily spent all His time alone, created miracles by himself, died on the Cross, rose from the dead, and that would have been it. However, He chose to surround himself with twelve other men whom He could pour His life into. He could converse, have fellowship, and not be lonely. Since Jesus was 100 percent God and 100 percent Man, He desired to have that fellowship. He also needed to impart wisdom to those that were around Him to carry His message to all the ends of the Earth.

There was an orphanage in Russia that had been very under-funded and neglected. When a news agency came in to see what was going on, they were amazed at the filth and neglect. But something more important caught their attention. The children had no one around them for days at a time, but every one of them had their arms wrapped around themselves. Since they could not get love from the outside world, they tried to get affection by wrapping their own arms around their little bodies. This is a gut-wrenching display of neglect, but one that shows us the necessity to pour our lives into others and not go it alone.

Exercise has to be a part of my life. When I was at the University of Maryland, we ran two times a day for over 100 miles a week. Even on Sundays, we would do an easy twenty-mile run. I look back and say, "What is an easy twenty-mile run?" But back in the 1970's, more was better. The problem with this was that as long distance runners, our bodies were accustomed to accumulating large amounts of endorphins each day. When I got this weird idea to quit running, I did not taper down; I just quit. When I look back, that is where the depression started. About three months after that, strange things, thoughts, and obsessive patterns stared to creep in. For ten years, I was in a downward spiral that took a lot of help to get stopped. The more I run now, the better I feel, so I need to run. Maybe not like Forrest Gump, but I need to run.

At Ironman Wisconsin last year, I received a DNF for the race. "Did Not Finish." At the time, I knew that I could not go on or I'd risk serious injury from hypothermia. The other determining factor was that my time was too slow. I would not have made the top five finishers for the championship in Kona, Hawaii, which was my goal. Looking back, if I had just spent an hour in the medical tent getting warm, I may have been able to go on. I should have tried to finish no matter what the time.

Suicide in this life is a "DNF." God has a race planned out for each of us and that race is the race of life. If we put unrealistic expectations on ourselves and set ourselves up for failure, we have a chance to get a "DNF." If you are a perfectionist and try to be perfect all the time, you will have trouble. If you try to win every race, every battle, try to get every promotion, and the plan you have dreamed about doesn't work, don't "DNF." Take the time to gather Christian friends, regroup, and pray about the direction the Lord wants you to go. All the experiences in our lives have made us more dependent on God. Don't get to the point in your life where you think there is no way out. When Daniel was in the lion's den, there was no way out. Daniel could have said, " Just kill me because I don't want to be eaten by a lion." Instead, he trusted God to deliver him and God did!

I don't know where you are in your life today. You may be at the end of your rope, thinking about a "DNF," but don't do it. Regroup, pray, take some time to get away from the situation, get around some godly friends, pray, open up, and get encouragement from others and, most importantly, the Lord. I guarantee that when the storm passes, you will see the brightest, bluest sky possible. If the sky were always blue, you would take it for granted. But when the darkness comes, the rain and wind gets too heavy, and fear sets in, pray. Then when the storm passes, you will see much clearer than before the storm. If you hang in there long enough in the Lord's strength, you will see miracles that you would have missed if you had a "DNF." Plus, you will be able to encourage others with the hope that you have been given by Jesus himself.

Don't ever give up, no matter how tough, how long the road, or how steep the trail. God is there, God is there, *God* is there. Pray that in the midst of the storm, you would sense His peace. Instead of the "DNF," you will come around the bend to a waving crowd at the finish line. Instead of breaking the tape, the Lord will speak to you saying, "Well done, good and faithful servant."

One step at a time, *one step at a time.* Have a great day in the Lord.

What Is Your Thorn?

Whether you know it or not, each of us has a "thorn in the flesh".

"To keep me from being conceited because of these surpassingly great revelations, there was given me a thorn in the flesh, a messenger of satan, to torment me. Three times I pleaded with the Lord to take it away from me. But He said to me, 'My grace is sufficient for you for my power is made perfect in your weakness.' Therefore I will boast all the more gladly about my weaknesses so that Christ's power may rest on me. That is why, for Christ's sake, I delight in weakness, in insults, in hardships, in persecutions, in difficulties. For when I am weak then I am strong" (2 Corinthians 12:7-10).

Yesterday was a tough day. But the Lord was not surprised. The day before, the leadership team for our Sunday School class had a meeting. We all look forward to this monthly meeting as over the years we have become like family. It is like the church of old, when people met in houses. We would do anything for each other and we truly share each other's burdens. These friends have been praying for me for months knowing about the depression that has been a severe burden to me. While we were going through prayer requests, my eye felt as though someone had cut my cornea.

I actually had to leave the prayer time to go and wash it out. Driving home was a challenge. The next morning I woke up and my eye was swollen, so I went to the doctor. Somehow, (the Lord knows) the cornea was scratched and I needed to go on antibiotic drops. While I was at the doctor's office, I realized I needed to talk to him about this depression. I realized then that my eye was the catalyst to get me to the doctor. The power of prayer the previous night! The doctor changed my medicine since what I was taking was not working.

God used the pain in my eye to get me to the doctor. Last night I prayed for relief. It has been thirty-four years of depression, but the last eight months have been a heavy burden. This morning at 4:44, I had a nightmare and woke up. When I woke up, it wasn't the evil one but the presence of Jesus himself calling me downstairs to do some business. I have been studying God's Word, but not praying like I should. What is true praying? Talking, yes, talking with God as you would your best friend. If you have never done that, you need to. I came down to my favorite spot and started praying. I still felt that I wasn't close enough to God and that real business needed to be done. So I lay prostrate on the floor and told the Lord, "God, You have me where You want me and I am willing to do whatever it is You want me to do." At that moment peace came over me, total peace, and a new, renewed spirit. Why did it take eight months for me to say, "Lord, You have me?" One reason is that the Lord wants to keep me from being conceited. Nothing good can happen when we are a conceited people. When we are conceited, people won't listen to us; churches end up splitting because of conceited people. When you think you can do something better than that which God has ordained, be very careful. Make sure it is God wanting you to change and not the evil one making you break ranks.

I think we can all relate to the Apostle Paul with his thorn in the flesh. Three times he pleaded. Pleading is not just asking God, but pleading is as if one's life is at stake. What did God say? God said, "No, My grace is sufficient. My power is made perfect in your weakness." You see, God's power cannot be made perfect when you are using your own power. Your power and my power *will never defeat the evil one*. The Holy Spirit working in us will defeat the devil. He is a defeated foe. But when we become conceited, arrogant, and prideful, then satan sees hope. He sees the fall coming and he doesn't discriminate.

I am thankful for my depression. I would rather be in trials and have God's abundant grace, than be conceited, have the world's accolades, and end up being an ineffective witness for Jesus. All I can say to satan is *bring it on!* I am not afraid of him, his schemes, or his demons. My fear is of the Lord, for God is just and will protect me in the valley of the shadow of death or on top of the highest mountain.

You may be in the valley of the shadow of death right now. Your spouse may have left you, your children may be sick, or have some tough issues that you are dealing with, your boss or job may be brutal and it may feel like a thousand pound weight. That is right where Jesus wants you. If you haven't done so, I ask you today to find a quiet place and lay prostrate before the Lord. Cry out to Him and give it all over to Him, *all of it!* No pain here on earth will ever be compared to the glorious riches that await us in heaven.

Most of you know what your thorn is. Whether you do or you don't, that thorn may not be taken away until the Lord calls you home. Just remember the Lord desires to complete a good work in you. Make it your motto to say and think, "Bring it on!" When your faith far outweighs the pain, then you will see God's glory and grace like you have never seen it before. All the things of this world will slowly fade away and you will live for the Lord. Nothing in this life is better than serving the King of kings and the Lord of lords no matter how big or deep the thorn. Keep on keeping on in the faith.

Take care and be courageous in the Lord today.

Please Give Me Another Chance

I think we can relate to those who fail and triumph, more than to those who seemingly always triumph. The ones who always triumph seem to always be on top. If they were to honestly open up, they would tell you that they have failed many more times than they have succeeded. When people asked Thomas Edison why he failed over 2,000 times in inventing the light bulb, he said, "I didn't fail 2,000 times. I found 2,000 ways the light bulb won't work." In life *we are all going to fail.* No one has it all together, no one. You see, people relate to suffering; they don't relate to someone who has it all together *because no one does.* Before someone will truly listen to us, we have to have a humble spirit. There are people who lead through fear and people who lead by example. While both may work for a time, the one who leads by example will always overcome the one who leads by fear.

The Apostle Peter denied Jesus three times before the rooster crowed. Then Peter wept. Can you imagine what he was thinking? "Lord, You showed me all these miracles, I lived with You for over three years and You encouraged me with lessons and even enabled me to walk on water. Why did I doubt? Why did I say I didn't know You when the going got tough?" I am sure Peter wished he could have had a second chance to make things right, especially after Jesus was crucified.

In life, I am sure each of us has done something where we thought to ourselves "If only I could get a second chance to make things right." It is almost like a bad dream. We have all had dreams where you get into an awful mess and them wake up and think, "Wow!" Then you will have a much better outlook on things. I don't care who you are, we have all wished at one point or another in our lives that we could have had a second chance.

I believe Jesus knew that He would be able to give Peter a second, third, fourth, and fifth chance even though Peter didn't know it. Can you imagine the joy Peter felt when he saw Jesus on the shore of the Sea of Galilee? Peter didn't wait until the boat got back to shore. Peter jumped into the water and swam to Jesus. Can you imagine the relief Peter felt when he could make amends?

Then Jesus spoke to Peter and asked Peter if he loved Him three times, the same number of times Peter had denied Jesus. In Peter's heart, it was a way to even things out for what he did wrong.

Each of us has sinned so many times against God that there is no way we should be forgiven, *but He does forgive us*. When we come to the Lord with an open, repentant heart, Jesus will forgive our sins and "remember them no more." We may forgive one another, but it is very difficult for us to forget. Fortunately, Jesus is God and He forgets totally.

I don't care where you are today. You may say, "If I only finished college; if I only finished trade school; if I only finished my commitment to my spouse and children; if I only …" When you come to God with a spirit of humility, hope, and repentance, then Jesus will give you another chance. I can't tell you in every instance how the Lord does it, but that is why God is God, and we are not. Many times we look down on the homeless or people in jail. I can tell you right now that you don't know how close you are to both of those places in life. Money is not security. No matter how much you have, it can evaporate in a night. A couple of bad decisions and you could be the next person carrying a cardboard sign. If you think, "not me," then you are a prideful person. The Lord controls how much money you make, it's not your own craftiness. You may also say, "I would never be in prison." All it takes is one poor decision. Have you ever been driving down the road with a cell phone to your ear and got close to hitting someone? All it takes is once and your life is changed forever.

"Do not judge or you too will be judged" (Matthew 7:1).

When we judge others, we are really saying that we are better than they are. We are then prideful and arrogant. Judging others means that they have fallen short of the standards we have set up. Stop judging anyone now. We sin so much in a day that if God were to judge us the way we judge others, we would never have a chance of eternal life. Instead of judging, give people a second, third, and fourth chance, not to live up to your standards, but for you to learn God's compassion. How arrogant and prideful it is for us to judge someone when Christ has given us a clean slate.

I don't care how many times you think you have failed or how many chances or opportunities you think you have missed. God doesn't make mistakes. All those missed opportunities give us a sense of urgency and drive that can make us better when we give it all over to God and trust in Him. The Lord will give you another chance. Pray that you see the opportunity and act on it in the His power and grace. Don't look too far down the road; one day at a time and the second chance will come again.

The Spirit Is Willing, But...

A few weeks ago I signed up for the men's softball league at church. Now the last time I played baseball or softball was about thirty-six years ago. Back then it was about perfection. Back then it was quite different. Now we had one practice before our first game. I had more aches and pains from this practice than from doing an Ironman. In an Ironman you don't sprint. But I was running to catch fly balls and throwing balls that I hadn't thrown in thirty-six years.

Our first game was last week. It was a double header. I knew my first problem was when the coach told me I was in right center field and I had to ask him where that was? I found my way out there and was actually a little nervous. I was nervous because my mindset went back to my younger years. When I was younger, I would be grilled if I didn't do it this way or that way. Sometimes I would get so worked up that I hoped the ball didn't come to me. That way I couldn't get in trouble. But this game was different from the start.

First of all, both teams stood on each chalk line and we prayed openly before the game. Then we went to our designated positions. I had gotten there a little late after getting lost, so I wasn't in on the selecting of the positions. Years ago our talk in the dugout was about the game, but it was also about our futures and our lives ahead. What we were going to do, the girls in the stands, the fun of building a tree house when we got home. Now the talk was, "I have to play right field because my knee won't go to the left." "I can hit, but I need a pinch runner because my left leg has a torn ACL." "I can't run fast anymore, so don't put me in the outfield." I was surprised how winded you could get catching a fly ball. I caught one ball and the second baseman said "When was the last time you caught a ball in a game?" and I said about thirty-seven years ago. The first two innings we ran out onto the field. The next two innings, we trotted and by the fifth inning, we were all walking out to our positions. And this was a double-header!

But we had fun and it was one of the few times I really had fun playing in a ball game. The fellowship was awesome and we got a little exercise to boot.

"Watch and pray so that you will not fall into temptation. The spirit is willing, but the body is weak" (Matthew 26:41).

Now when I read this verse, I know we can think we are young, but the body knows its age! Sometimes we can agree to something, not really calculating the cost. In the Garden before Jesus was captured, He had asked His disciples to pray. Jesus told them how distraught He was and He told them to keep watch and pray. What happened? They fell asleep not once, but twice. In the game I played, in my mind I was fifteen again, but my body is still fifty-one! I am sure as the season goes on, we will get a little stronger and a little faster, but not that much.

Today as you go through the day, remember that satan is around trying to make you fall. Trying to make you do something that you will regret later or even destroy your witness. In our spirits, we pray and can feel the power of the Holy Spirit. We can get ready to go, but then, whack! Satan does not want you and me to be effective witnesses to others. Satan wants us to keep our burdens to ourselves. When I shared about my problem with depression, it was amazing how many people asked me to pray for them and their loved ones who had the same disease. If I were not open, then others would not have been either. People can't relate to successes as much as they can failures. People will open up to you when they see you are transparent and that you are not trying to be arrogant or get one up on them. They will be open to you when you can show that you don't have it all together.

I said to one person, "I think the Lord let me go through this season of depression because He thought I might be running out of material to write!" Of course, humor is always good. I am truly thankful for all the trials I have gone through, because they continue to make me dependent on God and not on myself. When I do things in the flesh, I always fail, but when I do things in the spirit, I am usually much, much better.

We are in a war. Our souls are protected if you have accepted Jesus as Savior and Lord of your life. Satan can't take your soul, but he can try to make your life miserable so you are not effective for others. We all have things going on. We have to live in the Spirit, not in our weak bodies, and press onward for Jesus, not for ourselves. If you are in a trial right now, rejoice that satan sees you as a worthy adversary. Even though you may be down for a day, month, or year, don't fret. God is getting ready to put you back in the game much stronger, faster, and relying more on Him than on yourself. Pray more and then pray more again, that when the attacks come, you can continue to fight the good fight and finish the race strong.

We have another game tonight. I better take a nap and get some rest.

What Have You Done with Your Talents?

The parable of the talents is a very interesting one. For some reason when I read this passage, it always seems to apply to money. The other day I was reading this and it struck me that it also applied to our God-given talents.

"Again, it will be like a man going on a journey who called his servants and entrusted his property to them. To one he gave five talents of money, to another two talents, and to another one talent, each according to his ability. Then he went on his journey. The man who had received the five talents went at once and put his money to work and gained five more. So also, the one with the two talents gained two more. But the man who had received the one talent went off, dug a hole in the ground and hid his master's money" (Matthew 25:14-18).

When the master came home, he asked each one what they had done with what they had been given. The one who had five talents gained five more, so the master put him in charge of many things. The one with two talents gained two more. The master said that since he had been faithful with a few things, he would be put in charge of many more things and he would share the master's happiness. But the man who had one talent said that he was afraid he would lose the talent, so he dug a hole and hid it. The master said to this man:

"Take the talent from him and give it to the one who has the ten talents. For everyone who has will be given more, and he will have an abundance, whoever does not have, even what he has will be taken from him" (Matthew 25:28,29).

This could be summarized by saying, "Use it—or lose your talents."

"Talent" is a natural ability—an unusual natural ability to do something well.

Each of you, yes, each of you, has a natural ability that you can do well. Why? Because the Lord has given us talents, each one of us. Some of you have used your talents in a wise way and some have not. The reason some of you are saying now, "I don't have any great talent," is that you have not gone out into the world and used your talents. The man with five talents had to expend some risk and hard work to get five more. If you have not discovered your talents, then maybe you are not taking risks. If you have always wanted to paint, but never took the challenge, why not start today? If you have been hurt by a bad relationship, that doesn't mean that all relationships are bad. If you have a talent that you know is unused, *it is never too late* to start. The Lord gave you a talent to use, not to keep buried.

If you wonder why you do not have many talents, it could be because you have not done anything with the ones you do have. If the Lord sees that you do well with a little, He will continue to give you more. If He sees you are having trouble with a little, He may hold back until you get better. But the ones who were able to do more, " ... shared in the master's happiness." Unused talents will always bring guilt and despair. The devil does not want us to be effective witnesses. He does not want you to use your talents, he wants you to bury them and be idle.

Pray today that the Lord will reveal to you what you do really well. Each of us is great at something because the Lord does not make mistakes. You have to be very careful of what you do with your talent. Let me get back to talents as they pertain to money.

And He told them this parable. "The ground of a certain rich man produced a good crop. He thought to himself. What shall I do? I have no place to store my crops. Then he said, 'This is what I'll do. I will tear down my barns and build bigger ones, and there I will store all my grain and my goods. And I'll say to myself, You have plenty of good things laid up for many years. Take life easy, eat, drink and be merry.' But God said to him, 'You fool! This very night your life will be demanded from you. Then who will get what you have prepared for yourself?' This is how it will be with anyone who stores up things for himself, but is not rich toward God" (Luke 12:16-21).

Let me ask you this very important question. Are you holding anything back for yourselves instead of giving it to the Lord? God forbid any of us should do that because our lives could be demanded from us today if we do. Fortunately, if you come into the light and see your mistake, God will forgive, restore, and His grace will allow you to make things right. But if you keep on doing a wrong and know it, then God's will, will be done.

Many people say, "I need this to retire on," or "I want to be able to do this and that." If you are not rich towards the Lord, then God may take your life before retirement and give your money to someone who knows how to be rich toward God. Julie and I need to make sure that our house is in order in a godly way, *not in a worldly way*. Remember, God can confuse the wise and give many blessings to the poor at heart. Make sure today that your heart is right before God. Because when this happens then all your talents and resources will be used to further God's kingdom, not your own.

What Goes Up ...

. . .**m**ust come down! Where do we get these sayings? We have, "nothing ventured, nothing gained," "the early bird gets the worm," "where there's a will, there's a way," "when the cat's away, the mice will play," "a rolling stone gathers no moss ... "

A lot of these sayings come out of a Biblical context and especially from the Book of Proverbs. We tweak words a little to fit today. One that especially caught my attention recently is "What goes up, must come down." In our Sunday School class we are beginning a study of the minor prophets. Do you know the difference between a minor and a major prophet? It's the size of the book in the Bible. I didn't know that either! I have been studying the book of Obadiah, and something came to me, which I know we can all practice.

Because of Israel's rebellion against God, the Lord allowed the Edomites to seize Jerusalem. Even though the Lord allowed them to seize His people, the people of Edom became very proud of this fact. They gloated over all the power the Lord had given them. The Book of Obadiah is only one chapter, so the reference is to the verse.

"The pride of your heart has deceived you" (Obadiah 3).

"As you have done, it will be done to you; your deeds will return upon your own head" (Obadiah 13).

It says in the Book of Proverbs that pride comes before a fall. We are all deceived when we let our pride get in the way of our lives. It is like a cancer. Once pride starts in a person, it almost needs to be surgically removed in order to stop it. The problem is most of us don't see our own pride. We start to believe our own "press." We start to believe that we are really that good. We forget that *all we have and all we do comes from the Lord—all of it!*

So here comes the part that frightened me: "As you have done, it will be done to you."

This verse makes you want to be kind to others, doesn't it? God is a forgiving God when we come to Him with a repentant heart and ask Him to forgive our sins. Not only will He forgive our sins, but He also forgets them. But God is also just and must punish sin. God is perfect and He cannot let a wrong go unpunished. But He also forgives those who repent. Even though God forgives that doesn't mean we won't suffer the consequences of our actions.

Lately, I have seen some companies fall because of pride. Not only pride, but also because a lot of their people were mean-spirited. You can be good and still get ahead. The sooner we realize that God is in control, the sooner we will get rid of our prideful selves. Look at your life today. Nothing is sure in this life but death of the body. Don't be deceived by success if you are experiencing it, because success may drag you off to hell. Poverty has a way of humbling the proudest of the proud. I would rather have poverty and inherit eternal life, than have riches here on Earth and let that deceive me so I fall prey to satan's schemes. The Lord knows what will entrap us and what will not. Pray today that we will stop being deceived by the prince of this world, the devil. If you are successful in the world's eyes, don't gloat over it. Don't think you have done anything profound, because *you* have not done this. The Lord has just allowed it to happen for a time.

Live your life for others and, most of all, try to lead them to Jesus for "As you have done, it will be done to you."

Remember what goes up …

Let the Lord be on top of the mountain and let our hearts be humble. Pray today that the Lord takes away the blinders of pride and lets you see yourself as a sinner who needs Him and needs to be saved by God's grace and God's grace alone.

Watch What You Ask For

We are a lot like the Israelites. God had shown the Israelites many miracles. You would think that after seeing the Red Sea part so they could pass through, and then see the Red Sea swallow up the Egyptians, they would be trusting and faithful for the rest of their lives. Much like them, we easily forget the power, grace, and mercy of God each and every day. You and I have not seen the Red Sea part, but we have seen miracles that should cause us to live in victory instead of defeat. How many times has the Lord rescued you? How many times has the Lord shown you favor? How many times has the Lord poured out His blessings upon you? Far too many to count, I'm sure. If we were to journal all that the Lord has done for us, we would weep at the thought of our own doubts.

The Israelites had been rescued out of Egypt, the Lord drowned the Egyptian army in the Red Sea, and then the Lord promised to lead them to a land flowing with milk and honey. God performed many miracles in the desert by supplying manna, which was bread from Heaven. But that wasn't good enough, and they grumbled. They wanted meat. I am sure the Lord was thinking, "Okay, you want meat; here it comes."

"Where can I get meat for all these people? They keep wailing to me. Give us meat to eat" (Numbers 11:13).

"Now the Lord will give you meat and you will eat it. You will not eat it for just one day or two days, or five, or twenty days, but for a whole month until it comes out of your nostrils, and you loathe it because you have rejected the Lord" (Numbers 11:18,19).

"Now a wind went out from the Lord and drove quail in from the sea. It brought them down all around the camp to about three feet above the ground as far as a days walk in any direction" (Numbers 11:31,32).

Now that is a lot of meat! So why was it bad asking for meat? It wasn't just the meat, but it was grumbling about everything. Asking for meat was the last straw. To sum it up, everything God did for the Israelites was never good enough. Sound familiar? How many times does God do something great for us and then after a time we forget and want more. It is true that Jesus tells us to pray and we shall receive, but this has to be taken in the right context.

" ... whatever you ask for in prayer, believe that you have received it and it will be yours" (Mark 11:24).

The prayer Jesus is talking about is pure prayer, not something rote. Just asking for the asking usually won't get it done unless God wants to prove a point to us. Let me explain. If you pray, ask forgiveness of your sins, truly seek the Lord, and listen to His words, then you will ask what is in the Lord's will. Why wouldn't God give you what you are asking? On the other hand, if you heart is not right before God and you ask for something, chances are you are not asking for things that are in the will of God. For example, each time you pray maybe you are asking for more money to get out of debt. The Lord may get tired of this request and let you win the lottery. You may think that is good, but if you are not ready in your heart to handle that money, then it will truly be a huge curse on your life. Most of the lottery winners have become more destitute after they won, than before. Watch what you ask God for.

So how do we know what to ask for? If we pray with a pure, repentant heart that desires to know God, pray for others, seek to live a godly life and seek to do God's will, then chances are we will be asking for the right things. What are the right things? It is different for each one of us. If your treasure and motives are Earthly instead of eternal, then watch out. It is far better to serve others than to serve yourself and build up treasure here on Earth. If you are not rich toward God, you will suffer.

Let us all strive to get right before God. Pray that we would have the discipline to get up early and pray and put God first. Pray for an open, pure, repentant heart that looks to do more for others than for ourselves. Pray that we would be open to the Lord's leading instead of trusting in our own clever ways. The Lord wants us to ask Him for things. He desires to give us good things as a father or mother does. But giving too much of something can be more of a hindrance than a help. Just trust in God, pray, ask Him for guidance, and protection and then go about your day. The Lord will bring the right people and the right circumstances your way. Believe me you can *truly* trust Jesus.

Expect God's Favor

S atan wants us to lead miserable, defeated lives here on Earth. He will do everything and anything he can to make us doubt, our lives, our goals, our futures and ourselves.

That is not God's plan!

God desires to give you favor in everything you do. But there are a couple things we need to do in order to experience God's favor.

"For whoever exalts himself will be humbled, and whoever humbles himself will be exalted" (Matthew 23:12).

"Exalted"—high in rank, position, or esteem.

Our self-esteem can leave us as a shell or as secure as a fortress. If we are prideful and show it, eventually the Lord will bring about things or circumstances that humble us. On the other hand, if we have a humble spirit, the Lord will pour out His blessings. So what does living in humility to Jesus mean?

1. We need to give everything over to the Lord—yes, everything.
2. Whether good or bad, we need to praise the Lord. We can't see the whole picture so how do we know what is good or bad in an eternal sense?
3. We need to get rid of self daily by focusing on Jesus and His concerns instead of our own.
4. What is God's will for your life? Find it and take off.
5. For every compliment you get, say thank you; then silently thank the Lord and give Him the credit. He made you and will sustain you.
6. Ask the Lord to reveal to you anything that is not right between you and Him. Pray, be quiet, and be right with God.
7. Trials are a time to learn to trust in God's goodness, not a time to fret. If we can get this one right, our lives will be much more at peace.
8. Realize that all we have is from the Lord. Nothing is ours, so please don't take credit; give all credit and praise to God.

When we can start to do these things, we will become humble servants of the Lord. When we are humble ourselves and let God be God in our lives, we will experience God's favor. If we do the opposite of all the things above, become prideful, arrogant, and not give any credit to God, we will experience God's judgment. I am sure we want God's favor instead. This day you can repent and humble yourself before the Lord. You can have a great life and expect God's favor in all you do when you have a humble, repentant heart.

The Lord does not want us to lead a defeated life, but a victorious life. *Expect good things to happen.* Expect to get that promotion, expect to have a good doctor's report, expect to have God's favor in everything you do and say.

Let today be the day we stop living defeated lives, cowering in the face of danger, and start leading a victorious life with great expectations from the Lord. Live like the child of a King, instead of a defeated foe.

Let's all expect greatness in our lives through Jesus.

Will God Always Fight For Us?

Yes and no!

"In spite of this you did not trust in the Lord your God, who went ahead of you on your journey...." (Deuteronomy 1:32).

The Israelites finally were about to inherit the land that the Lord had told them they would occupy. But before they went in, they convinced Moses to send out one person for each tribe to take a look. Twelve men went out to spy on the land. When they came back, they gave a report on how great the land was, but they also gave a report on how fortified the cities were and how big and tall all the men were. So they became afraid and did not go into the land. God became furious at them and told them that they would wander in the desert for forty years and not one man now living would enter the Promised Land.

"Do not be afraid of them, the Lord your God himself will fight for you" (Deuteronomy 3:22).

This was the time that the last of those men from that generation died. This new generation of men trusted in the Lord and went out to defeat the enemy and occupy the land that the Lord had promised them. So, what was the difference? The new generation of men did not go out beforehand and look at the land. The Lord said to go out and occupy the land and they obeyed God without question.

The cities may have been fortified and the people may have been bigger and stronger, but these men trusted in God instead of their own strength. God did the fighting for them. *They did not get in God's way!*

Are you getting in God's way today? Has He given or shown you His greatness, but you choose to disobey and worry? Maybe you have a huge task ahead of you; what should you do? Let me tell you this, it does not matter how strong, how clever, how wealthy, or how powerful you are. If the Lord wants you to do this you will, and if the Lord does not, then no matter what you do, you will *not* succeed, no matter what. If I have ever said anything to you, trust me on this one. The Lord will fight your battles when you are right with Him. So what does "right with God" mean?

It means that there is no blatant sin between you and God. If you feel that God wanted you to go right and you have gone left, the Lord will not bless that. Politics in life *will not work*, period! You can stay twenty-four hours a day at work to show someone that you are committed to your job. You can stay late to make sure no one talks about you. You can make friends with the right people and the powerful people. But in the end, if your heart is not right with God and you are not doing what He asks of you, then *you will fail*. Oh, you may succeed for awhile, but that is just going to cause a bigger fall when it happens. Nothing in this world is secure except your relationship with the Lord Jesus Christ.

God will always fight for you and me when we are trusting in Him instead of trusting in our own talents. In effect, we don't have any talents since they are on loan to us from God. Our lives, our children, our homes, money, and everything we have are on loan. Since we lose all this when we leave this world, what are you doing today?

Are you furthering your kingdom, or the Lord's?

If God has given you a great land to inherit, don't question it. If you have been given talents to do something, don't question your ability—go! If you are always asking "what if," then you have actually told God you do not trust Him.

Let us all believe that God will fight for us when we trust and obey Him. Don't trust or obey the world, but the one who created the world. This should enable us to not fret about what we do, but drive us closer to the one who desires to protect and sustain us for now and forever.

Chasing After the Wind

"Now this is what the Lord Almighty says: 'Give careful thought to your ways. You have planted much, but have harvested little. You eat, but never have enough. You drink, but never have your fill. You put on clothes, but are not warm. You earn wages, only to put them in a purse with holes in it" (Haggai 1:5,6).

The prophet Haggai was speaking to the top political leaders about their motives. The Temple that Solomon built had been destroyed and was still in ruins. The people of that day were more concerned with building lavish places for themselves and letting God's Temple lay in ruin. To say their priorities were skewed was an understatement. Sounds familiar, doesn't it?

This above passage is what the Book of Ecclesiastes says is, "a chasing after the wind." Have you ever felt like your life was like chasing after the wind? You would look at me as though I were out of my mind if I asked you to chase after the wind, but that is what most of us do everyday—chase after the wind.

We do things that have no end, have no purpose, have no plan, and certainly aren't for God. They are all for ourselves. Don't you sometimes feel that "… you have planted much and harvested little, and you earn wages only to put them in a purse with holes in it?" This is the meaning of the verse: God controls everything, *everything*. When we are rich towards ourselves instead of God, then we may find ourselves drinking but never having our fill.

If things are falling apart at the seams in your life, and you are running from morning till evening with no contentment, this may be the problem. Are you trying to store up treasure on Earth or Heaven?

"The ground of a certain rich man produced a good crop. He thought to himself, 'What shall I do? I have no place to store my crops.' Then he said, 'This is what I will do. I will tear down my barns and build bigger ones, and there I will store all my grain and my goods. And I'll say to myself, You have plenty of good things laid up for many years. Take life easy, eat, drink and be merry.' But God said to him, 'You fool! This very night your life will be demanded from you. Then who will get what you have prepared for yourself?' This is how it will be with anyone who stores up things for himself but is not rich towards God" (Luke 12:16-21)

Are you rich toward God or yourself? Ouch! When we politick at work, when we scheme, when we put financial gain before God's gain, *we will always fail.* Oh, maybe not right away, but it will come when we least expect it. The human heart is not any different now than it was in Haggai's time. A lot of us are still chasing after the wind; and it's something that will *always* be elusive. To be sure, we need to do the best that we can with the talent the Lord has given us. We need to work as hard and as diligently as we can at our jobs. But in the end it is not your talent that will make you successful. It is God allowing you to finally " ... *eat and be full, to finally put clothes on and be warm.*" If we are rich toward God and not self, then we will live a spirit-filled, contented life. When we are not and store treasure here on Earth, then our contentment will be fleeting—a chasing after the wind.

You do not have the Lord's power when you are not a believer in Jesus Christ. The forces of the evil one are much stronger than anyone who does not have Jesus in his or her life. But Jesus died and rose again so that all those who believe in Him will have everlasting life and the power to fight evil. All you have to do is confess that Jesus died on the Cross and rose from the dead to pay the penalty for your sins. If you believe that in your heart, confess your sin, and ask Jesus to come into your life, then you will be saved for eternity. Remember Luke, chapter 12: If your life is demanded from you today and you have not made that decision, you will spend eternity in hell. It isn't about how good or bad you are because Romans 3:23 says that we have all sinned and have fallen short of the glory of God. Make this the day that you not only have eternal life guaranteed in Heaven, but that you now have the power to lead a spirit-filled life here on Earth.

Make this the day that you stop playing company and family politics and trust in Jesus instead of your own calculating ways. What good does it do to own many things on this Earth only to give them away when you die? Wouldn't it be better to lead others to the Lord where eternity is at stake? You will never see anyone in Heaven holding onto something they acquired here on Earth. *Think about that*—how you live your life and how you conduct yourself.

We can all stop chasing after the wind and chase after Jesus instead. When we seek the Lord with all of our heart, soul, and mind, then the things that are currently entrapping us will fade away and our lives will take on a whole new, wonderful meaning. Make this the day you change to follow the way of the Lord instead of the way of the world.

Why Am I Failing?

How you ever wondered why you seem to do all the right things, be in the right places, and work as hard as you can, and then fail? It doesn't seem fair, does it? But in this life there are billions of things beyond our control. Since that is the case, why do we try to keep those billion things under our power? The farther we are away from God, the more control we want, the more we need to have things planned out and in order. The closer we are to God, the more we realize that God does have the billion things under control and all we have to do is walk with Him. So why do most of us trust in ourselves, instead of in God? Now when I say trust in God, I mean trusting in God for *everything*. You may be saying, "I trust in God and things just aren't turning out right." Let me ask you this: What is turning out right? Are things turning out right for your glory or God's?

When Joshua took the Israelites into the Promised Land across the Jordan River, the Lord said that He would give their enemies into their hands. The story of Jericho is a great one. If I was the leader of the army and the Lord had told me that the wall around the city was going to come down by walking around it, blowing a trumpet, and shouting, I would have been a little worried. Why? Because I would have thought that fire and battering rams would have been a lot more effective. But God wanted to show His children and their enemies that the Israelites served the God of Heaven and Earth. The only true God. The Lord, at times, will wait until the last minute to help us so we realize that the only way things could work out is that God intervened. God does not want to share His glory with anyone or anything, *anything!* So why do we spend most of our days trying to get the glory and the credit?

We all know the story—when the Israelites gave a loud shout, the walls came down, the Israelites went in, and conquered Jericho. They were to kill every, man, woman, child, and livestock and not take any plunder. They were to burn it all. Later on, the Israelites wanted to conquer Ai. Joshua sent spies out and the spies came back and said, "Send two or three thousand men to take it and do not weary all the people, for only a few men are there" (Joshua 7:3).

So what is wrong with this? They had just routed Jericho, and they were to keep on with the conquest of Ai. However, there was one big problem. The problem was that one of the men, Achan, had stolen some of the devoted things brought back from Jericho, against the Lord's instructions. The Lord's anger burned and He let the two thousand Israelites get routed by the men of Ai.

Joshua fell facedown and asked the Lord, "Why?" So often we don't ask the Lord why; we just keep going and suffering defeat after defeat.

"I will not be with you anymore unless you destroy whatever among you is devoted to destruction" (Joshua 7:12).

Here is the answer to some of your pain. You may have tried everything under the sun to succeed, to try to gain favor, to try to have peace, but when you think you get close, the carpet gets pulled out from under you every time and you have to start all over. Horrible, isn't it? *This is what you have to do.*

"Search me, O God, and know my heart; test me and know my anxious thoughts. See if there is any offensive way in me, and lead me in the way everlasting" (Psalm 139:23,24).

When we search *our own* hearts, we start believing in our own press clippings. We think we are the masters of our ship and in control. But we are not; we're actually far from it. There may be something that satan has blinded you about that is keeping a barrier between you and God. It may be an impure thought life, selfish pride, wishing destruction on others, making idols of *things*, instead of serving God first. Most of the time we don't know because the things of this world will entrap us and make us think we are all right, but we are not.

"All have sinned and fall short of the glory of God" (Romans 3:23).

We have a sin nature that needs to be kept in check. We need to find a quiet place, be still and quiet before the Lord, and ask *God* to search our hearts. When you do this, the Lord will reveal to you anything that is a barrier between you and Him. The problem is we are too busy to be still. God wants to be first in our lives, not second, third, or fourth. If you want to stop being anxious, put God first. If you want to succeed, put God first. If you want to get off the roller coaster of life's ups and downs, put God first. When you do, you may find yourself in some dark places you may not want to be in. You may not like what the Lord reveals to you, but it is the only way. We need to get rid of all that satan has entangled us in and come clean before the Lord. We need to quit holding onto the things of the world and only hang onto God, our Redeemer and Savior.

The Lord has a perfect plan for each of you and that plan does not include being afraid, anxious, or a failure. You are a child of a *King*. Let us all start living like one by casting all our worries and concerns at the feet of Jesus and *pick them up no more*.

Have a great day and make this the day you change forever to really follow and trust the Lord.

Lord, Why Are You Waiting?

Do you ever get tired of waiting for God to deliver you from a trial? We all go through trials, and the main reason is to test our faith. Most of the time, the reason our trials last so long is that God wants to show us that *He* is the deliverer, not us.

The Israelites needed judges to rule over them after Joshua died. The generation after Joshua had forgotten about the Lord because the fathers of Joshua's generation did not pass on the great deeds of the Lord to their children. Are you taking time each week to pass along truth about God to your children? Are you planting seeds that God will water, or are you planting worldly seeds that will be destroyed in the fire?

Gideon was raised up by God to deliver the Israelites from the hands of the oppressive Midianites. The angel of the Lord had appeared to Gideon and Gideon asked the Lord many times to do something to show him that God had truly called him. The Lord told Gideon to put meat on a staff and the Lord consumed it with fire. That wasn't enough for Gideon, so he told the Lord he'd put out a fleece. The first night, the fleece was damp and the ground was dry, but that was not enough for Gideon. He asked God to try it again. The next night, the ground was wet and the fleece was dry just as Gideon had asked. This story gives me comfort because it shows how the Lord put up with Gideon's initial lack of trust. How many times does God tell us to do something in his Word and we just do not trust Him, because we think it is impossible. Gideon's real test looked impossible.

Gideon finally got up the nerve to fight against the Midianites. I am sure he was thinking about how many men he had, how they had been trained, and where he was planning to do battle, but God had another plan. God wanted to get the credit; not give it to Gideon. God wanted to bring the people back to Him by using Gideon.

The Lord said to Gideon, "You have too many men for me to deliver Midian into their hands. In order that Israel may not boast against Me that her own strength has saved her, announce now to the people, 'Anyone who trembles with fear may turn back and leave Mount Gilead.'" So twenty two thousand men left, while ten thousand remained But the Lord said to Gideon, "There are still too may men. Take them down to the water and I will sift them for you there" (Judges 7:2).

The Lord eventually chose those men who had drunk the water from their hands, instead of putting their faces in to drink. Gideon started out with 32,000 men. How many men did God leave him with to fight the Midianites, who had over 120,000 men? Three hundred men! Yes, 300 men. Now how could 300 men possibly defeat an army of 120,000? Certainly not in their own strength. The Lord had said, " … for Me to deliver." God confused the entire army of the Midianites. When Gideon's men surrounded the camp at night, blew their trumpets, and broke glass jars, the Midianite men were afraid and started to turn on each other. In the end, Gideon's army (the Lord's army) had slain over 120,000 men.

It took many, many years of my life for me to realize that God is God. He is the Creator of billions of stars. He holds them up with His hands, and knows how each day is going to go for us and everyone else on the planet. He sees our hearts and orchestrates everything in the world and the heavens. So doesn't it make sense to turn your insurmountable problems over to God and trust Him, instead of trying to get out of your mess yourself? Of course it does. But we have been trained in this world to trust ourselves, to go it alone, to gather up treasure on Earth, and to enjoy life at other's expense. We want it all and we deserve it all. No, we *deserve* hell. That is where we were all headed until Jesus came to this Earth as God in the flesh, to lead a prefect life, then die on the Cross for our sins. He conquered death so those who believe in Him will have eternal life. That is the miracle of this life.

Do you feel today that you are outnumbered 32,000 to 300? Do you see no way out, no hope, no future, and no escape? Then *good!* That is exactly where God wants you. You see, God created you and me. Somehow along the way when we drift from God, we take on the majesty of the Creator instead of the created. It takes everything being stripped away to see that we don't have control of anything except our desire to follow Jesus. But that is enough. When we set our hearts, souls, and minds on the things of God instead of the things of this world, then God will do battle for us.

Don't be afraid to let everything you have go so that you will be free to serve God. Don't let anything be a stumbling block to your relationship with Jesus. Satan wants to entrap us to where we think we are the masters of our ship, deserving of our own praise. Don't you believe it. Jesus died a horrible death for you and for me, so that we could inherit eternal life. Not only that, but also so we could lead victorious lives here on Earth. If you are outnumbered today, good! Start relying on God because you have nowhere else to go. Then you will see the true power of God and the love and peace that come from following Him, instead of leading and failing. Today, no matter what you have done in your past, let God forgive you. Then, with a repentant heart, attack this life in the Lord's strength, wisdom and mercy.

The Distraction of Materialism

Whether we like it or not, our nation is on the verge of crumbling. As I pray, read God's Word and try to listen to the Lord, there is a one thing that is evident in this country. Besides the moral decay, the biggest threat to all of us is the "Distraction of Materialism." In foreign countries, satan uses demonic influence because he does not have a lot of other tools to use to stop the spread of the gospel. In our country, satan has an easy road. The people who lived during the Great Depression *never* bought anything until they had the cash to pay for it. They realized that it all could be gone in an instant. Our society, on the other hand, is all about leverage. We mortgage our house again and again and again to buy more things. We borrow, not thinking how we are going to pay it back, because we think we will always have enough money to take care of things.

Lately, I have seen so many people in debt that I know satan is laughing all the way to the depths of hell. He doesn't need demons to stop us from sharing the gospel and from getting close to the Lord. Satan has this country right where he wants us. We are slaves to the lender; we are slaves to debt and we worry night and day because there's no way out. Some of you, who do not have the Lord as Lord of your life, buy things to make yourself happy. Satan loves that one! You may say you have the Lord, but think again; you have let the evil one take control of your life, not Jesus. Jesus' example was that He could have lived in a mansion, but chose to not have any place to live that He called his own. Materially, the clothes on His back were all Jesus owned. Those of you who are choked by debt today have made some bad decisions. Having someone bail you out is not the answer. You need to learn the sting of this horrible weight so that you never want to be in debt again. So how do you get out of debt?

The most obvious way is to make more than you spend. That may mean selling your house, car, boat, and down-sizing. I know that seems drastic. The reason it seems drastic is because of our pride. Pride is that horrible monster that says, "If I start selling things, people will think that I am not doing well; that I have failed and that I am worthless." Somehow in this world we have equated success with material things and not the things of the heart. True success in this world is a heart issue, not a bank issue.

"What good will it be for a man if he gains the whole world, yet forfeits his soul" (Matthew 16:26).

Yes, what good is it? Does satan have a hold on you even though you think you are righteous? Thinking you are righteous can be a very deceptive pit.

"There is no one righteous, not even one" (Romans 3:10).

We have to live this life as if we are in a war, *because we are*. We are in a war for our souls. If you are saved and are known by your fruit, then satan cannot get you; you are the child of a King. If you think you are saved by the grace of God, but have no outward fruit, you have to have a serious talk with Him and find out why. Do that today if you have a question. If you are a believer and have no fruit, something is seriously wrong. When it comes to debt, this is the whole heart of the matter. If you are saved and have an inheritance in Heaven, then *you should be storing up treasure in Heaven, instead of here on Earth.*

Those of you who are trying to store up treasure for yourself are for the most part being choked to death because of it. You have not obeyed the word of the Lord, and now satan is choking you to death. Debt is a cancer that, if not taken seriously, will keep you immobile. You have to take drastic measures to get rid of debt, and the first step is that you have to get right with Jesus. Those of you who are in debt and do not have a plan to get out, are own your own, far from the Lord. Debt is a heart issue, not a financial issue. Let the Lord be your portion in life, not the things of this world.

Seek the Lord and have Him heal your heart. Ask Him to make you see things as they are, instead of as a sugar-coated hook. Wouldn't it be nice to not owe anybody? This country can only be saved one soul at a time. You are not too far gone when the Lord gets involved. Ask the Lord to reveal to you any unconfessed sin today and ask the Him to help you get out of this mess, which seems insurmountable. God knows the way out; we do not! Stop acquiring and start giving. That is it, isn't it?

Have a great day and don't let the evil one win this battle in your heart.

Expectations

We all have expectations; some are real and some are way out there. Expectations could probably be considered hope. When our son Chase was first diagnosed with autism, our hope was shattered. What hope, you may say? I guess a selfish hope that he would be the top of his class, the best athlete, and the most well liked. As parents, we always want what is best for our children. So when we got the news four years ago, it shocked Julie and me. How could this be? Our plans were set for him, his future planned out, no problems, just successes. As most of you know, life doesn't always go as planned. In other words, life very rarely goes as planned.

Chase is now eight years old. The Lord has done not only miraculous things in Chase's life, but also our lives as well. *Our expectations have changed, but not our hope!*

Chase was like any normal boy playing and talking until he received his immunization shots. The day after the shots, he stopped talking and started to get a blank stare on his face. It was as though someone came in the middle of the night and stole our boy. But through much prayer and God's unfailing love, Chase has been able to talk, read, know who we are, and show a love without holding anything back. Chase doesn't understand the evil of this world, so he only sees the good (except when Bryce steals his Legos!). He doesn't understand that we live in an evil world. Your life would be changed if you could hear his prayers at night. We kneel beside his bed and he thanks Jesus for everything he did that day. I can just see Jesus calling His angels around to listen.

Chase is now eight years old and we signed him up on a soccer team at the church we attend. I had some trepidation until I met his coach. The Lord really put a godly, compassionate man with Chase. Julie and I couldn't have asked for anything more. Last night was the first scrimmage and my mind went back to my first scrimmage. Would Chase steal the ball, make the winning goal, and surprise all that watched? As the game started, my expectations quickly faded. Chase just stood in the middle of the field, as the kids were running back and forth kicking the ball. He was more interested in blowing the coach's whistle, than playing the game. I could tell he was overwhelmed with it all, but his coach had compassion. I felt sorry for Chase, or did I feel sorry for myself? The only interaction Chase had with another player was when another child fell to the ground and Chase helped dust the little boy off.

"But God chose the foolish things of the world to shame the wise; God chose the weak things of the world to shame the strong" (1 Corinthians 1:27).

In reality, Chase has changed more hearts than most of us. Chase isn't out to impress anyone, to get the next best deal, to do what it takes to trample his competition; Chase is Chase. I would like Chase to be like other boys, but my expectations have changed. God does not make mistakes. The Lord has given us Chase for a reason. I can see how Chase confuses the wise at heart. It isn't Chase who is handicapped; it is most of us who view him the way we think he should be, instead of the way God made him.

Today, who do you have unrealistic expectations for? Is it your spouse, children, co-workers, or is it your own ability? At some point in our lives, we have to come to grips with the fact of who we are *in Jesus*, not who we think the world wants us to be. Have you ever considered who you are in Jesus? As you get out today into the soccer field of life, are you going to trample over and kick everyone you come in contact with? Or are you going to pass the ball to others. There is not much glory in passing the ball, as most of the praise goes to the one who gets the goal. But we need to be willing to play the game like Chase. Look for that one person who has fallen and help dust them off even though what may seem important is passing you by. The game of life will keep on going when the Lord has called the end to your days on this Earth. While you were on this Earth did you look for opportunities to help people who fell, or were you more interested in scoring the goal and getting the glory?

Ask the Lord today to help you search your heart so that nothing is hidden. Let the Lord be your God, your Redeemer, Savior and Hope. Our faith is in things unseen and our hope is eternal. Let us trust in the Lord and live the life that the Lord has prepared for us with a joyful outlook, no matter what the circumstances. Remember one day at a time.

If I Only Had ...!

Right now as you are getting into your day, your hope may be in that big deal you are trying to close at work. It may be in corporate politics. "If I can get my person in this position, then I may have a chance to win." "If I can work hard enough, I may be able to afford that new ..." "If I only had a different ... , my life would be so much better." "If I only had ten kids instead of twenty in my class, my life would be so much easier!" If, if, if. Life is full of "if's," isn't it? Fortunately for us, Jesus is not in the "ifs" business.

"May integrity and uprightness protect me, because my hope is in you" (Psalm 25:21).

The reason we all get the "ifs" is because our hope is in our own talents instead of our hope being in God.

It is easier to do something ourselves even if it is wrong than to wait on God!

I always take a road map with me when traveling. No so much to know where I am going, but in case there is an accident on the interstate, I want to know where I can get off and find another route. That may sound good, but in some cases it is not. I would rather go fifty miles out of my way as long as I am moving. Why? Because I hate to wait.

The Lord is in everything and I believe He is amused at my hectic lifestyle. Why would God be amused? Because sooner or later He knows that I will get it. The light bulb will come on and I will figure "it" out. No matter how much we wiggle, scheme, get off the beaten path, play politics, try to get one up, God will be God and *nothing* we do will change that. We try, but in the end God's will, *will* be done.

In the Twenty-third Psalm, there are many verses that are so meaningful. The problem is that the Twenty-third Psalm is so familiar, that we just glaze over it. Jesus is our only shepherd and we are His sheep. Sheep need a shepherd. They can't see very well. They can't defend themselves, and they are very skittish. Well, I have all three of those traits, especially the skittish part. My nickname in college was "Hectic." Not much changes.

"He makes me lie down in green pastures; He leads me beside quiet waters" (Psalm 23:2).

You see, we get to running so fast in our lives that, in order for the Lord to get our attention, He *has to make us lie down.* You may get some strange injury, illness, defeat, money issue, or get fired from your job. That gets our attention, doesn't it? The Lord has been getting my attention lately in many areas. One of the areas where the Lord has gotten my attention is that there are no gray areas in life. What is right is right and what is wrong is wrong. There are no half-truths if you want to live a godly life. God has shown me recently that the time is short, the workers are few, and building our treasure on Earth is totally futile. Treasure on Earth should be people's souls, not a larger bank account. You see God does not desire our money, He desires our hearts. I am seeing that if I do not send out devotionals, share the gospel, build up my family in the Lord, and take care of the things in front of me, then I have wasted my God-given talents. Isn't it horrible to waste something that God has given you?

If I only had more love for Jesus, my life would be a whole lot better. I would quit chasing after the wind and start doing what matters for eternity. That's the answer to "If I only had … !" Think about your life today. Think about your hopes, dreams, and plans. If they are not based on an eternal perspective, then they will ultimately fail. If what you are striving for is not for the Lord, it *will never be enough.*

Make this the day that you would trust and hope in the Lord and put away the foolish things of this world.

Have a great day, make the most of it, and make the most of encouraging others without expecting anything in return.

Are You Stuck?

This life we are in today is meant to be *lived.* How many of us just exist, trying to get through the day and then collapse? I would have to say most of us do, but God desires more for us. For those who have accepted Jesus as their Savior and Lord, Heaven is guaranteed, but in the meantime, what are you going to do with that assurance? Are you going to be so thankful for Heaven in your future that you will be kind to others, share the good news about Jesus, and have a smile on your face and a bounce in your step, or are you going to fall back into the world's schemes?

The Lord has been showing me lately that the business world is a futile place. I see God changing the way I view things. I am starting to get a glimpse of people's hearts instead of how they can just further our business. The Lord can change your vision also. When you are willing to let go of whatever it is that's keeping you from the Lord, then God will open your eyes to a new world. That new world is seeing souls instead of the mentality of "What can you do for me today?" How many of us approach the day with "How will you serve me," or "What can I get from you?" When our hearts are set on the things of this world, we are traveling at light speed in the opposite direction of God. I know in my heart that those reading this today want to be closer to Jesus. I know it. However, the devil has created ways to make you feel comfortable to the point of being paralyzed so you can't make a stand for Jesus. Would you be willing to give up the things that entrap you in order to serve Jesus? I am not talking about some things, but all things? Would you be wiling to give up the comfort of where you live, work, and play to serve the Lord. If the answer is no, then you have some praying to do.

You see, we will never be free until we are willing to *let go!* You know what you are holding tight to. It is a snare that is comfortable or a snare that has you so entangled that you can't turn to the left or right. Jesus never makes the first move. All throughout the Bible when people act first, then God pours out tremendous blessing and power. In order for the Lord to allow Peter to walk on water, he had to get up and get out of the boat. In order for Moses to part the Red Sea, he needed to raise his staff. Now you may not think that is such a big deal, but let me explain this in more detail.

The Israelites had left Egypt after the last plague—the death of the firstborn sons. Pharaoh finally let the Israelites go. But after he had let them go, he decided he made a mistake and then chased after them. Moses is standing on the side of the Red Sea with over a million Israelites, and the Egyptian Army coming after them. Now it would have been easy to trust in self and start fighting, but the Lord said to raise his staff. Now I don't know about you, but I think I would have started fighting instead of raising a stick. Can you imagine if raising the staff had not worked and the army started destroying them? Moses would never have lived that down, even if his life had been spared. But He trusted in what God had told him, even though it didn't make much sense.

What and who are you trusting in today? Are you trusting in the known, instead of the unknown? Are you content in a paralyzed state or do you want more out of life? The only way to get more out of this life is to be in the will of the Lord by doing what He wants you to do. Many of us serve the Lord after we have served ourselves. I have a horrible sweet tooth. If I order an apple crisp ala mode and Julie tries to take the first bite, look out! But after I am almost full, I don't mind if she has a little bite. That is the same way a lot of us are about serving God. I will do this, this, and this, and *then* I will do a little serving of the Lord. But what would happen in our lives if God came first, truly first? The first step is letting go of all the things that you are entangled in. It may not make much sense, but neither did Moses raising his staff to part the Red Sea. It didn't make sense for Peter to get out of the boat. You know Peter was the only one who got out and he was the only one who was able to walk on water.

I know each one of you would love to get out of the boat you are in and *be free to walk on the water.*

"For whoever wants to save his life will lose it, but whoever loses his life for Me will find it. What good will it be for a man if he gains the whole world, yet forfeits his soul?" (Matthew 16:25,26).

Are you willing in your heart, mind, and soul to give it all up for the Lord? Our time on this Earth is very short, so if you are building your treasure here, you are greatly mistaken. Think about what you are doing today. Is it lining your own pockets or are you helping others to see the love of Jesus? Do not be deceived by others and by the evil one. Ask the Lord today to start freeing you from being enslaved by the evil one. Pray that you would see the plan that the Lord has for you. Isn't that exciting? The Lord of the universe has a plan *just for you.* When we stop trying to fulfill our Earthly pleasures, we will stop the snare of the evil one and we will be able to clearly see Jesus. Let us all pray that we would have the faith to first stand up, and then step out of the comfort of the boat. Once you do, you will never look back. Stop the cycle of being always stuck and *live.*

The Spotter

I have been fortunate to work in the sport of NASCAR racing for the past ten years. No I am not a driver, crew chief, or crew member. It would take me fifteen minutes to change a flat tire, and if you were to open the hood and ask me a question, you would see a blank stare. I am a licensing agent for the companies that retail NASCAR products, so I don't have to fix anything or drive fast.

I don't even like to go fast, but I do like to watch others go fast. In order to go fast, each driver needs a spotter to tell him the condition of the track and who is around him. The new HANS (Head and Neck Restraint System) device does not allow the driver to turn his head very far to the left or right, which makes the role of the spotter even more important.

A spotter tells each driver if he is clear to the left or right, if there is an accident up ahead, or where to go if an accident occurs. Now I could not be a spotter. I hate heights, and I am dyslexic. The spotters are always on the highest perch of the track, and that wouldn't be for me. Also, I would say clear left when in actuality they would probably be clear right. I will stick to consumer products; it's far safer. But as I was thinking of the spotter, I realized that each of us needs a spotter in our lives. Most of us try to go it alone. While this may work for awhile, we usually do not see trouble until we are upon it.

Most of us don't like being told what to do or how to do it. In order to live a godly life, we all need someone to look out for us. We may not see things about ourselves that others see. Right now you may be in the middle of a huge wreck with smoke all around you. You may think there is no way out. In your own strength you are probably right, but our ultimate spotter is the Lord. The Lord sees the beginning and the end and knows each step we need to take. The next time you are in a crisis and you can't see in front of you, instead of going full steam ahead, stop and ask the Lord for help.

"In his heart a man plans his course, but the Lord determines his steps" (Proverbs 16:9).

You and I can make all these elaborate plans, but in the end the Lord's will, will be done. Wouldn't it make sense to get directions first? Of course it would, so why don't we? Control is something very difficult to give up.

We like going our own way even if it is the wrong way. Why do most of us start building a toy for our children, then when we have ten pieces left over, we decide to look at the directions? Since I am not mechanically inclined, I was very nervous about installing dimmers on our lights. I read and re-read the directions, but still was a little unsure. I made sure the current was off, not on the light switch (I made that mistake before), but the circuit box. Then I went to work. When I got finished, I had Julie gather the boys together and had them stand near the front door. If flames started shooting out of the dimmer switch when I turned on the breaker, I wanted them to have a fighting chance! I did a little dance when the thing worked. I actually couldn't believe it.

The next time you are in need of help, please ask if you are clear left, clear right, or clear all around. We cannot see even though we try, but the Lord can. The race we are in is called life. It can be a great experience or an act of futility. The Lord knows the right way. Please ask the Lord for help, rely on Him, and you will finish the race.

"You were running a good race. Who cut in on you and kept you from obeying the truth?" (Galatians 5:7).

The evil one doesn't want you to finish the race; worse yet, he wants to injure you so you have no chance of being an effective witness. The only way to finish the race of life is to listen and trust the words of God. Do not give in to chance to finish this race. Yes, listen to the Lord.

Are you listening to your spotter? How can the Lord help you with this?

"Whoever calls on the name of the Lord will be saved" (Romans 10:13).

What Are Your Plans Today?

By the time you read this, most of you are already starting to put out "fires." Each day has a ton of problems of its own, but with those problems is a chance to shine for the glory of the Lord. On the other hand, those problems can make you shine and even impress satan. How will you handle yourself today? If you are not a believer in Jesus Christ, and you have not put your full faith and trust in Him, then you do not have the power to fight evil (far from it). But if you are saved and have the Holy Spirit living in you, you do have the power, through Christ, to overcome evil.

So what are your plans today? Are you on your way to building the biggest personal empire possible or are you trying to fit in a little bit of eternity also? Let me explain. You may be off and running from meeting to meeting, discussing how your brand is going to be the best ever. You may be deciding how you are going to get one up on your competition; you may even be deciding how you are going to get one up on a co–worker, so that you may look better in the boss's eyes. It may be all about you! You may also say, "My job is to make money for the kingdom of Heaven". The only way this is a noble gesture is that you do not keep the majority of the money for yourself. Many people hide behind this umbrella in order to make money for themselves and not to do the work of the Lord. Listen to me very carefully: *Jesus does not need your money; He desires your heart.*

If you are planning on this way of giving to the Lord and that is your ministry, then if you are willing to give away 90 percent to the Lord's work and keep 10 percent for yourself, then that would be appropriate. Anything less is hoarding and keeping treasure on Earth.

All of us have the same twenty-four hours in a day. Most of us get to the end of the day and what have we done? We have fought and schemed to store up treasure for ourselves and have had no thought of the kingdom of Heaven. Why? Because we feel that the kingdom of Heaven has no power here on Earth. But you are wrong in that thinking.

Jim Elliot, one of the missionaries killed by the Auca tribe in Ecuador many years ago, said this:

"He is no fool who gives up what he cannot keep to gain what he cannot lose."

What does this mean? It means that if you go through the whole day and do nothing for eternity then your day has been a waste of time. You may say I have to earn a living, feed my children, and provide for others. Have you every truly lacked for anything? Of course not! So why do we try to hoard, scheme, and tell half-truths to get ahead? If you have not figured it out by now, no matter how clever, smart, devious, or hard working you are, if the Lord wants you to have something you will get it and if the Lord does not, you won't no matter how hard you try.

You may also say I have a financial responsibly to my company to do the best job I can. That is true, but if you are a Christian, you have a greater obligation to the one who saved you from hell. That obligation is to store up treasure in Heaven, instead of storing up treasure for yourself here on Earth. You may pass along a Christian book to a co-worker, pray silently for them, pray for an opportunity to share, or just be a light in a dark world. That is storing up treasure in Heaven. If we go through the day with our temporal eyes instead of eternal eyes, *our day has been a complete waste.*

What will your day be like today? *It is your choice.* Will you start sharing the only thing that will last or will you trust in self and try to stuff your pockets with things that will rust and turn to dust?

"He is no fool who gives up what he cannot keep to gain what he cannot lose."

Please, please, please do things for the Lord today and pray for one another.

Live today in the Lord's strength, mercy, and wisdom.

I Don't Want to Pray

Through the Lord's grace, mercy, power and my email ministry has grown quite large. But with that has come some challenges. My email address is sometimes viewed as spam and then I am blocked by other service providers. I have been on the phone constantly with people from India to the United States to determine and help fix the problem, but to no avail. It has affected my business, so at times I have a hard time even getting one email through.

Yesterday was the last straw. I had spoken to everyone I could think of and my last call I wanted to tell everyone that I was switching providers. My wife Julie could tell I was frustrated and mad, all right, furious. She said, "Before you call anyone else, let's pray." I told Julie, "I don't want to pray." I wanted to continue to be mad. Now there is some spiritual maturity. So I said, "All right, you pray, because right now I can't." I was just like Jonah, who knew that the Lord would save those evil Ninivites, so "Why go?" In my heart I knew that if Julie or I prayed, then my heart would be softened. You know what? I didn't want it to be softened. I wanted to be mad so I could let people know how frustrated I was. Now that kind of thinking is from a non–believer, not someone who has seen miracle after miracle happen in his life. What was going on with me?

So Julie prayed and once I let myself hear her prayer, I started to soften, my blood pressure decreased, and I was back to normal. I got on the phone with the next agent and this is what happened. I said that I had an email ministry that goes out to a large number of people. Somehow my own provider is seeing my email address as spam. He told me, "I am a believer and I can help you." At that moment my thoughts went back to the prayer Julie just prayed. A miracle just took place and I wasn't going to forget that God is God and always on the throne. My pride had gotten the best of me, but fortunately Julie's prayer started a healing in my heart. The technician and I talked about various devotional web sites and had a great conversation. Oh, by the way, he fixed the problem!

"See to it, brothers, that none of you has a sinful, unbelieving heart that turns away from the living God. But encourage one another daily, as long as it is called today, so that none of you may be hardened by sin's deceitfulness" (Hebrews 3:12,13).

Living the Christian life is not a one-shot deal. We have to pour ourselves out daily if we want to be close to Jesus. I know by experience and the testimony of others, that if you do not pray daily and read God's Word *you will have problems*. Going to church on Sunday is to worship God, not to be fed. We are to feed ourselves daily at home. If we only ate once a week what would that do to our bodies? That is why so many people keep switching churches. They want one that is just right for them. So instead of going to worship God, they want to just feel good by their own merits.

My heart was hardened yesterday morning because I got up later than usual, sent out a quick devotional, and didn't pray. I can tell you right now that if you don't start your day out with prayer, then you will have problems. Trust me on that one. Some of you may say, "Come on, pray every day?" Who gives you breath? Who gives you protection? Who holds up the stars and keeps the oceans back? Should we come to the Creator of the Universe, our Savior, each morning and ask for forgiveness, direction, and help? Of course, we should.

So if today has already started out as a four-alarm fire, stop, find a quiet place, and pray. God will rescue you and get you back on track. Do this before the evil one gets a foothold and you say something you shouldn't. We are here to encourage one another in the faith and to lead others to Jesus. When we have hardened hearts, we will not be effective to anyone. Let us be a light in a dark world, instead of contributing to the dark.

Have an awesome Spirit-filled day. Ask the Lord of the Universe to give you His passion and mercy to handle everything that comes your way today.

How Can I Be a Kid Again?

"I tell you the truth, unless you change and become like little children, you will never enter the kingdom of Heaven" (Matthew 18:3).

In this verse, Jesus is talking to His disciples. Most of us, at times, struggle with our faith, but children don't. I could tell my son that we were getting an elephant today and he would believe me. There are a couple reasons for that. I haven't lied to him on previous occasions and his mind has not been tainted yet by the evil in the world. He has not been told one thing and then had his hopes taken away. As we get older, we start to see the reality of this life. We start to get into competition, whether in the workplace, athletics, or raising children. It is every man and woman for themselves. You quickly see that if you don't take care of you, who will? Our faith in man becomes tainted, but Jesus wants us to see Him as we did when we were children. That's when we had complete faith and trust without doubting. The reason we doubt at times today is because we have been told one thing and something else happens. All of us have had the rug pulled out from under us when we least expected it. It is very difficult to trust the Lord when we rely on our past situations. But thank the Lord, God is not like man.

It is true that Jesus was 100 percent man and 100 percent God, so that He could feel our pain, know our trials, and also be the ultimate sacrifice for us. All we have to do is believe. *All we have to do is believe.* You may think, "Okay, this will be easy," but let me give you a trial. Things are going great in your life, bills are paid, money in the bank, kids are healthy, and things are good. Why wouldn't faith be easy, right? You get a call from the doctor's office that you need to come back in. Your last blood test revealed something abnormal. All of a sudden those material things that you equated to faith and security seem to pass into the heavens at light speed. Your life comes to a standstill and nothing else matters but this test and the results.

Why do we worry when we should know that the Lord is on the throne? I can say that because I forget Jesus is on the throne and it is easier for me to worry than to trust many times. When I worry, I am doing something. When I trust, I am trusting someone or something else. *I am not in control.* Remember our past and how many people have failed us. We start to equate Jesus with one who can fail us because we make the mistake of treating Jesus like a man. We forget the faith we had as a child and rely upon our tainted past of missed opportunities and broken promises. So how do we rest when the waves of life are crashing over us?

Most of us would say that the one thing we fear is death, believer and non-believer alike. That is just human nature. I was reading in a commentary last week and a man made a statement that caught me off guard, but also made a huge impact on me. He said, "For the Christian, death is the ultimate healing." A lot of us are afraid to leave this world, because we haven't seen Heaven. Most of us when we go on a vacation have seen pictures of where we are going. If you were going somewhere that you have never seen, you would be a little uneasy. Now if you had to die to get there, then you might really be afraid. But if you were a child and your parents told you that it would be okay, you would trust and not doubt.

Jesus is telling you now to trust like a child and not doubt His forgiveness, salvation, and eternal security. Since our ultimate healing is death, don't worry. Jesus does have your life covered if you are a believer. The only things in this world we are told to worry about are the souls of others who don't know Jesus. If we were to start living like children again, this world would be a lot different.

1. You may squabble with someone, but then you would be playing with them a couple minutes later.

2. You wouldn't worry about yesterday or tomorrow; you would be having fun now. We lose joy because we can't live in the now!

3. You wouldn't be worried about your appearance because your childhood friend takes you as you are.

4. You have parents to trust in for everything you need (God wants to be your parent—will you let Him?)

5. As a child, you forgive and forget. Now, we may try to forgive, but rarely do we forget.

6. Last but not least, you can wear what you want. As a child, I could stay in my pajamas all day and not too many would laugh at me. If they did, who cares? Most of the kids would go home and get their pajamas, too.

Lighten up a little. Quit taking life so seriously and try to get back to the mindset of a child. Try to forgive, forget, and trust in your eternal parent, God. One day every knee will bow and tongue confess that Jesus is Lord. If you have done that before your last breath, you will enter Heaven; if not, no matter what you have done on this Earth, you will end up in hell. Those are not my words, but the words of Jesus in the Bible. Make this the day you *trust Jesus like a child and don't waver in your faith.* I was going to say get some Tinker Toys and play with them, but the last time I did that, some kid shoved one up my nose and I had to have my mom come and get me. I guess there are some things you just can't get over!

Have a great day today and try to have some fun out there.

Take care,
Brad